VINTAGE CLOTHING

The
Official® Identification
and Price Guide to
VINTAGE CLOTHING

Cynthia Giles

First Edition

House of Collectibles • New York

© 1989 by Cynthia Giles

All rights reserved under International and
Pan-American Copyright Conventions.

Published by: The House of Collectibles
201 East 50th Street
New York, New York 10022

Distributed by Ballantine Books, a division of Random House, Inc., New York, and simultaneously in Canada by Random House of Canada Limited, Toronto.

Manufactured in the United States of America

ISBN: 0-876-37771-1

First Edition: August 1989

10 9 8 7 6 5 4 3 2 1

These I have loved:
White plates and cups, clean-gleaming.
. . . grainy wood; live hair that is
Shining and Free; blue-massing clouds;
    the keen
Unpassioned beauty of a great machine;
The benison of hot water; furs to
    touch;
The good smell of old clothes, . . .

RUPERT BROOKE, *The Great Lover* (1914)

Contents

Preface

I've been collecting vintage clothes for many years now, and I can testify that it's a most delightful thing to do. But like most people who just start collecting, without much knowledge and usually without any kind of plan, I've wasted a fair amount of time and money. In the beginning, I felt that a romantic fondness for the past, and an enthusiasm for the wonderful look and feel of clothes from those bygone days, were enough to make me a collector. Knowledge didn't seem very necessary, just a love of adventure and a willingness to spend time looking through piles of dusty old clothes in search of treasure.

In fact, I felt that a more serious approach to collecting would spoil the fun. But as I see it now, nothing could be further from the truth. The more I learn about fashion and its history, the more exciting the vintage quest becomes. And the more I know about values of clothing collectibles, the more use I get from the money I spend. Plus, I have far fewer regrets and "if-onlys" to detract from the pleasures of looking at my collection.

With all this in mind, when I began the task of designing a *really useful* guide to vintage clothing and accessories, I decided that it ought to meet three criteria. First, it would have to be easy to use. Second, it would have to be filled with information. And third, it would have to convey at least some of the fantasy and fun of collecting vintage clothes.

The test for the first criterion would be whether someone who's found, for example, a floor-length, black crêpe skirt with a side drape and a back zipper, could, within a very few minutes, identify the item as an evening skirt of the 1940s, and know that a skirt in this style (of either better or worse material, construction, etc.) had recently been offered for sale by a flea-market dealer for about $40.

In order to make this ease of use possible, I decided the book would be best arranged by style and type of item, rather than by period, because after all, you could tell by *looking* at the item that it was a floor-length skirt, even if you didn't have the faintest idea whether it was Edwardian or maybe even something from the sixties. So for a first step, you could look the item up under "Skirts, floor-length," quickly scan the listings for a similar item, and if you found something that sounded like your mystery skirt, have a value indication to go by.

If you *didn't* find a similar item, or if you weren't sure your item matched a given description, then it would be useful if you could skim through a table of period information which would tell you: 1) that zippers were widely used as fasteners only after 1935, and 2) draping was a popular detail of the 1940s. Once you had identified the skirt as a forties piece, you could then get a rough value indication by looking up any skirt from the same period.

Now, for the second of the criteria I decided on: lots of information. The test for this point is whether, for example, if you found a skirt labeled "Hobble skirt, 1910, $140" in a vintage clothing store, you could quickly find out whether this identification was correct, and whether or not the price was realistic. The best way to do this would be to have complete glossaries of fashion terms so you could find out just what a "hobble" is and when it was being worn; then you could turn to the price guide, skim the periods listed, and check out some prices for skirts of the teens.

If you decided to collect the item, you might want to know what other items from the same period would complement it. Then you could return to the table of period information, scan the section on 1910–19, and find out what type of blouse or jacket might have been worn with it, as well as what accessories might have been added to the costume.

In addition to information about identification, a good book would also have to illuminate some other aspects of collecting. It would need to give an overview of the clothing collectibles field, plenty of hints on building and displaying a collection, helpful tips on care of vintage clothing, and some suggestions for further reading. It should also offer a list of dealers selling vintage clothes, either by mail or in retail stores.

Which brings me, finally, to the third criterion I think a good book on vintage clothing should meet, which is to convey the fantasy and fun of this delightful collecting field. The test for *this* criterion would be whether or not the book was entertaining to read, and I decided that in order for it to be entertaining, the book should: have wonderful descriptions and interesting illustrations sprinkled through it; tell some of the fascinating stories that make up the history of fashion; quote a few of the witty and insightful things people have said about clothing; and offer some surprises along the way.

After coming up with all these ideas about what a *really useful* guide to collecting vintage clothing should do, I've tried to create a book that would live up to my own expectations. Now, I hope it lives up to yours.

Acknowledgments

The following people have all gone out of their way to be helpful in the preparation of this book:

Myra Walker, Director of the Texas Fashion Collection, who gave generously of her very valuable time.

Dr. Mary Lou Hoyle, who read the manuscript and made many helpful comments.

Mary Hansen, of the Phillips auction firm, New York office, who was most gracious in providing material.

Barbara Kauffman, owner of Bon Ton Vintage Clothes, who gave me access both to her delightful store and to her collection of vintage magazines, books, and catalogs.

Margy Self, my tirelessly helpful mother, who has found in her treasure-hunting a variety of materials which have aided me in the study of vintage clothing.

Robert Alexander, who helped me grasp some of the subtleties of men's fashions.

Special thanks are due to Siri and Patrick Ahearne, owners of Puttin' on the Ritz, an elegant vintage clothing boutique in Dallas, Texas. Not only did they provide many of the wonderful clothes which appear in the book, but they also helped with the photographing and made constructive comments on various aspects of the project.

Finally, great appreciation goes to George Holman, who did several drawings for the book, helped extensively with the photography, and offered invaluable support in many ways throughout the project. And last in the list, but first in order of those to whom thanks are due, is Charlotte Gordon, without whom this book would never have existed.

Color photographs are courtesy of the Texas Fashion Collection. Black and white photography was done by the John Walker Studio in Dallas, Texas.

P A R T
O N E

The Basics of Collecting

Trust not the heart of that man for whom old clothes are not venerable.

THOMAS CARLYLE

American Indian motifs were fashionable in the 1920s.

Why Collect Clothing?

Three hundred dollars for a 1930s evening gown. One hundred dollars for a Hawaiian shirt. Thousands for an original Poiret or Fortuny.

Why on earth are people spending that kind of money for old clothes? The first and most important reason is . . . romance.

These days, when new clothes are designed by the cookie-cutter method (and are often cheaply made even if the price tag is staggering!), it's not surprising that so many of us look back longingly to a time when clothes were created with care and imagination. We miss the delicate detail and generous line of Victorian and Edwardian clothes; the outrageous wit and the flattering fit of clothes in the thirties; the ultra-sophistication of high fashion in the fifties; and the experimental passion that hit the streets in the sixties.

Perhaps just as much as we miss those wonderful clothes, we're nostalgic for the whole aura of glamour and individuality that once characterized the world of fashion, when clothes were often custom-made or made at home by inventive hands, and when personal life was wonderfully accoutered in every way—from shoe horns that were actually made of horn, to fetchingly decorated hatboxes, to elaborate silver and gold dresser sets.

"Back then," ordinary middle-class ladies could step out of their satin slippers, slide off their silk stockings, and have the maid hang their handbeaded chiffon dresses in their mahogany armoires, next to the summer tea gowns of handkerchief linen trimmed with handmade lace, the featherweight cashmere shawls, and the violet-black mourning dresses of paper-thin watered taffeta.

Those days are gone, it's true. We've traded away the availability of sumptuous fabrics and luxurious designs for more important things, such as social equality, better health, the wizardry of computers, and dozens of other innovations that make today's world in many ways a far more desirable place to live than the world of our grandparents. But still . . . the fancies of those bygone times linger in the imagination.

Those marvelous vintage garments are collectible because they are symbols of a way of life that will never be recaptured. And they are also things of beauty in themselves, made in a time when creative imagination could be expressed almost without limit in fashion because labor was incredibly cheap and fabulous materials were plentiful.

But it's not only the Chanel suits and the broderie anglaise petticoats and the silk-velvet evening capes that have become collectibles. Even everyday clothes, work clothes, play clothes, children's clothes—all can have great interest for the collector, because in their lines, colors, and textures they reveal a great deal about how people saw themselves at a particular time in history. Clothing expresses the values and customs of a society, and so is collectible from an historical, as well as an aesthetic, point of view.

There is also an economic aspect to collecting clothes. Vintage clothing is in limited supply, and without careful preservation, what remains will deteriorate. Therefore, well-chosen items that are also well-preserved will generally appreciate in value—which makes vintage clothing potentially a good investment and, therefore, an attractive collecting field.

It's also still a relatively open field. Until fairly recently, vintage clothing was looked upon by almost everyone as merely old and out-of-fashion, rather than "collectible," so the countryside hasn't yet been thoroughly scoured for every last remnant. There are still plenty of treasures—from both an aesthetic and a financial standpoint—left to be found at affordable (even bargain) prices.

Besides a yearning for the romantic past, or an interest in the art of fashion and the attitudes of society, or an eye for investment potential, there's one more reason—a very personal one—why people collect vintage clothes: to wear them! If worn carefully and sparingly, many vintage garments can continue to lead a fashion life, just as they were meant to do.

Your reasons for collecting probably include several of the above, and that's just fine. You may buy one piece of vintage clothing because it's an unusual specimen of the fishtail hemline, another because it *might* turn out to be a valuable Poiret original, and another because you've always wanted a silk negligée and, at today's prices, you haven't a prayer.

But, ultimately, if you wish to get the maximum satisfaction from your collection, it's helpful to focus your collecting efforts. That doesn't mean you can't pick up a few things just for love or because they're irresistibly priced. It does mean, though, that overall, you set some limits and priorities. The object is to *create* your collection, rather than just letting it grow like Topsy. And the first key to achieving this object is to understand the field you are working in.

There are many clothes out there. You can't collect them all, and anyway, some aren't even worth collecting. So where will you start— and where will you *stop?* The next section offers some basic information that will help in making these decisions.

An afternoon dress and lavish hat of the 1900s.

What Clothing is Collectible?

If your approach to collecting is very casual, anything you like and can afford is "collectible." But if you are a bit more serious—and especially if you want to build a collection that will appreciate significantly in value—it's important to be aware of the factors that make some clothing items highly collectible, and others less so.

I should warn you that there is no simple, agreed-upon set of rules about what makes clothing collectible. The point of view on which this book is based is the one I've developed for myself through the study of fashion history, observations of the vintage clothing market, and conversations with collectors. Though my ideas about clothing collectibility shouldn't be taken as the final word, by any means, they are the ones that organize this book, so I will present them in some detail.

The first factor that makes a clothing item collectible is, as you might expect, its age. Since fabric is subject to a natural process of decay, most of the clothing made in the long history of mankind has by now vanished without a trace; only a small number of things remain from before the nineteenth century, and those are here by accident of climate or of fortune, not because there was ever any intent to save items of clothing for posterity. Clothes were usually worn until they fell apart, or they were cut up and made into other things.

Because it is true that the further back in time you go, the fewer items of clothing survive, it's obvious that the older clothes are, the more rare and precious they become. Generally speaking, items from before the nineteenth century belong in museums and cannot properly be thought of as collectibles; they are very few, very fragile, and must be protected as part of our common heritage.

The nearer we come to our own time, naturally, the more things survive, just because they haven't had time to disintegrate. But while there is quite a bit of clothing available from the nineteenth century, much of it is not, strictly speaking, collectible. Clothing from the first two-thirds of the century compares with *really* antique furniture, china, and so forth, in the sense that you *could* have a whole collection of it, but only if you had quite a bit of money to spend or were fortunate enough to inherit the whole lot.

More clothing remains from the last third of the nineteenth century, however, in part because daily life became easier and cleaner, and clothing was subjected to less wear and tear, so it lasted longer; also, as the process of change speeded up, more people developed a sense that "history" was being made in their own time, and clothing began to be purposefully saved and passed from generation to generation. As a result, clothes from this period *can* be collected, and so they may be considered "vintage" rather than "antique."

For the purposes of this book, the definition of "vintage" is more or less identical to the designation "collectible," and the two terms are used in a similar way. This tactic isn't a hundred percent accurate of course; it *is* possible to collect antique clothing, with enough time, money, and expertise. But only a very few people can do that sort of collecting, while almost anyone who wants to can acquire and enjoy a delightful array of vintage clothes.

There is, however, a good deal of disagreement among the many people involved in the buying, selling, and collecting of vintage clothing on the question of when is—and isn't—"vintage." Some people would say that the term "vintage" encompasses anything that's still intact and on the market; some would say that the vintage period doesn't begin until 1900, with the end of the Victorian era; others would contend that the vintage period ends with World War II; and still others would insist that the end of vintage coincides with the demise of high fashion in the late sixties.

My choice of dates to enclose the vintage period is dictated by practical considerations of what is actually available in the marketplace, as well as by the interests and capabilities of the majority of collectors. Since the average person, with an average amount of time and money to spend, can reasonably expect to acquire one or two garments from as early as the 1880s, that seems a sensible starting point for the vintage period. It makes sense in another way as well, for in the 1880s, fashion turned decisively away from the high Victorian style and began to make its way toward the dawn of modern dress.

Now—where to stop? For the purposes of this book, the line is drawn at 1969, and that choice is open to at least a couple of criticisms. For one thing, the period 1880 to 1969 covers nearly a century, and while that isn't a very long time in the great scheme of things, this particular century saw the most rapid and drastic changes in the whole history of fashion, making it a great deal of territory to cover. For another thing, this dating brings the vintage period very close to our own time; the clothes of the fifties and sixties, after all, are clothes that you may very well have worn, thinking they were the height of fashion—and ten years later, groaned with retrospective embarrassment as you dropped them into the Salvation Army box. Can these recent decades really be called "vintage"?

A simple reply is that the word "vintage," whether it's applied to clothes or to wine, simply means "of a particular time." And among the things that make clothes collectible is the *particularness* of the way they represent their times. Clothes from the fifties and sixties can achieve this level of representation just as well as Victorian apparel can, after all.

But the word "vintage" is also used to mean "special" and "of high quality," and there is debate over whether fifties and sixties (or even forties) clothing ought to be considered "vintage" in this sense. One argument is that vintage clothes are special precisely because they have qualities of craftsmanship and imagination which can't be found in the mass-produced and minimally designed clothes of the fifties and sixties. Another contention is that vintage clothing represents a lost era of elegance, and ought not to include the kitschy poodle skirts and vinyl micro-minis of a later and less tasteful time.

My own attitude is that these points of view actually limit the term "vintage" to make it mean something more like "picturesque." They assume that *prettiness* is the chief value in clothing design, and it seems to me that such an assumption leaves out some of the most fascinating aspects of fashion! Furthermore, narrowing the vintage field to before World War II would take away the excellent opportunity that still exists to create very fine collections of later clothing.

Actually, some marvelous clothes were made in the fifties and sixties. It's just that the marvelous qualities of those clothes are of a different kind than the marvelous qualities of Edwardian whites and beaded flapper dresses. Clothing of the fifties and sixties rarely can boast the romantic delicacy or vivid dash that marked earlier periods;

nor does it display the bounty of detail that is found in hand-finished garments. But many items from the later decades *do* have highly sophisticated design values, and many others capture the culture of their times like snapshots in fabric.

There are all sorts of fascinating garments to be found from the fifties and sixties: the last *authentic* imported, ethnic, and regional clothes (dramatic Hawaiian shirts, richly embroidered rodeo outfits, and handpainted Mexican skirts are just a few examples); carefully beaded cashmere sweaters; fabrics that capture the art of the Abstract Expressionists; simple suits that are masterpieces of cut and proportion, along with sultry cocktail dresses that fit as no garment made today can ever seem to do; painted denims, gloriously tie-dyed T-shirts, neo-Edwardian dresses home-made from scraps of silk and velvet and lace.

The surprising thing is, however, that these treasures are not necessarily much easier to find than Edwardian whites or beaded flapper dresses. It's true that the closer we come to the present, the easier it is to find and acquire clothing items. But! It simultaneously becomes *more difficult* to find clothing that is well made, well designed, or even interesting. Though the reservoir of available clothing is large, the pool of truly *collectible* clothing makes up only a very small proportion of the total amount.

For this reason, as we come nearer to our own time, the nature of collecting changes from the hunt for remnants of an elegant past to the search for a few fine things that are afloat in a sea of—to put it bluntly—junk. Nearly a hundred percent of the clothing that remains from the 1880s is collectible, simply because of its age; but at the other end of the scale, probably only between five and ten percent of the clothing from the sixties is really collectible, and those items are distinguished by their special qualities of design and/or historical significance.

Now, look at the marketplace. Most of the really good examples of pre–World War II clothing are already in the hands of collectors or dealers; to acquire a substantial collection you will have to be either rich or very resourceful and very lucky. But there are still a lot of collectible postwar items out there, waiting to be bought at reasonable prices. Creating a really good collection with a relatively small investment is still possible—*if* you learn about the period, develop your design sensibilities, and think creatively.

To sum all this up: 1) Anything you love is collectible *for you.* 2) If you want to form a more serious, and potentially valuable, collection, there are some specific considerations which govern the desirability of particular garments. 3) Age alone can make a garment collectible, but only if it is *both* at least fifty years old *and* in good condition. 4) Garments less than fifty years old should have significant design values and/or obvious historical interest. 5) Collecting from the later vintage period is no less a challenge than collecting from the earlier decades, and the rewards are potentially substantial.

The tonneau silhouette of the late teens.

Shaping a Collection

Because collectors are, by nature, an individualistic lot of folks, no two collections will ever be created just alike. But there are certain patterns which have been tried by many collectors and found useful. The first, and most obvious, is collecting **by period.**

Conveniently enough, over the last hundred years, periods have generally coincided with decades. The first of these periods really to stand out as having its own special fashion identity was the "Mauve Decade" of the 1890s. Since then, each decade—the Edwardian aughts, the World War I teens, the roaring twenties, the "modern" thirties, the wartime forties, the "normal" fifties, and the revolutionary sixties—has had a style all its own.

Of course the clothes of different periods overlap, and there are even revivals (like the late-sixties vogue for thirties-style clothing), so a garment doesn't necessarily belong to a certain period or come from a particular decade just because it fits a characteristic style. But by and large, periods can be defined, and focusing a collection by confining it to a specific period is an excellent approach.

But . . . you may like *both* the Edwardian period and the thirties (they do have some similar characteristics). Or you may be interested in evening gowns, no matter what their period. In such cases, a collection could be organized **by type of garment or accessory.** Lingerie, hats, sweaters, sporting clothes, aprons—any choice can be a good one. And this sort of organization is especially interesting because it allows you to see more clearly the evolution of fashion.

Swimsuits, for example, run the gamut from Victorian woolens that swathed the swimmer completely, to Rudi Gernreich's infamous topless suit. Between these two extremes lie the classic maillot, the sarong suit made famous by Dorothy Lamour, and the first timid bikinis of the fifties (which were actually introduced to the fashion world not by surfers, but by the elegant Paris designer Jacques Heim). A collection that included all these swimwear styles would make the whole fashion journey of the twentieth century wonderfully visible.

However, you may be more interested in fashion as art than in fashion as history—in which case a collection organized *by design or designer* would suit you well. Perhaps a whole collection of Poirets or Fortunys or Vionnets? Well, probably not. Even if there were enough original designer clothes available, the cost would be prohibitive for most people. But you don't have to have originals. Most designers were widely copied, by private seamstresses and mass manufacturers alike, so although you may not be able to have a collection of real Poirets, you might hope to gather a whole selection of Poiret-*type* clothes.

Or, you could focus on a single design, rather than on the designer. Chanel's "little black dress," for example, was worn by all sorts of women, in endless variations, for decades; it's a classic design idea, which could easily be the starting point of a dazzling collection. Similarly, Schiaparelli's famous trompe l'oeil sweater could serve as the inspiration for a collection of fool-the-eye garments and accessories.

But there are still plenty of other strategies. You might, for example, set out to build *a complete "wardrobe"*—the clothes one bride might have chosen for her trousseau, perhaps, or everything one traveler might have packed for a Grand Tour of Europe. This is really a fantasy approach to collecting, one which can include the creation of a whole imaginary character, with likes and dislikes, expectations and activities.

You could even collect a synopsis of one life—with representative samples of all the clothes that might have been worn in a lifetime by a woman who was born, say, in frontier Kansas at the turn of the century, and who died in Philadelphia, 1959. Or perhaps a whole family's wardrobe, from baby clothes to Papa's velvet smoking jacket.

If these collecting scenarios are too fictional, return to real life, where a *materials* collection can be based on fabrics, trimmings, and decorative details. Beading, for example, could form the basis for a collection that included hats, evening gowns, handbags, and sweaters. Exotic buttons offer another fascinating choice. How about unusual prints? (Several designers commissioned well-known artists to produce fabric designs, which were widely copied and could form a stunning collection.) Or pleats—all kinds of pleats, from delicate accordion-pleated ruching to knife-pleated kilt skirts.

The ideas offered above are just a few of many which could be used as the creative spark for a collection of vintage clothing. But a collection doesn't *have* to have a definite set of limits. You could use the **eclectic approach.** That doesn't mean, however, just picking up anything that strikes a fancy and throwing it all together in a jumble. Even an eclectic collection can have form and balance.

To achieve success with the eclectic approach, be sure that the various pieces in a collection complement one another in some way, rather than clashing. When you are considering a purchase, imagine how it will look with the other things you own. Will it harmonize, or stand out like a neon sign?

An eclectic collection might have several different centers of interest—for example, it could contain a micro-collection of designer dresses, another of sports costumes, yet another of fancy feather trimmings. Or, it could be made up entirely of unique items, having nothing in common except quality and visual interest. However it might be composed, the eclectic collection can still have a coherent personality if it is thought of *as* a collection, rather than as an assortment.

The nature of the collection is one of many things the collector must keep in mind, even when hot on the collecting trail. The next section will discuss the basic strategies of collecting, as well as offering some ways to organize your treasure-hunting for maximum efficiency and minimum stress.

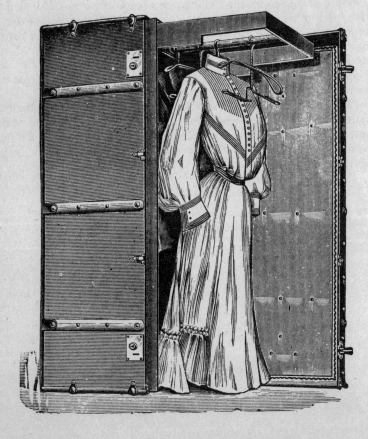

The pigeon-breast bodice, on a sailor-influenced dress of the 1900s.

Building a Collection

First thing to consider—just where does one *look* for all these vintage clothes?

Some sources are perfectly obvious. Pull out the Yellow Pages, look under "Clothing—Used, Retail" (or some similar listing) and see if there are any vintage clothing stores in your area. If you live anywhere near a middle-sized or bigger city, there probably is at least one. (Some well-established stores are listed in Part Four.) Also try stores listed under "Antiques."

Dealers who sell from retail stores are usually the most expensive of all sources of vintage clothing. They've put in the time to find, evaluate, restore, and display the items, and the buyer must pay for that service, as well as make a contribution to the overhead and return a fair profit to the dealer. Though the services and expertise that can be provided by a good store are valuable indeed, most collectors cannot afford to make all of their acquisitions in this way.

Dealers who sell from their homes, through the mail, or at antique fairs and flea markets don't have as much overhead, so they usually offer somewhat lower prices. But the prices are still substantially more than the amount *they* paid for the garments. Unless the dealer is providing restoration services, you are essentially paying the dealer to find garments for you, and, in a way, that can be a bargain, considering the time and effort (as well as knowledge) that goes into ferreting out good vintage items.

At the same time, the thrill of the hunt is part of the pleasure of collecting, and many collectors want to do their own discovering. If you are willing to spend time studying fashion history, searching out sources, sorting through boxes of junk, and mending ripped seams, then you can try being your own dealer, at least partially.

Nightdress, 1900.

As a rule, it takes many different acquisition strategies (including knowledgeable buying from dealers, hunting on your own, bidding at auction, and wheedling clothes from friends and family!) to build a good collection. So there are several avenues you will need to pursue. One is to establish a relationship with local or mail-order dealers, and learn the ins and outs of the vintage clothing market so that you can buy effectively.

Another important strategy is to master the art of finding and buying vintage clothing on your own. Start with the fact that there are clothes out there. Now—how will you find them?

Since you can't go door to door and ask people about their old clothes, you have to wait for them to put out a sign or take out an ad—and happily, thousands of people do just that every weekend. All over the country, people are having garage sales, estate sales, rummage sales, and so on. If you're interested in collecting, you are probably already quite familiar with the sale circuit in your own town.

A warning is in order here. Good vintage clothing is not often found in neighborhood sales. You will strike out far more often than you will find something worth acquiring, and most of what you might find will be post–World War II. But the heart of the collector is charmed by the thrill of the chase, and looking can be half the fun. If you have, as many collectors do, more than one collecting interest, the chances that you will reap sufficient rewards to justify your treasure-hunting time are increased.

So—forewarned and undiscouraged—where will you go? Estate sales are obviously the most likely source of vintage clothing, since most people die when they are at an advanced age, and so are more likely to have left behind clothing from previous eras. Older parts of town are also better hunting grounds than the newest suburbs, where sales are likely to focus on baby clothes and lawn furniture. Older, *wealthier* parts of town are better still, since people tend to keep expensive clothes much longer than inexpensive ones (and well-made clothes of good-quality fabric hold up a good deal longer anyway).

But then, as you might guess, the more sophisticated the sellers, the more likely that they will recognize the real value of things, so bargains are less frequently to be found in upper income neighborhoods than in declining ones. It's worthwhile to keep in mind, however, that a good collection can rarely be built from great bargains alone; most collectors will have to pay reasonable prices for things a good part of the time, whether that means buying from a dealer or paying near-dealer prices to an individual.

The competition at estate sales is keen. Dealers and pickers (people who scout for vintage items and sell them to dealers) get to the promising sales very early, purchase decisively, and are gone with the good things before the amateurs can struggle out of their cars. So if you want to have a fairly consistent chance in the competition (rather than just hoping for a burst of luck), you have to spend some time patiently familiarizing yourself with different parts of town and finding out where signs for sales are usually put up; check the classified ads not only in your town's main newspapers, but in neighborhood papers and tradesheets as well. Plan an efficient route beforehand to save time, and get an early start.

Always be sure to take a reasonable amount of cash so as not to miss any grand opportunities because the owner won't take a check. And form the habit of quickly sizing up each sale, leaving promptly if it doesn't look promising (rather than wandering around among the Fry Daddies and Weed Eaters, thinking "there *might* be *something* here"). The more sales you attend, the more educated and reliable your intuition will become.

Beyond the estate sale is the rummage sale. This is a sale given by a church or charitable organization to raise money, and it usually features a lot of merchandise from different sources. The sheer quantity of goods is appealing, but here again, in an organized sale run by many volunteers, there's a good chance that someone knowledgeable will have weeded the "vintage" items from the merely "old" clothes, and sold the more valuable things to a dealer beforehand.

This same type of weeding will almost always have been done by charitable outlets, such as Salvation Army or DAV stores, so these sources (although they are fun places to look for real bargains in recent wearables) are not usually steady sources for the collector. The one exception is in the area of sixties clothing, which is not yet considered by everyone to be of vintage value, and so may make its way onto the hangers of these outlets. There will also be the occasional overlooked gem, but in order to be the one to find it, you need to go by these outlets frequently and learn to peruse them very efficiently so you won't spend too much time hunting through the polyester pantsuits.

There is, by the way, one chance to take advantage of the weeding process done by institutions that receive donated clothing. Theaters often receive donations of old clothes for costume use, and duplicated or unwanted items are sold off. Take the time to make some friendly contacts with local theaters, and you may get a chance at these items.

A little time can also be profitably invested in driving around. The further you go from a large urban center, the less likely people are to be thinking much about the price of vintage clothing. Pick out some smallish towns within a comfortable driving radius and try them out. If you want to maximize your chances, call beforehand and try to find out if there are any sales planned for a given weekend; try calling the churches, the women's club, or the Chamber of Commerce for suggestions.

There is another rich category of sources to be considered next, one which includes everyone you know—and everyone *they* know. Your own family may be a great potential source of vintage clothes. Don't assume that you would be aware of it if they had any vintage clothes. Many's the collector who has heard her mother say, "Why, dear, I had no idea you'd want those old things of Granny's! And we did get fifty cents apiece for them at the rummage sale—even those tacky things with the bustles."

Be *certain* that everyone you're related to knows you would like to hear about any vintage clothes they may have or discover. You can make it clear that you don't necessarily expect to be given the clothes, just a first chance to buy them if they are going to be sold. And tell them what your period of interest is; don't just say vintage and leave it at that, or people will often assume you mean only *very* old things.

You needn't limit yourself to relatives you know well. Every collector has to be a little nervy once in a while, and that can apply with relatives as well as strangers. There's no reason not to write to distant cousins and great-aunts, introducing yourself and explaining that you're a collector, and that you are especially interested in acquiring things from your own family heritage. Most of those kin will be glad to know about you.

Why stop with relatives? Tell all your friends, and ask them to mention your interest to *their* friends and relatives. Talk about your collection at parties, on planes, or wherever you can slip it into a conversation gracefully. The next thing you know, some stranger will say, "Well, my word, my sister's got a ton of that stuff. Why don't you give her a call?"

Remember that although *you* may be captivated by vintage clothes, to many people they're just more junk, which they will get rid of one way or another, and often as not, by throwing them away or using them for scraps. It's not pushy to give people an opportunity to make a better disposition of things they have no use for! And if you don't tell them you're interested, how will they know?

Taking the same principle a bit further, you don't have to wait for other people to advertise. You can place ads yourself. Put a note on the bulletin board at church or at work; ask to have your collecting interest mentioned in a club or employee newsletter; put up a sign at your *own* garage sale saying, "I'd love to hear about it if you have any vintage clothes." And you might offer to show off some items from your collection at the local library or community center, or even do a vintage style show for the PTA or some other group; when people see your collection, they're likely to remember things in their *own* attic and tell you about them.

Finally, there are two other opportunities for buying vintage clothes which should be mentioned. The first is buying by mail. Part Four of this book contains a list of some of the dealers who will sell by mail. Some will provide periodic lists of their stock, and some will take your order for a particular type of item and let you know when they have something similar. Before you order from any mail-order dealer, be sure to determine that they have a reasonable return policy.

The other source is auctions. Many people are intimidated by auctions, but actually, auction-going can be a good deal of fun. Check the classified ads for auction ads that look promising; it's rare to find one that says "vintage clothes," but look for things like liquidation of estates (for example, farm estates, where the attention will be centered on tractors rather than on a lot or two of old clothes), antique auctions (where vintage clothes may be among the miscellaneous categories), and auctions of the unclaimed contents of warehouses, condemned buildings, etc.

Call ahead, if possible, and try to determine if clothes will be among the items offered; if there's a preview scheduled, be sure and attend. To participate in the auction, you must first get a bidding number (usually a paddle or numbered card), and, as a rule, you must demonstrate ability to pay. Although credit cards are increasingly being accepted, checks frequently are not; on the whole, cash is the rule.

You should decide ahead of time which items or lots you're interested in, and how much *maximum* you would be willing to pay. Write down the lot number *and* your high amount for each thing you plan to bid on. Hang onto this list for dear life, and stick to it religiously, because it will help you avoid the two great dangers of auction-going: confusion and enthusiasm.

Determine your top price for each item as a function of how much you think the item is worth and how much—total—you have to spend. Plan your *whole* auction strategy in advance, or you may end up spending all your money on one thing, when you would much rather have had a shot at some others.

In deciding on each item's value to you, set the figure somewhat lower if you think you might want to resell it than if you are buying for your own collection. Knowledgeable buyers can sometimes finance their own acquisitions by picking up some good buys for resale, but this works only if: 1) you are accurate in gauging the value of the item, and 2) you know how to get the right price for it, either from a dealer or from another collector.

A few further practical tips: Bidding is usually done by showing your paddle *clearly* or raising your hand *firmly*; don't worry, a twitch of the nose won't be mistaken for a ruinous bid anywhere but in the movies. If yours is the highest bid, you are obligated to purchase the item at that price, and you will be expected to do so immediately after bidding on the item is completed or at the end of the auction.

Once you've found and attended a couple of auctions, you'll probably have a steady supply of opportunities because you can get on mailing lists, which are shared among various auctioneers and auction houses. Auctions are entertaining, and can be good sources for collectors, but vintage clothes are not as frequently found at auction as are some other collectibles. So consider this an adjunct to the many other approaches mentioned previously.

No matter where you hunt for vintage collectibles, from retail store to estate sale to auction house, there are a few things to keep in mind. I mentioned above the importance of thinking of your collection *as a collection* rather than just as an assortment. It's equally important to think of the process of building your collection as a vital, creative activity, and not just as an occasional amusement. To get the most out of collecting in the long run, it takes a little strategizing in the short run.

First of all, you may want to make a budget (quarterly or yearly) of both the time and the money you want to spend on your collection. Figure in time and costs for mending, maintenance, etc., as well as for shopping. Also decide on the *number* of items you can acquire, from the standpoint of storage/display space.

This kind of plan is very, very useful in successfully developing a collection. Not only will it help you distribute your resources optimally, it will also radically diminish the guilt feelings that so often accompany impulsive spending. But to keep the whole thing from being oppressive, be sure to build a splurge factor into the budget. That is, plan the number of times and the amount of money that can be allowed for exceptions (things you fall in love with, or values too good to pass up).

With a budget firmly in mind, you're prepared to go forth in search of collectibles. But you will also need a plan for actually *implementing* budget considerations—in terms of both time and money—when you go out into the field. One way to organize a hunting expedition is to set a price ceiling (per item) in advance. Then, at a store or sale, you can look through everything rapidly from the standpoint of price. Find the items that are under your price ceiling and, if possible, separate them into one group.

Then, make a quick division of that group into two categories— things you like, and things you don't like. Don't spend much time thinking, just trust your intuitive reactions. Once you've decided which things you don't like, forget them, no matter what bargains they might be. The cardinal rule of successful collecting is *if you don't love it, don't buy it.* The one exception to that rule is the case in which you absolutely know, without a shadow of a doubt, where you can resell the bargain item immediately.

As for the things you *do* like, look through them first in terms of condition, and reject anything which you can't reasonably expect to mend or clean successfully—given your level of skill and the time you're willing to put into it. Don't fool yourself! Many people become ex-collectors because they have nothing to show for their collecting efforts but a pile of bargains waiting to be repaired.

By now you should have the items for consideration down to just a few. Which, if any, of the things would give you continuing pleasure to own? Which would compliment pieces you already have? Which, if any, is such a standout that it overcomes all other considerations? If there is nothing that fits any of these categories, move on.

But if there are several things that make the cut, and your budget forces a choice of one from among them, consider next the price/value relationship. The item whose price is the smallest percentage of its value is generally the best buy. In fact, it's usually better to spend a bit more on an undervalued item than to spend less on an item that is priced at-value.

This systematic approach to hunting is an especially good one in the early phases of collecting, when you're building a foundation and exploring your collecting interests. It will allow you to look through everything without spending an eternity and ending up too dazed by possibilities to make a decision. And, it will prevent an early case of "collector's burnout," which is caused by looking at too many "things" for too long.

As your collection begins to take shape, and your specific needs and interests become more defined, you can organize a hunting trip by identifying ahead of time a particular period or category of item you want to focus on. Get in the habit of sticking with that decision, and don't even *look* at anything that doesn't fit the shopping list.

Most of the time, that is. Of course collecting shouldn't become so serious and so rigidly organized that it's no fun anymore. But it is particularly true with vintage clothes, because there are so many possibilities—so many fabrics, so many designs, so many combinations of trimming and color and on and on!—that you can become depressed (because you can't have them all) or satiated (in which case the sight of even one more Victorian nightie will be too much to stomach). To avoid losing the spontaneous joy of collecting, it's best to choose some limits to work within.

Besides that, it's important to leave some time, money, and energy available for all the other matters that go along with successful collecting. As the next section will reveal, there is much more to collecting than just buying.

Considerations for Collectors

One of the first decisions a collector has to make is: ***To wear—or not to wear?*** To a certain extent, buying vintage clothes to wear is incompatible with building a successful collection. For one thing, it restricts your choices significantly. If you're buying to wear, you're limited to things in your own size, which may eliminate a great many interesting items. You will also be limiting yourself to things which might conceivably be worn in today's society.

Furthermore, every time you wear a vintage garment, you risk decreasing its value. Accidents happen, and old textiles are fragile and more easily torn or spotted than new fabrics. Of course, the older the garment is, the more this is a concern; clothes from the fifties and sixties are much more safely wearable than things from earlier periods. But even if a garment isn't damaged in wearing, you will still be faced with the need to clean and press it after wearing—which can be time-consuming and even risky when you're dealing with old and/or unknown fabrics.

But although everything said above is true, still, there is a special pleasure in wearing beautiful vintage clothes. The best answer for many collectors may be to acquire a few special wearables, which may or may not be considered part of the "official" collection. Outerwear, and accessories such as scarves and hats, are generally more durable than clothing, and can be worn more safely. Similarly, winter clothing—which is heavier and more sturdily made as a rule—will stand up better to wearing than delicate summer garments will.

There is something of an art to wearing vintage clothing well, but it's an art that can be learned. In general, it works best to combine vintage items with contemporary ones, to avoid a costume look. Try

From the forties: a pinafore dress, a cartwheel hat, and T-strap wedgies.

wearing vintage accessories with modern clothes, and modern accessories with vintage clothes. But be sure that the whole outfit works together, and flatters your personal shape and coloring.

Also, keep in mind the way vintage styles were meant to be worn; the Chanel suit, for example, looks marvelous heaped with costume jewelry (as Chanel intended it to be), but rather dowdy when left all by itself. The trick is to understand the *spirit* in which clothes were worn in their own time, and when composing an outfit, be true to that spirit. This approach usually turns out to be much more attractive and comfortable than trying to copy an exact outfit of the period.

Whatever vintage items you do decide to wear, you will want to protect as much as possible. Generally speaking, expect to be able to wear a pre-war item in good condition about six times before the risk (which increases with each wearing) becomes too great. Limit your vintage clothes to relatively short and inactive outings—dinner, yes, dancing, no. And as soon as you remove the garment, check it over

The classic robe de style, popular from the 1900s through the
1920s.

for any problems—pulled seams, disintegrating fabric, loose trimmings—which might have developed.

One of the keys to safely wearing vintage clothes is to remember
that perspiration is incredibly bad for virtually all fabrics, and *especially*
old ones. If there's any likelihood of perspiring while wearing the
garment, consider wearing dress shields (not too uncomfortable once
you get used to them) and absorbent cotton underwear; when that isn't
possible, be sure the anti-perspirant you wear does *not* contain alumi-
num salts, which will only make matters worse if perspiration does get
on the fabric. A garment that is perspired on should be rinsed out
immediately if the fabric is washable, or taken straight to the cleaners
the next day.

Which brings us to the next consideration: ***The care and feeding
of vintage clothing.*** This is—literally—a delicate topic, and one which
is a source of aggravation for most collectors. There are two basic

reasons why the cleaning of vintage clothes is such a problem. First, you usually have no idea what the fabric is or what the right way of cleaning it might be. And second, whatever you come up with as an approach to cleaning a piece of vintage clothing, it's going to take either a lot of time or a chunk of money.

There are, remember, no fabric content tags or care labels on most vintage clothes, so there are no instructions about what to do, and more important, *not* to do, to clean them. Worse yet, many of the fabrics used in vintage garments are so unfamiliar that you can't even guess at what the fiber content might be. And on top of *that*, a wrong guess about washing or cleaning the fabric may permanently ruin it.

It would be nice if there were experts to help you solve these problems, but if you find a cleaner who is knowledgeable about vintage clothing, you should be incredibly grateful for your rare good luck. Most cleaning establishments today are franchised factories, and they will not even notice the difference between your precious vintage garment and any other thing that comes into the store. Even if you carefully tell them about your garment and how you want it to be handled, they will not necessarily do what you ask. *And*, if they carelessly ruin your garment, they may not want to reimburse you for its true vintage value.

Grim as that may sound, it's an advantage to be aware of the truth. The best approach is to talk to several cleaners, pick one that seems sympathetic, and patiently try to develop a good relationship. If you're lucky, you'll find an ally who will become interested in your collection, and will even go out of the way to help you.

Your other best bets are: 1) to become as knowledgeable as possible about your garments and the care they need, and 2) to do as much of the care as possible yourself. There are several books listed in the bibliography which offer guidance in both areas. But here, in the meantime, is a synopsis of must-know facts and techniques.

First, avoid buying things which can probably not be cared for successfully. There are several such pitfalls to keep in mind:

- "Weighted" silk (in which the silk fiber has been mixed with metal salts to increase its fabric yield) was used very frequently early in this century. It does not age well; in fact, it shreds very readily. Learn to recognize its distinctive brittleness—and always test the condition of any silk by stretching it gently from side to side.

- Any lightened or discolored areas, especially near the underarms, can signal perspiration damage. It may initially seem possible to live with the blemished appearance, but the catch is that the fiber in these areas is so damaged that the first cleaning or wearing will usually cause the fabric to disintegrate.

- Similarly, major moth damage may not show up *until* a fabric is cleaned. The one or two moth holes which can be seen are often harbingers of dozens more which will appear when the garment is washed or dry-cleaned.

Garments that fall into any of the above categories are very questionable purchases. Buy them only if you're prepared to write them off after one cleaning attempt, or if they have particularly wonderful trimmings—and the price is cheap enough to allow you to salvage the good parts and discard the rest.

The initial step in caring for vintage clothing should be to do any mending that is necessary. Washing or cleaning a garment with a pulled seam or frayed hole can be disastrous. So, examine the article carefully, and if any problems are found, fix them. Be sure and hold the garment up to a bright light, one thickness at a time, to reveal any tears or holes that are not easy to see. (This is also a good test for the overall condition of the fabric; if many spots appear thinner than the rest, or if there are numerous pin-prick-type holes, the fabric is in very fragile condition.)

Match thread, fasteners, and so on as closely as possible with present-day materials; better still, you might consider picking up when you see them cheap vintage pieces which are not themselves salvageable, but which can be "scavenged" for hooks and eyes, snaps, and buttons. Though you won't be able to make exact matches, you *will* be able to mend the garment much as the original owner might have, using what was available then.

Split seams, loose trimmings, pulled hems and the like can all be mended in the obvious ways. But small tears and holes are a frequent problem in vintage clothes, and they require greater skill to mend discreetly. Making a small seam to conceal them is usually more desirable than darning or patching.

Once the garment is as sound as you can make it, you have to decide whether it can stand a bath or must brave the dry cleaners. A great many fabrics—more than most people realize—can be washed with the proper care. Fabrics which usually *can't* be washed successfully include nap or pile fabrics, metallic fabrics, very heavy fabrics (satins, tapestries, and the like), and very crisp fabrics (such as organza or taffeta).

There are also several kinds of construction which make washing impossible or at least very inadvisable: 1) two or more different fabrics used in one garment; 2) trim which cannot be removed; and 3) elabo-rate seaming (the seams may tend to draw up when washed). There are also certain kinds of dyes which cannot be washed without running; they are especially likely to be found in imported clothing and in unusual, handmade items.

If neither the construction nor the fabric of a garment clearly rules out washing it, test a small, inconspicuous spot, using tepid water and mild soap. Wet it thoroughly, scrub gently, rinse completely, and let it dry. If it looks very stiff or very wrinkled, try a warm iron with a steam cloth. Then, if you're satisfied with the result, go ahead and wash the whole garment.

Be sure first to remove the trimmings. You may also need to remove metal fasteners, since old button shanks, hooks, and so on often were not rustproof. Close zippers. If the garment is at all fragile, place it in a mesh lingerie bag before washing. And *never* pick up a wet garment, as the weight of the water may pull seams or rip the fabric; always let the water drain out of the fabric first.

The process of washing vintage garments has to be a balance be-tween what is needed to get the garment as clean as possible, and what is realistic in terms of the garment's age and condition. In general, it's safest to wash everything in lukewarm water and use a very mild, neutral soap. But some fabrics—such as white cotton—will not look very clean with this kind of washing. As a rule of thumb, remember that plant-based fibers, such as cotton, linen, ramie, and rayon, can be washed in warmer water and with a stronger soap. Protein-based fibers, on the other hand—which include silk, wool, and animal hair—need cool water, very mild soap, and very gentle handling, since they are easily stretched.

Very heavily soiled washables may benefit from pre-soaking in one part glycerin and four parts lukewarm (about 90 degrees) water. Soak only about ten minutes, and then if the water looks dirty, change the solution and soak again. Do this until the water is clear, and then wash. If bleaching of white cottons or linens is required, try one tablespoon-ful of lemon juice to one gallon of water. (And by the way, dry cleaning may make white cottons and linens look dingy, so you're better off washing if you possibly can.)

Always wash by hand, of course, squeezing rather than lifting the garment. And *always* dry flat. In fact, if you do very much of this sort of thing, you may want to invest in a drying screen, which will fit across the bathtub and allow air to circulate around the drying garment.

As for ironing—don't. You can *press,* though. Pressing differs from ironing because the iron touches the fabric only lightly, and is never moved across the surface of the fabric. Just lift the iron and move it from one place to another (following the grain of the fabric), then lower it very gently, leave it a moment, and move on; press bias fabrics along the straight of the grain.

The pressing method takes a while, but it's much better for the garment. Use the lowest effective setting on your iron, and if steam is needed, be *sure* to use distilled water in your iron; the minerals (and who knows what else) in tap water may leave deposits in/on the fabric of a garment. Press on the wrong side, and be absolutely certain the bottom of the iron is clean!

For a garment which simply cannot be washed, very sincerely ask the dry cleaner to place the item in a mesh bag, and to clean it only in *clean* solution. (Offer to wait until the solution is replaced, whenever that may be next.) If you want to be extra careful, and you have both the patience and the technique to do the pressing yourself, ask them to return the garment to you cleaned but not pressed.

This advice should see you through most of the routine cleaning needs of your collection. But of course one big reason for collecting vintage clothing and accessories is that they are *not* routine. So there are some special requirements for the care and cleaning of particular items which should be briefly mentioned.

First, lace. Not all old lace is handmade, by any means. But almost all of the handmade lace there is or ever will be *is* old. So you will want to take especially good care of any handmade lace which comes into your possession. Do not dry clean it. If you can find a professional who knows how to *wash* it, by all means take advantage of your good fortune. But most likely, you'll have to do it yourself.

First, remove it from the garment and trace its shape on a piece of paper. Wash it very gently (don't rub!); rinse in several changes of distilled water. Then smooth the lace onto the paper pattern you've been prudent enough to make beforehand and pin it to the paper— through the openings, needless to say, not the yarn. If you must press, use a thin presscloth over the lace while it's still damp. Stiffening can be achieved, if desired, by spraying fabric sizing on a damp presscloth.

If you come across white cotton or linen lace that is very discolored or has become brittle, it's worth a try to boil it in soapy water. And black lace can often be brightened by dipping it in a solution of three parts water and one part white vinegar; squeeze gently and rinse.

Like handmade lace, feathers are rarely seen these days on clothes or accessories, but they used to be an enormously popular trimming. After lightly brushing away any loose soil, try refreshing feathers with steam. Single plumes can be washed by dipping them in mild suds and rinsing. Dry feathers can be recurled by warming them (gently), and then drawing the feathers from the quill out, between the thumb and the blunt edge of a knife.

As for vintage furs and leather goods, the principles of caring for them are generally the same as for their modern-day counterparts. Use a good leather conditioner as soon as you acquire a vintage leather piece, and continue to use it at regular intervals. (Unlined smooth leather gloves, by the way, can be gently washed.) Furs should be professionally cleaned, glazed, and stored every year if possible—and since vintage furs are comparatively inexpensive, there may be enough money left over to take good care of them!

Now for the last collecting consideration: **What's to be done with them all?** A collection has to be somewhere, and vintage clothing can pose more problems of storage and display than, say, paperweights or shaving mugs. Textiles are very fragile, and they require special care if they are to survive, and remain beautiful, for a long time. As for display—you can't put clothing on shelves or tables, you can't readily hang them on the wall, and you can't practically keep them in file drawers.

So if you want to collect vintage clothing, and you haven't a museum-sized house, you will probably have to resign yourself to keeping most things under storage conditions, and rotating them among one or more display areas. Objects which can help with displaying include: mannequins and dressmakers' dummies (popular ways of displaying dresses); hat-racks and hall-trees (excellent for showing off hats and coats); shadow-box picture frames (which can hold blouses or jackets carefully pinned to a padded backing); antique or vintage store fixtures (such as glass-front display cases or revolving chrome racks); and armoires or wardrobes (which can be left open to show off the contents).

If you are so lucky as to have a spare walk-in closet, by all means turn it into a micro-sized museum gallery. If not, commandeer a corner of one room, or scatter groups of items through several parts of the house. A guest bedroom is an especially prime place for housing your collection, but almost any room can accommodate a few more wonderful things to look at. The only places it is not a good idea to display vintage clothes are in the kitchen (too much grease in the air and danger of spills) and in the bathroom (too much moisture in the air).

If you do incorporate your collection into living areas of the house, take care to preserve some continuity between the display and the rest of the room's decor by choosing things that harmonize in color and texture. Or, if the things to be displayed have a very different feel from the rest of the room's furnishings—say, Victorian clothes in a contemporary room—locate a few items at different places in the room, for a counterpoint effect.

Deciding *where* and *how* to display collectibles is just the first step, of course. Displayed items should be shaken, dusted, or brushed—as appropriate to the item—once every week or two, and then arranged differently, so that folds don't become set. Be sure that displayed items aren't exposed to strong sunlight, even for an hour or two a day. And change the display regularly (every two or three months is about right), both to allow for the best care of the items and to keep the display from becoming dulled by familiarity.

For things being kept in storage rather than on display, there is another entire set of concerns. The first cardinal rule of storing vintage clothing is *use no plastic.* Plastic—whether boxes or bags—can deteriorate and give off exudations dangerous to textiles. So when things come back from the dry-cleaners, remove those plastic film bags right away and discard them. The second cardinal rule—believe it or not—is *use no regular tissue paper.* The tissue used in department stores or sold in dime stores is acid-based and will be harmful to fabrics. *Acid-free* tissue paper is required.

Every collector of vintage clothing should also be a collector of two other things: stout boxes with lids and sturdy hangers. Don't use the flimsy, and often rough or rusty, wire coat hangers that accumulate from the dry-cleaners. When you buy hangers, spring for the thickly padded ones sold in specialty and closet shops, if you possibly can. If you possibly can't, though, try the discount stores for specials on molded plastic hangers; but be *sure* to inspect every hanger for jagged bits of plastic which might snag a delicate fabric (try a nail file for smoothing these away).

Which things hang and which things fold? Heavily beaded items and anything with the least bit of stretchiness should be folded; ditto anything with signs of weakness in the shoulder seams or fabric. Fold anything in which the skirt fabric is heavier than the fabric used in the shoulders. When you do hang a garment, be sure that the edges of the hanger don't extend past the shoulder seams and poke out the sleeve fabric.

Folded things should ideally be placed in roomy individual boxes, wrapped in layers of (acid-free!) tissue. Every two months or so, take them out, shake them, and refold them, to prevent lines from setting. This will also give you a chance to check for any evidence of moths, silverfish, or crickets—the three insect banes of textile collectors.

Wools should always be stored with moth protection (try the better-smelling herbal moth bags now widely available). Bear in mind that all insects, especially crickets, are attracted to the residue left by perspiration, so be sure clothes are clean prior to storage. (Silverfish, by the way, often hitchhike into your life via old books or other papers, so be careful not to store these near your vintage clothing.)

All in all, the guidelines for care and storage of vintage clothing are not extremely different from the good-sense rules most people observe for all clothing care. *But*—and this is an important "but"—extra attention, concern, knowledge, and effort are required. Vintage clothes are far more vulnerable than modern ones; a small mistake, or a little carelessness, can do a large amount of damage. And once damaged, these irreplaceable garments are gone forever.

So be careful. But don't allow worry, drudgery, or guilt to spoil the fun of collecting. The vintage clothing collector is not supposed to be a museum curator, just a person who loves beautiful things and has an affinity for the past. With that said, on to Part Two, and a survey of important background information for fashion collectors.

P A R T
T W O

A Collector's Guide to Fashion

If I were permitted to choose from the rubbish which will be published a hundred years after my death, do you know which I would take? . . . I would take simply a fashion magazine in order to see how women will dress themselves a century after my death. And their fantasies would tell me more about future humanity than all the philosophers, the novelists, the preachers, or the scientists.

ANATOLE FRANCE

An Overview of the Vintage Century

One of the important pleasures of collecting is recognizing and appreciating the distinctive qualities of vintage clothing. In order to enjoy that pleasure to the fullest, it's very helpful to understand just how the fashions of the last century fit into the whole epic story of how human beings have covered and decorated themselves.

Besides that, a general knowledge of fashion history helps a great deal in understanding the special characteristics that make garments of interest to the collector. This is particularly important if you intend to be even moderately serious about collecting; the more knowledge you have, the more successful you will be, both aesthetically and profitably.

If you want to learn more about the historical backgrounds of vintage clothing, Part Four of this book contains "A Quick Tour of Fashion History" which will take you through some highlights in the evolution of fashion from prehistoric times to the eighteenth century; there are also a number of fine books on fashion history listed in the bibliography. Meanwhile, here's an overview of the major periods for clothing collectibles:

In the 1870s, women's fashions were in a state of transition, for the hoop—which had been the centerpiece of high Victorian fashion—was giving way to the bustle. Throughout the decade, skirts were sometimes full, sometimes narrow, longer one year, shorter the next, but the overall trend was toward a silhouette that was flat and narrow in the front, projecting out behind in elaborately decorated swathes of material. This tied-back style remained the principal line until the end of the 1880s.

The "train" came and went during this period, and when it was in fashion, it trailed the ladies even along the dusty streets of America's still-developing frontier towns, prompting one Texas editorial writer to make this observation: "It is hardly worthwhile to tell our fair friends that men do not admire the revival of long skirts and the hitching gestures which they entail upon women. Nature has given but one animal a train and that is a peacock. The bird is not compelled to kick its appendage into shape behind and therefore wears it gracefully."

More serious efforts were already being made to reform women's dress, having begun in mid-century America with Mrs. Amelia Bloomer's infamous split skirts (which looked rather like harem pants). By the 1890s, uncorseted clothes were worn by "aesthetic dressers" in England, and throughout Europe the rational woolen clothing promoted by Germany's Dr. Jaeger had a modest following. Many ladies of the American West had already adopted their own practical styles of clothing for frontier life.

For most women, however, extreme and uncomfortable fashions remained the norm as the nineteenth century closed, with laced-in waists and enormous sleeves (each one sometimes requiring two yards of material) creating the hourglass figure.

In America, progress and prosperity marked the last decades of the nineteenth century, and as always when times are good, fashions were extravagant. The wealthy now began to patronize the first generation of Parisian couture salons (most notably, the influential House of Worth), where they purchased the latest fashions. And very quickly, the same styles, done up in less expensive materials, could be worn by the middle and even lower classes; patterns were published in the *Delineator* and elsewhere, to be made up on the by-then widely used home sewing machine. Mail-order catalogs also strove to offer the newest looks, bringing fashionable, affordable clothes to even the remotest parts of the country.

So fashion became more democratic, but not more comfortable. For five hundred years, women's figures had been squeezed, pinched, and puffed into all sorts of shapes, concealed under layers and layers of hot, heavy clothing, and generally treated in every unnatural way that could be devised. Since all this was done in the name of "fashion" or "propriety," most women (men had always got themselves into more comfortable outfits!) believed they had no other choice than to dress in this miserable way.

The beginning of the twentieth century, with its curious "S-bend" silhouette, was no exception. The bosom was puffed out in one unbroken, drooping line from high neck to cinched-in waist, and the behind was emphasized, resulting in a sway-backed look. Though the Victorian period had ended with the turn of the century, the Edwardian era was almost as fussy in its decorative style, and for the most part, women's garments were covered with frills and furbelows.

A trend toward tailored styles that had begun in the Gay Nineties was also continuing to gather strength, however. The American Gibson Girl, with her crisp shirtwaist and sensible skirt, became the prototype of the New Woman—who rode a bicycle, played tennis, perhaps even went to work (although she still did these things garbed in yards of heavy material).

Then, about 1908, a new fashion concept arrived, courtesy mainly of couturier Paul Poiret. When Poiret threw away the corset, very quickly other designers, along with women by the droves, did just the same, creating a new natural silhouette that generally followed the normal lines of a woman's body. To prevent fashion from becoming dull, however, Poiret introduced two popular new curiosities: tunics (including wired "lampshade" versions) and hobble skirts, so narrow at the hem that women had difficulty walking in them unless kick pleats and discreet slits were added. Exotic details and Oriental decorations also contributed to the fashion revolution that opened the teens.

This novel look was part of a whole burgeoning of energy and experimentation in the new century. The age of technology had begun to dawn, and people could see a near future of talking on the telephone, riding in automobiles, and even flying. Freud had revealed the existence of the unconscious, Picasso was painting in the shocking Cubist style, and Isadora Duncan was dancing barefooted. So it was not surprising that something radical should arise on the fashion front.

In world politics, however, the same old conflicts were wearing on, and in 1914, the "war to end war" began. Although the effect of World War I in America was not immediate or direct, the changes in European fashion quickly began to influence dress in this country. Wartime scarcity dictated shorter, trimmer, and less ostentatious clothing; and the new roles taken by women while the men were away at war created a demand for more comfortable, practical dress.

When the war ended, the world was in a state of shock over the grim carnage which had decimated a whole young generation of European men, including some of the most talented. Although there was a brief reappearance of the high-waisted, long-skirted pre-war silhouette, there was to be no return to the period of creative energy that had been interrupted by the war. The twenties would become, instead, a time of cynicism, when people were determined to "live it up" in a spree of free-spending and free-living.

The most obvious—and scandalous—fashion change was in the length of skirts. Hemlines rose, and by mid-decade, knees were bare, hair was bobbed, and the flapper was smoking in public. The Jazz Age-look was more than a style; it was a statement, one which (purposefully and successfully) nettled the older generation. It said plainly that women were no longer content to be prisoners of their clothes; with the advent of the flapper regime, underpinnings were reduced to a minimum, and the figure, rather than being shaped, disappeared entirely under the popular, unfitted chemise dress.

There was a heady sense of freedom about the new clothes, but there was also a feeling of something lost. In the past, lamented London hostess Mrs. Claude Beddington, "a woman's greatest charm was her unattainability. Whoever enjoyed hitting a low-flying pheasant?" Many other women must also have wanted a little of feminine mystery back, for by the end of the twenties, clothes were once again beginning to hug the figure and cover the calf, bringing in a new decade which was to see the height of sexiness in long, lean, fluid, and elegant clothes.

Fashion in the thirties was inspired by the same fascination with streamlined, speed-loving progress that brought us skyscrapers and sleekly futuristic cars. The clean, geometric lines of Art Deco were everywhere, including the couturier's salon, and in spite of the Depression, the high fashion industry thrived. New drama was added by assertive, imaginative designers like Schiaparelli and Rochas, while Chanel, Vionnet, and other brilliant couturiers continued to exercise a powerful influence not only over the wealthy women who wore their original gowns, but over the millions of women who saw and copied the latest styles from fashion magazines and movies.

Again, war. The German occupation isolated Paris, and rationing in England and America restricted the amount of fabric which could be in a dress or suit, the number of trimmings, and even the types of fasteners. (Sequins were one of the few unrationed decorations, and so became a frequent feature of forties clothes.) Five years of violence overshadowed fashion, as it had two decades before, but this time, when the war was over, there was no desire for a revolution in style. People wanted to forget the bomb and turn backward, to a more innocent and peaceful time—which is exactly what Dior's postwar "New Look," with its romantically full skirts, nipped waists, and picture hats, enabled them to do.

In the fifties, the exaggeration of the New Look subsided into a more controlled approach to style, and the couture had its last great fling. This was the age of Balenciaga and Givenchy, Balmain and Dior. But the architectural, even sculptural, looks created by these great designers depended almost completely on perfect cut and construction. When the same styles filtered down into mass production ready-to-wear, the result was often dull and even dowdy.

So the rich looked ever more spectacular in the fifties and early sixties, while the middle classes became increasingly locked into styles which amounted almost to uniforms: sweater sets and circular skirts for the teenagers, Ivy League coordinates for the college crowd, house-dresses and carcoats for young suburban matrons, safe little suits with white gloves for going into town. As for the poor, mass production allowed them to wear very cheap versions of these same clothes; social critic Michael Harrington observed, "It almost seems as if the affluent society has given out costumes to the poor so they would not offend the rest of society with the sight of rags."

Little wonder that one point of attack in the youth rebellion of the sixties was fashion. A new generation of designers brought out fashions that broke the old conformist molds; mini-skirts and go-go boots, pantsuits and hiphuggers became the "hot" fashion items on Paris runways. Many young people, however, rejected the whole idea of couture-inspired fashion, buying their clothes in flea markets and concocting vaguely tribal costumes that made much use of blue denim, bits of leather, and copious strings of beads.

The result of all this was an unprecedented fashion anarchy that permanently changed—both for better and for worse—the way clothes are made, sold, and worn. A great age of fashion was over, while a new era of individual creativity in dress was beginning. Ironically, perhaps, among the other consequences of the sixties, the seeds were sown for this book. In the sixties, clothes were suddenly revealed as expressions of the ways people think of themselves and their lives, and since then, old garments have been seen as more than merely relics of an outworn style. Now, clothes of the past are recognized as valuable social and aesthetic statements, worth preserving.

The Great Designers

Leading the way as fashion evolved between 1880 and 1969 was a form of creative expression called "haute couture" in France, "alta moda" in Italy, and in America and England, "high" fashion—or simply, "the couture."

The couture was a way of life. For the fashion-minded woman, it meant sitting in tasteful salons, as mannequins paraded the latest styles; it meant having whole wardrobes custom-designed and perfectly fitted; it meant having the serene assurance of the "right" look, or the provocative thrill of discovering the "latest" designer.

For designers, the couture was an exciting art form, with almost endless possibilities. While even the most talented painters and sculptors struggled in poverty, creative couturiers could readily achieve a substantial income, along with significant social status. Their monied clients were prepared to pay for the finest workmanship and the most exquisite materials, which meant that the great designers had virtually carte blanche in developing their ideas.

There will probably always be a strong debate as to whether clothing design can truly be classified as a fine art. But even the most stubborn opponents of this idea will have to admit that there are certain garments—the quintessential Chanel suit, for example, or a Charles James ballgown—which must be described as masterpieces. In line, color, and texture, they are perfect in their expression of the relationship between creative imagination and human form.

There was, of course, another side to the couture, and that was the business of making rich women happy and socially secure. Certainly *that* aspect, with all the money and prestige it produced, was just as important to most couturiers as the aesthetic side. But in looking back at the age of the great designers, we see that their ideas did far more than merely amuse the rich; the couture penetrated (over a period of time) almost every level of society.

Women everywhere—in small towns, on farms, on military posts—looked forward eagerly to receiving the latest issue of *Godey's* or *Harper's,* with the fashion news from Paris. Before ready-to-wear, women copied the new styles at home, or had them made by seamstresses. And by the twenties, a great many women could dress in ready-made clothing inspired by Paris designs. Certainly the construction was not as fine, nor the fabrics and trimmings as luxurious; but the pleasure of wearing something *à la mode* (in the current fashion) was attainable, all the same.

The fashion ideas created by the great designers trickled down into the mainstream of society fairly rapidly and quite pervasively. And for this reason, it's very worthwhile to study the couture. By understanding the principles of fashion which were developed in the salons of Paris (and later London, New York, California, Italy), every collector can gain a much greater skill in identifying clothing styles and periods.

It's also possible that as a collector, you will occasionally discover designer garments. The output of some of the great couture houses was quite large, and though most of the surviving examples of elaborate, custom-made originals have long since been donated to museums and fashion collections, some lesser items remain out there somewhere, waiting to be found. The couture was not limited to the production of one-of-a-kind ballgowns. In the early days, houses like Worth, Doucet, and Paquin created everything from nightgowns and simple shirtwaists to wedding gowns, mourning clothes, parasols, and hats. As the century progressed, couturiers established *prêt-à-porter* (ready-to-wear) lines which offered designer style and quality in more accessibly priced garments.

But in order to recognize such a treasure if you should come across one, it's important to be familiar with the major designers and their labels. The following guide gives basic information about most of the well-known designers who influenced the period from 1880 to 1969. Included in each listing is the active period of the designer, the name(s) of the house(s) he or she designed for, and a brief explanation of the designer's importance to fashion history. Also included are remarks on special items which might be of particular interest to the collector.

The dates given begin with the year the designer's name first appeared on a label—even if it was someone else's label (for example, "Norman Norell for Teal Traina"). The closing date is the date of retirement or death. In many instances, the house label continued under the direction of other designers after the death or retirement of the original designer, but as a rule, the most valuable collector's items are those produced during the active period of the principal designer.

Along with the names of fashion houses, the listings also give addresses by dates. (All French addresses are in Paris and all American addresses are in New York, unless otherwise stated; other addresses are identified as to location.) Because labels and boxes sometimes bore the address of the salon, this information could aid in dating a garment. If you do find a designer treasure, be sure to inquire after the box or any other items, such as receipts, sketches, etc., which might have been connected with it. Designer "packaging" was often wonderful enough to be kept; Fortuny's exquisite tea gowns, for example, were twisted like skeins of yarn, nestled in Fortuny-watermarked tissue, and packed into cream-colored boxes tied with black ribbons.

A designer label does not, of course, mean that a particular garment is a couture "one-off" (that is, unique, custom-made original). Particularly with the post-war designers, it's important to keep in mind that the appearance of a designer's name on a garment or product may not have much real meaning. After World War II, the couture became far less important (and profitable) than it had been, and it was necessary for most of the design houses to broaden their marketing bases. Many designers took to "licensing" their products—and eventually their names—to manufacturers who wanted to use the designer mystique to promote their mass-manufactured goods.

Today, designer names like Pierre Cardin, Oscar de la Renta, and Yves Saint Laurent appear on everything from sheets to luggage, and many designers lend their names to relatively inexpensive off-the-rack clothing lines. The collector should not confuse these popular items with those from the couture production of the same designers. Couture quality is recognizable in the use of superior fabrics and fine methods of construction. (The label itself may give a clue, since the label in a fine garment is usually tacked on separately, rather than sewn into a seam; labels are by no means always present in designer garments, however, so the absence of a label is inconclusive, particularly in early items.)

The great designers are not all great for the same reason. There are several different aspects of high-fashion creativity; cut, coloring, detail, and innovation are the most important—and only a few couturiers (Vionnet? Dior?) were masters of all these, while most excelled in one or two areas. Charles James will always be remembered chiefly for his sublime cutting, Schiaparelli for her daring innovations, Jeanne Lanvin for her superb way with color and detail. So the following entries try to specify a designer's greatest strengths and most significant contributions to the couture.

Designer clothing is an exciting area of collecting, and these items are more than worth hunting for. But even if you never find a real couture garment, getting to know the work of the great designers is an excellent—and thoroughly enjoyable—investment of time. There are some beautiful, informative books on the subject listed in Part Four.

Adrian
Period: 1941–52
House/labels: Adrian, Ltd., Beverly Hills

Adrian is the designer who brought together Hollywood and haute couture. Throughout the 1930s, he created many of the most memorably fashionable wardrobes in film. In the 1940s, he moved away from the movies and opened his own salon, but his designs continued to influence the movies, and vice versa. The Adrian suit (long jacket with little or no collar/lapel, single button or tie closure at waist, wide shoulders, and long, fitted sleeves, worn with a narrow skirt) became a fashion standard. Adrian also created theme collections, including one of "Greek" dresses (columnar white dresses with Greek key designs), and another of "Americana" dresses (gingham, patchwork, Pennsylvania Dutch motifs used as decoration).

Augustabernard
Period: 1919–35
House/labels: Augustabernard, rue Rivoli; after 1928, 3, rue du Faubourg St-Honoré

Augustabernard is best remembered for her skillful treatment of the long, very slim, bias-cut dresses we associate with the early 1930s. Her dresses, whether for evening or day, were perfectly poised; the fabric itself, in the form of scallops, loops, belts, scarves, and so forth, created the essence of the dress, and these self-details were used in lieu of the elaborate embroideries or printed fabrics popular with other designers. The result was a distinctive Augustabernard look which earned her many patrons, especially from South America. Ironically, it was mainly the monetary crisis in South America which ruined her business in the mid-1930s, in spite of the great admiration for her designs.

Balenciaga
Period: 1937–68
House/labels: Balenciaga, Avenue Georges V

This uncompromising Spanish designer actually began his career in Spain, in the 1920s, designing under the name "Eisa," before opening his Paris house in the late 1930s. His work is known for its pure, sculptural lines, precise details, and strong colors. Balenciaga introduced the stand-away collar, the three-quarter sleeve, and the sack dress. His designs—especially his evening dresses and suits—were considered to epitomize the elegance of haute couture; in fact, it was Balenciaga who heralded the end of the high-fashion era, when he closed his house in disgust during the Paris protests of 1968.

Pierre Balmain
Period: 1945–82
House/labels: Balmain, rue François Premier

Balmain brought a special kind of glamorous femininity to the generally rather architectural lines of the high-fashion 1950s. There was also just a touch of the offbeat (which perhaps accounts for the surprising fact that radical poet Gertrude Stein was a loyal supporter of Balmain, and even wrote about his first collection in an article for *Vogue*). Among the most characteristic of his designs were dresses and suits with unusual skirt treatments and/or fur trimming; he was also noted for elaborately embroidered evening dresses.

Boué Soeurs (Sylvie Boué Montegut and the Baronne D'Etreillis—nee Boué)
Period: 1899–1931
House/labels: Boué Soeurs, 9, rue de la Paix (also New York branch after 1916)

A much-loved Paris design house (with an even more popular American branch), especially noted for beautiful lingerie, lingerie dresses, and robes de style; the signature of the Boué sisters' romantic garments was the use of folded silk-ribbon rosettes to trim designs which featured delicate colors, sheer fabrics, and the frequent use of gold and silver in many forms, including cloths, laces, and embroideries. Among the many types of lace they used was their own floral-patterned *filet Boué*. Although Boué Soeurs was never considered among the top couture houses, the designs were so distinctive and so delightful that they may be considered especially collectible.

Callot Soeurs (Marie Callot Gerber, Marthe Callot Bertrand, Regine Callot Chantrelle)

Period: 1895–1937

House/labels: Callot Soeurs, 24 rue Taitbout; after 1914, 9-11 Avenue Matignon; from the 1920s, branches in Nice, Biarritz, Buenos Aires, London

The Callot sisters created fashions widely noted for their unusual character and exotic beauty. Their early dresses were designed in the style of Louis XV, and they continued to develop this theme into the 1920s, in the form of robes de style. Equally famous were their Orient-inspired creations, which began in the early teens with "robes pheni-ciennes," evening dresses with oriental motifs, colors, details, etc. Their use of unusual fabrics and combinations—stamped leathers, wool trimmed with organdy—as well as their flair for inventive coloring and detail, found an eager audience and influenced many young designers.

Roberto Capucci

Period: 1950–

House/labels: Capucci, Rome; 1960–66, Rue Cambon; 1966–present, Via Gregoriano

This Italian designer has the same architectonic approach that characterized Balenciaga, but his clothes are more daring in color and cut. He sees the form of the dress as independent of the shape of the body—so his designs often go off in inventive directions! Capuccis are relatively few and far between, since he prefers not to duplicate his creations, but each one is a work of art.

Pierre Cardin

Period: 1950–

House/labels: Cardin, rue Richepanse; Eve boutique, 118 rue du Faubourg St-Honoré from 1954; Adam boutique from 1957

Cardin has involved himself with so many enterprises that his place as a couturier has been somewhat overshadowed. However, he has an excellent fashion background; he trained with Paquin and Schiaparelli, among others, and has made real contributions to the couture. In the 1950s, he brought a simplified, forward-looking style to conventional clothes. And his very avant-garde designs of the 1960s—vinyl dresses, ribbed body-suits, space-age tunics—are widely regarded as some of the most significant statements of the period.

Bonnie Cashin

Period: 1949–

House/labels: Bonnie Cashin Limited (from 1953); the Knittery (from 1972)

Bonnie Cashin's clothes are noted for their functional, comfortable purity. They have an organic quality—nothing out of place, everything logically and gracefully interconnected. Many sportswear styles we take for granted today (easy-fitting jersey dresses, soft leather and suede garments, the layered look) were pioneered by Cashin, who designed for quite a few Hollywood movies before beginning her own fashion line.

Chanel

Period: 1912–71

House/labels: Chanel, 21 rue Cambon; branches opened in Deauville (1913), Biarritz (1916); house closed from 1939–54

Coco Chanel is probably the best known of all couturieres—in part because of her enormous impact on twentieth-century fashion, and in part due to her colorful personal life. Looking back on the way Chanel took the fashion world by storm, Paul Poiret remarked, "We should have been on guard against this miss with the head of a young boy." Chanel created two enduring fashion concepts: the Chanel suit (boxy cardigan jacket, straight skirt with walking pleats; braid and buttons used extensively), and the "little black dress" (a dressy fabric done in a simple, tailored style which could be dressed up or down). She also introduced the idea of "costume" jewelry, which she advocated wearing in large quantities with her fashions to create the total "Chanel look."

André Courrèges

Period: 1961–

House/labels: Courrèges, 48 Avenue Kleber; from 1965, 40 rue François Premier; labels: Prototypes (couture), Couture Future (deluxe ready-to-wear), Hyperbole (inexpensive ready-to-wear)

Although his stardom was brief, Courèges created such a sensation with his bold, original designs in the mid-1960s that he is still regarded as the quintessential designer of that period. His clothes were vivid, geometric, and pared down to bare minimums. It was Courèges who defined the mini-skirt, the pant-suit, and the hip-hugger—as well as popularizing his trademark, white "go-go" boots.

Oscar de la Renta

Period: 1963–

House/labels: "Oscar de la Renta for Elizabeth Arden" (1963–65); "for Jane Derby" (1965–67); Oscar de la Renta

Opulence is the key word for de la Renta's designs. His famous late-1960s collections had a completely different feel from those of most other designers, featuring renditions of counterculture clothing fads (such as hot pants, bandanna prints, and hippie-style costumes), done with luxurious fabrics and trims; elaborate caftans; and—most famous of all—his dramatic, romanticized Russian- and gypsy-inspired "peasant-look" creations.

Jean Dessès

Period: 1937–63

House/labels: Jean Dessès, Avenue Georges V; 17 Avenue Matignon (from 1948); No. 12 Rond-Point-des-Champs-Elysées (from 1958); Diffusions ready-to-wear line (from 1955)

Dessès produced softly feminine clothes in numerous fabrics and styles, but he was especially well known for his use of chiffon; this fabric—often ombré—he twisted, plaited, and draped directly on a dummy to produce intricate evening gowns.

Christian Dior

Period: 1947–57

House/labels: Dior, 30 Avenue Montaigne

Dior's originality is shown not so much in the introduction of specific garments as in the creation of a total "look." He introduced two new collections every year, each with its own distinctive silhouette and its particular type of accessorization. The most famous of these lines were the 1947 "Corolle"—called the "New Look" (cinched waists, full, ballerina-length skirts)—and the 1955 "A-Line" (narrow shoulders and wide hems creating a triangular shape). However, some of his other collections—such as the 1948 "Envol" which added asymmetry to the New Look, and the 1955 "Y-Line" which turned the "A-Line" upside down—were even more inventive.

Jacques Doucet
Period: 1871–1929
House/labels: Doucet, 21 rue de la Paix

Jacques Doucet was the first to merge the role of couturier with that of connoisseur; he became renowned not only for his elegant fashion creations, but for his art collection, which was composed of the most avant-garde paintings—including Picasso's revolutionary *Demoiselles d'Avignon,* which Doucet bought and housed in a specially designed wing of his house. Perhaps ironically, Doucet's clothing aesthetic was just the opposite of his taste as a collector. Doucet's designs were delicate, romantic, and opulent, making use of exotic, and expensive, materials—from Alençon lace to chinchilla and paper-thin chamois. His approach to fashion remained very conservative, and his popularity declined after the Poiret revolution, but from about 1880 to 1910 Doucet was, after Charles Frederick Worth, the most influential couturier in the world. Doucet popularized the tailored suit for women, and introduced the "fur-side-out" coat.

Jacques Fath
Period: 1937–54
House/labels: Jacques Fath, 32 rue de la Boëtie; rue François Premier (from 1940); Avenue Pierre Premier de Serbie (from 1944)

Fath's designs were distinguished by being showy and yet thoroughly elegant; he was noted for skintight dresses and plunging V-necklines that were the epitome of sophistication, never becoming vulgar. (The fact that Rita Hayworth was a devoted client of Fath's says a good deal about this style.) His clothes emphasized the figure in a flattering way, and he made frequent use of diagonal lines, angled pockets and collars, and huge buttons. Unfortunately, Fath died of leukemia at the height of his career.

Mariano Fortuny
Period: 1906–49
House/labels: Mariano Fortuny, Venice; shops in Paris and London

Fortuny's clothing is almost legendary today because of the mysterious pleating process which achieved the unique look of his designs. Fortuny's method of pleating natural materials has never been satisfactorily duplicated, but some processes for man-made fabrics have come close (particularly the fabric called "marii" used by Mary McFadden). Fortuny specialties included the Knossos scarf, a long sheer silk rectangle; the Delphos gown, a columnar pleated dress; and the Peplos gown, which added a hip-length tunic to the Delphos. Though most of his clothes were constructed in one of a few simple designs, every garment was distinctive because of the beautiful fabrics used, and the distinctive trimmings, which frequently included beads of Venetian glass or terra cotta. In addition to the pleated fabrics, Fortuny also created stenciled fabrics, especially silk velvet.

James Galanos

Period: 1951–

House/labels: Galanos, California

Galanos is today still among the most successful designers; his clothes—especially his evening gowns—fill the wardrobes of very wealthy women. Since his debut in the early 1950s, he has maintained the same extremely high standards of cut and construction, which has put him in the top rank of American designers. His clothes are generally lean and controlled, with the focus on perfect fit, often achieved through bias-cutting, luxurious fabric, and arresting detail.

Gallenga

Period: 1914–?

House/labels: Incorporated signature into fabric designs; during the 1920s, sometimes used printed labels

Maria Monaci Gallenga was an artist, and not really a part of the couture establishment, but her creations were so beautiful and unusual that they command a place in the history of fashion. Her specialty was gold patterns stenciled on black silk and velvet in an unusual technique which made the pattern seem to "float." These fabrics were often used in the creation of the most distinctive Gallenga garment, a medieval-style tabard tea gown (two rectangular panels, the back one long enough to form a train).

Givenchy

Period: 1952–

House/labels: Givenchy, Avenue Alfred de Vigny; 3 Avenue
Georges V (after 1957)

Hubert de Givenchy's name is almost synonymous with haute couture. A close associate of Balenciaga, Givenchy shared the latter's
insistence on purity of line, but added his own note of gaiety. His first
great success was the widely copied Bettina blouse (white cotton with
bishop sleeves ruffled with black and white broderie anglaise), and
probably his most famous association is with the chemise (sack)
dress—straight with a slightly bloused back. Givenchy's clothes are
perfectly ladylike, but with a youthful excitement that exactly fitted his
two most famous models—Jacqueline Kennedy and Audrey Hepburn.

Grès (Alix Barton)

Period: 1934–

House/labels: Alix, 83 rue de Faubourg St-Honoré; Grès, 1 rue de
la Paix (from 1942); the Alix label continued under another
ownership

A designer who has steadfastly followed her own sense of style, Grès
is known especially for her draped, sculptural dresses of silk jersey;
these famous gowns are perfectly fluid, suggesting a Greek inspiration.
She has also created other distinctive looks, using paper-thin taffeta in
a variety of designs, leather and soft wools for hooded and caped day
dresses. Most of her clothes are monochromatic.

Jacques Griffe

Period: 1942–mid-1960s

House/labels: Jacques Griffe, rue Gaillon; 29 rue du Faubourg
St-Honoré (from 1946); 5 rue Royale (from 1950); boutique line
Jacques Griffe Evolution

Griffe was known as a master of cutting, and all of his designs are
marked by this skill in one way or another. He was best known for
evening gowns with simple bodices and elaborate skirts featuring giant
bows, shirring, bias-cut spirals, etc.; boxy, unfitted suits, among the
first introduced in the 1950s; flowing, bloused or draped dresses.
Griffe's work was influenced, and later supported, by Vionnet.

Norman Hartnell

Period: 1924–79

House/labels: Norman Hartnell, Ltd., 26 Bruton St., London; briefly in the late 1920s, a Paris branch, rue de Ponthieu; ready-to-wear line (from 1963)

Best known as a favorite designer of the British royal family, Hartnell is usually associated with conservative, ceremonial evening dresses, generally with simple lines, much beading. In fact, however, his whole career evolved from his interest in theatrical costuming, and most of his creations—from early robes de styles to the Queen's coronation dress—were more costume than fashion. For this reason, he was most successful with wedding dresses and other special occasion gowns, though his couture suits and coats were well respected. His clothes are remarkably unstuffy, all things considered—perhaps owing to his own admission of being "more than partial to the jolly glitter of sequins."

Jacques Heim

Period: 1923–67

House/labels: designed for Heim (his parents' house), 48 rue Lafitte; Avenue Matignon (#50 after 1934, #15 from the 1950s); Heim Jeunes Filles (wedding dresses); ready-to-wear line Heim Actualité

Heim began his career working in the fashionable fur salon of his parents, and he soon produced interesting geometrically pieced suits and coats, often incorporating fur. But this Cubist-inspired approach was only the first of his innovations, which influenced the entire fashion industry. He introduced the sarong-style bathing suit in the 1930s, and in the process legitimized cotton as a couture fabric, as well as establishing the second area of fashion emphasis at Heim—bathing suits and beachwear. Indeed, it was Heim who, in 1950, introduced the daringly bare two-piece suit that was to become the bikini. In 1937, Heim began the first line of fashionable clothing for teenagers, and the house became well known for its presentation dresses and wedding dresses.

Charles James

Period: 1924–58

House/labels: Boucheron (millinery); from the 1930s, designed clothes under different versions of his own name in various locations (first New York, then London, occasionally Paris, finally New York again—and permanently—from about 1940)

When asked what fashion meant to him, Charles James replied, "what is rare, correctly proportioned, and though utterly discreet, libidinous." He was absolutely rigorous in his pursuit of design perfection, which he achieved through masterful cut and construction, sometimes working for years on the details of a design. James' output is so small, compared to that of other couturiers, and so rarefied that anything he made is of great value. His best-known designs were architectural/sculptural evening gowns made from many yards of perfectly cut and draped satin. Other James trademarks were the juxtaposition of contrasting fabrics, such as velvet with starched cotton, and the use of asymmetry and abstraction in his designs.

Jeanne Lanvin

Period: 1890–1946

House/labels: Lanvin, 22 rue du Faubourg St-Honoré; first millinery, then (by 1900) ladies' and children's clothing; opened Lanvin Tailleur for men in 1926; in 1929, fur salon, Rond-Point-des-Champs-Elysées

Lanvin first created for her own daughter clothes which were (in contrast to prevailing children's styles) young in spirit—fresh, innocent, and playful, yet still refined. Soon she was approached to dress her daughter's friends, then their mothers, and in the end, her beloved fashion house offered distinctive, high-quality garments for every member of the family (hers was the first house to open a men's boutique) and for every occasion. The hallmark of her designs was always the creation of a youthful feeling that could be carried with a woman through all of life. Lanvin's designs reflected inspirations drawn from her art collection, which included the works of Redon and Renoir, and from medieval images; her famous "Lanvin blue," for example, captured the blue of stained glass. She followed her own path, no matter what the prevailing mode, and her specialty robes de style remained popular through the 1920s and even the 1930s. Lanvin trademarks include the use of appliqués and embroideries; she rarely used printed fabrics.

Louiseboulanger

Period: 1923–39

House/labels: Louiseboulanger, 3 rue de Berri; 6 rue Royale (from 1934)

Marlene Dietrich was one of the cool, adventurous women who found Louiseboulanger's thoroughly modern fashions well suited to their tastes. Louiseboulanger, who, like Augustabernard, elided her two names into one streamlined statement, was known especially for her excellent sense of color and fabric; she made much use of printed fabrics rather than embroidery or appliqué to achieve pattern, and she employed such interesting and innovative fabrics as moirés and organdies, flowered taffeta, and painted chiffon. She also, however, introduced two influential cuts, the "pouf" evening dress (closely fitted around the torso, bouffant fullness at the back of the hips), and the uneven hemline (knee-length in front, longer at the back or sides).

Lucile (Lady Duff Gordon)

Period: 1894–1930

House/labels: Maison Lucile, Old Burlington St., London; 14 Georges St. (1898–1900); 23 Hanover Square (1900–18); Lucile, Ltd., 1903; New York branch (1910, W. 36th St.; from 1913, W. 57th St.), Paris (1913), Chicago (1913–18)

"Hesitate No Longer" and "His Lullaby" were the kinds of names given by Lucile (later Lady Duff Gordon) to her dramatic, seductive, and utterly luxurious fashions. First, last, and always theatrical, Lucile began her fashion business in the midst of the Mauve Decade and continued with headlong success through the teens, creating clothes that were very much an expression of their time. Though she designed everything the rich and fashion-indulgent might desire, her specialty was elaborate tea gowns, generously garnished with silk roses. Lucile was noted for her stage designs (including the immensely influential *Merry Widow* costume), and her clothes were worn by Irene Castle in her dance shows and featured by Florenz Ziegfeld in his revue.

Mainbocher

Period: 1930–71

House/labels: Mainbocher, 12 Avenue Georges V.; 6 E. 57th St. (after 1940); 609 Fifth Ave. (after 1960)

Sally Kirkland, the former *Life* fashion editor, said of Mainbocher that "he not only made a woman look like a lady, but as if her mother had been a lady too." His designs are distinguished by their elegant simplicity. He introduced the strapless evening gown, and pioneered the use of unusual fabrics—such as checked gingham—for evening dresses. Among the most typical Mainbocher garments are dressmaker suits, often worn with Peter Pan-collared blouses, and beaded evening sweaters.

Vera Maxwell

Period: 1947–85

House/labels: Vera Maxwell Originals (no production from 1964–70)

Another of the pioneering women designers who created the American ready-to-wear look, Vera Maxwell contributed whatever Bonnie Cashin and Claire McCardell didn't. Her clothes were always practical above all, but with a sporty flair and distinctive personality. She is known for suits and ensembles, often in a streamlined version of the Chanel look, employing a lining for coat or jacket which matches the dress or blouse beneath. Her wartime suits—with no lapels, self-buttons, and channel seaming—were models of fashionable austerity, and throughout her design career she showed a marvelous ability to use strong fabrics—tweeds, loden cloth, flannels—and yet achieve an easy, graceful silhouette.

Claire McCardell

Period: mid-1940s–1958

House/labels: Claire McCardell for Townley

Much of what is today taken for granted in American sportswear was initiated by Claire McCardell (and much of the rest by Bonnie Cashin!). Her special insight was that mass-produced clothing could and should be well designed; she brought to "ordinary" clothes—like housedresses and simple separates—the same conscientious use of fabric, cut, and detail that marked the great couturiers; as a result, she is revered for having developed the first truly American style. Among her best-known creations are the "monastic" dress, a flowing robe-like design that the wearer shaped to her own waistline with a sash or belt, introduced in 1938, and the 1942 "popover"—a wraparound casual dress which has been worn ever since.

Edward Molyneux

Period: 1919–74

House/labels: Molyneux, 14 rue Royale; 5 rue Royale (1921–50); branches Monte Carlo (1925), Cannes (1927), London (1932); house inoperative during World War II; returned from retirement in 1965 with Studio Molyneux prêt-à-porter

Noel Coward's sleek, astringent feminine characters might have been models for the perfect Molyneux woman. Indeed, Molyneux designed the costumes worn by Gertrude Lawrence in the smash 1930 production of *Private Lives.* And as a mark of his diversity, three years later he created the costumes for a French production of *The Barretts of Wimpole Street.* Molyneux was a genuine Renaissance man—British war hero, art collector (Cezanne, Van Gogh, Degas, and more), nightclub owner (in partnership with Elsa Maxwell!), and designer of clothing which achieved sophistication through simplicity. His streamlined, backless, white satin evening dress became a symbol of the 1930s, and his soft tailored suits, often with pleated skirts, were the mainstay of many fashionable wardrobes. The mark of Molyneux's fashions was that they were neither outrageous nor dull, but simply "right," no matter what the occasion, and therefore adored by women who wanted to wear their clothes, and not the other way around.

Norman Norell

Period: 1940–72

House/labels: Norman Norell for Traina, 1940–60; Norman Norell

The New Yorker equated Norell's influence with that of Balenciaga, and it is certain that Norell is widely regarded today as the patron saint of American fashion design. Yet it's very hard to describe what made his clothes so singular. He used a very limited repertoire of basic shapes and details, but he somehow achieved great variety with them; he was noted for his prescience, introducing many innovations the year before they appeared in Paris. A good deal of his production was based on two themes: first, mixing day and night—with sportswear styles (trench coat, turtleneck, trousers) done in luxury evening fabrics, or sporty fabrics such as wool or tweed made up for evening, with sequins, organdy trim, etc.; and second, his signature masterwork, the "mermaid" sheaths, skintight neck-to-toe swathes of sparkling paillettes.

Paquin

Period: 1891–1920

House/labels: Paquin, 3 rue de la Paix; branch Paquin London, 39 Dover St. (1898); all other branches were opened in the 1920s, after Madame Paquin's retirement

Although the house of Paquin remained open until 1956, its great period was during the reign of its founder, Madame Paquin, who retired in 1920. Arguably the first woman who could truly be called a major couturiere, she brought to fashion design her own feminine experience, and designed clothing which women could wear with comfort and pleasure. She created wonderful exotica (for example, a lace headdress shaped like butterfly wings, with birds-of-paradise for antennae) which competed favorably with the fantasy concoctions of Poiret, but she also produced elegant tailleurs, often with fur trimming.

Jean Patou

Period: 1912–36

House/labels: Maison Parry; Patou, 7 rue St. Florentin (from 1919); branches in Deauville and Biarritz (1924), followed by one in Monte Carlo

Jean Patou was one of several gentlemen couturiers whose reputations were based as much on their social lives as on their designs. In keeping with his own adventurous approach to life, Patou designed for the active, sophisticated woman. He offered sports clothes (fishing and hunting outfits, tennis clothes, bathing suits) and efficiently coordinated travel wardrobes. But his designs were always elegant and finely made, as well as dashing. His perfectionism was exemplified in the fact that he insisted on having fabrics made for him dyed in the thread—an expensive and time-consuming practice—in order to achieve the delicate and absolutely distinctive hues (such as Patou blue, a dark blue with violet rather than navy overtones), which were among his hallmarks.

Poiret

Period: 1904–32

House/labels: Paul Poiret, 4 rue Auber; 26 Avenue d'Antin (from 1909); 1 Rond-Point-des-Champs-Elysées (1925–29); Passy 10-17 (1931)

Paul Poiret's impact on the history of fashion was so great that the period from 1906 to 1914 is often called the "Age of Poiret." His designs turned totally away from the artificial "hourglass" silhouette which had become the standard fashion look; Poiret advocated instead a waistless, natural line. He also created such playful garments as the lampshade tunic, wired at the hem, and promoted the use of oriental exoticism in fabrics and trimmings. Poiret was responsible for the impractical but very dashing hobble skirt, as well as for the popularization of the harem trouser. Although he continued to design for some years, his work was never as fashionable after World War I as it had been before.

Nina Ricci

Period: 1932–70

House/labels: Nina Ricci, 22 rue des Capucines; Ricci designed only until 1954, but continued to oversee the business

Rather than setting trends, Nina Ricci concentrated on producing well-made and elegant versions of whatever the mode might be. Her designs were always extremely feminine, with emphasis on detail. One special quality of Ricci clothes came from her inclination to let the dress evolve from the fabric—for example, constructing a bodice to echo some detail of the print in the skirt fabric. Mme. Ricci offered insight into her design philosophy when she spoke of her aim to find for a dress the special, elegant detail that would make it a favorite of its owner.

Marcel Rochas

Period: 1925–54

House/labels: Marcel Rochas, 100 rue du Faubourg St-Honoré; 14 Avenue Matignon (from 1931); New York branch, 32 E. 67th St. (1937 on)

Phosphorescent lamé? A dress trimmed with stuffed bluebirds? Rochas. Consistently one of the most dramatic of couturiers, Rochas was noteworthy for his ability to incorporate novelties into his designs, and still produce an elegant result. In some ways, it seems as if his designs herald the innovations of thirty years later—he produced in the 1930s such items as see-through crochet beach shorts, and beach pajamas with godets of pleats inset at the knees, which look for all the world like bell-bottoms; he created blouses to be worn with men's neckties, long before *Annie Hall*. But his clothes were unmistakably couture: carefully cut, with the finest of fabrics and workmanship. His motto— *"Jeunesse, Simplicité, et Personalité"* (Youth, Simplicity, and Personality)—captured the attention of many patrons, and the most famous story about Rochas is that in 1931, eight stylish women showed up at the same party in exactly the same Rochas black satin dress.

Maggie Rouff

Period: 1929–48

House/labels: Maggie Rouff, 136 Avenue-des-Champs-Elysées

Maggie Rouff was actually a name coined when designer Maggie de Wagner took over the House of Rouff. As Maggie Rouff, Mme. de Wagner designed stylish clothes that epitomized the 1930s. Her relaxed, feminine daywear often featured collars made of shawls or scarves; her evening dresses frequently were wrapped in slanting tiers of ruffles. Organdy was a favorite fabric, and color—chosen in relation to the texture of the fabric—was one of her special interests. Maggie Rouff's designs definitely reflect the intelligence for which she was widely noted; they are very clearly resolved and notably wearable. In addition to her success in fashion design, she published two interesting books, one based on her observations of America, the other, *The Philosophy of Elegance*, offering thoughtful commentary on style.

Yves Saint Laurent

Period: 1962–

House/labels: Yves Saint Laurent, rue Spontini; first ready-to-wear boutique opened in 1966; couture house moved to 5 Avenue Marceau in 1974

Year by year, since taking over as head designer for the House of Dior in 1958, Yves Saint Laurent has introduced fashion looks that reshaped the way women dress. His first collection focused on the "Trapeze," narrow shoulders, with a closely cut bodice and flaring short skirt; subsequent collections for Dior included the "bubble dress," gathered into a band at the knees, and a "beatnik" look that introduced motorcycle jackets (made of alligator!) to haute couture. On his own, he began to establish the Saint Laurent look that has continued to develop for the last twenty years: a "masculinized" look for day—pants, blazers, tailored shirts—and a bright, romantic approach to evening wear. Among his most famous innovations were the

1965 Mondrian-patterned dresses; 1966 "smoking suits," evening pantsuits derived from the tuxedo; and 1968 safari-style jackets.

Elsa Schiaparelli

Period: 1927–54

House/labels: Schiaparelli, 4 rue de la Paix; 21 Place Vendôme (from 1934); London branch, 36 Upper Grosvener St. (opened 1934); closed during part of war, reopened 1945; quit couture in 1954, though continued to design other things

Balenciaga is said to have remarked: "Coco [Chanel] had very little taste, but it was good. Schiap[arelli], on the other hand, had lots of it, but it was bad." History, however, has turned the tables; many of Schiaparelli's boisterous, whimsical designs are much closer than those of Chanel to the tastes of today. Among Schiaparelli's legendary designs: trompe l'oeil knits, such as the black and white wool pullover with knitted-in bowtie design which was her first success, in 1928; wraparound sundresses composed of different colored sections; and whimsical accessories, such as a hat made to resemble a lamb chop. Schiaparelli was also famous for her introduction of "shocking pink" (a bright magenta), and her use of fabulous buttons and unusual, often surreal, fabric patterns, as well as manmade fabrics that did not look like textiles.

Pauline Trigère

Period: 1942–

House/labels: Pauline Trigère, 18 E. 53rd St.; E. 47th St.; W. 57th St.; 550 Seventh Ave.

"A walking column, slim and loose at the same time." That is how Pauline Trigère described the look she wanted her clothes to achieve—a look that made her a very popular designer for women who want to be both graceful and comfortable in their clothes. Her way with wool was exemplary, and she was especially successful in creating beautiful evening clothes in wool. Boldly patterned fabrics were frequently chosen by Trigère and used in creative ways, since she worked directly with fabric on a model to achieve complex constructions that resulted in deceptively simple and fluid looks.

Valentina (Schlee)

Period: 1928–57

House/labels: Valentina Gowns Incorporated, 145 W. 30th St.; 27 E. 67th St. (from the 1940s)

Valentina was a one-woman fashion industry. She designed all the clothes produced by her New York couture house, and modeled them all herself, as well as costuming many plays. Her dramatic clothes— often severe, but always with a great deal of flair—were especially popular with the theater set, both on- and off-stage. But she also attracted a following of other fashionables with her emphasis on practical travel wardrobes, comfortably chic daywear (especially capes, skirts, and blouses), and soft, distinctive evening wear, which often featured echoes of her Russian heritage, such as ballerina skirts and slippers, or peasant-style aprons.

Valentino (Garavani)

Period: 1959–

House/labels: Valentino, Via Condotti, Rome; Via Gregoriana (from 1967); prêt-à-porter and other lines began in 1969

From the early 1960s, Valentino became a favored designer of the very, very rich. He is widely considered the foremost Italian couturier, one who brings the quality and elegance of France (where he was trained) to Italian design. His most famous collection was the "no-color" offering of 1967, in which all the designs were shown in shades of white, from chalk to ecru. From the mid-1960s, a "V" has frequently been incorporated into Valentino's designs, often in the form of hardware buttons.

Madeleine Vionnet

Period: 1912–40

House/labels: Vionnet, 222 rue de Rivoli; closed during World War I, reopened 1919; 50 Avenue Montaigne (from 1922)

Although it seems perfectly obvious today that cutting fabric on the diagonal can produce all sorts of wonderful results, the principle was actually discovered by Vionnet in 1926. The concept came to her as a result, first, of her method of working, which involved creating in the round on a miniature figure, and second, of her philosophy of design; Vionnet believed that good design meant fitting the fabric to the body, not the other way around. Through her mastery of cutting and her understanding of fabric, she created clothes that were intricately shaped, and yet could be worn on the natural, uncorseted figure. Frequently seen in Vionnet's designs are the use of triangular gussets, cowl necklines, very pale colors, handkerchief hems, and designs created by pintucks.

Worth

Period: 1858–1954

House/labels: House of Worth, 7 rue de la Paix

The first modern couturier, Charles Frederick Worth originated the presentation of annual collections: he developed the idea of the mutable silhouette, and with it, effectively, the concept of the "new" in fashion. His son Jean-Philippe took over the main activities of design from the mid-1870s on, although C. F. continued to contribute until his death. The House of Worth produced extensive wardrobes (including mourning dresses, maternity clothes, christening dresses, and fancy-dress costumes) for a large clientele for nearly a century, and all of its products (prior to World War II) are well worth collecting. The late nineteenth-century "princess dress," a one-piece, curve-seamed silhouette created by Worth, is a noteworthy example of Worth style.

Couture in the Sixties

The sixties was a decade of upheaval in the fashion industry, just as it was in almost every other aspect of society. Although by the end of the decade the couture would be declared "officially" dead, neverthe-less, many couturiers opened their salons during this period, and some survived—though not without developing other sources of revenue to support the luxury of producing couture clothing.

This trend toward multiple lines and products had been developing since the twenties. One of the most common sources of extra income for couturiers in those days was perfume, and many of their famous fragrances—*My Sin, Chanel No. 5, Shocking, Joy*—did yeoman's duty in keeping the great couture houses financially afloat. Boutiques for acces-sories, and partially ready-made clothes also provided revenue.

As the costs of labor and materials increased, while the demand for couture diminished in a more and more casual society after World War II, many fashion houses added high-quality ready-to-wear lines. In 1960, eleven couture houses formed a group and began to offer their less expensive prêt-à-porter collections a fortnight before showing their couture lines. These Paris ready-to-wear lines were: Carven, Claude Riviere, Grès (the "Grès-Special" label), Guy Laroche, Jacques Griffe (the "Evolution" label), Jacques Heim ("Vedette"), Jean Dessès ("Dif-fusion"), Lanvin-Castillo, de Rauche, Maggie Rouff ("Extension"), and Nina Ricci. Exclusive Paris stores, like Maria Martine, sold the couture prêt-à-porter lines to the same patrons who also bought one-offs in the couture salons.

Within a few years, the prêt-à-porter collections were a more impor-tant part of the Paris fashion scene than the haute couture, and many of the designers who became important in the sixties went directly into the production of the ready-made lines. At the same time, mass manufacturers were introducing expensive, high-style ready-to-wear lines, further blurring the old distinctions of the fashion industry.

It's difficult, therefore, to divide the following list into categories, but in the first group are designers who generally sought—and achieved—entry into the fashion establishment during the sixties, while the second group includes the pop designers who made more radical (even "anti-fashion") statements.

Couture Designers

Adolfo: Opened his own house in 1962 and has continued to design chic, upper-echelon wardrobes.

Geoffrey Beene: Presented his first collection in 1963, and has continued to produce clothes that are both relaxed and stylish.

Rudi Gernreich: Another of the designers who were in the 1960s spotlight, Gernreich produced futuristic, daring designs.

Jean Muir: London designer famous for her work with jersey and suede, which began under the label "Jane & Jane" in 1962; she started her own company in 1966.

Thea Porter: Beginning in the mid-1960s, Porter created high-quality ready-to-wear and custom designs distinguished by a fantasy-oriental approach, with lavish fabrics and trims.

Paco Rabanne: Designer noted for his use of alternative materials (such as plastic and metal) for garments in the 1960s.

Zandra Rhodes: Rhodes' designs are artistic and individualistic (in the extreme). Although most of her work was done after 1970, any examples of her design are probably worth collecting. Prior to 1970, she made some clothing from her own fabrics for sale in the Fulham Road Clothes Shop, a boutique in which she was a partner.

Sonia Rykiel: Her sweaters (especially very tiny fuzzy pullovers) were offered in her husband's Laura boutiques in the early 1960s, and by 1968, her knitwear designs were featured in a Galeries Lafayette boutique.

Pop Designers

Laura Ashley: Beginning in the late 1950s, she produced a popular line of clothes that feature nostalgic, romantic styling: soft floral prints, ruffles, etc.

John Bates: His sexy designs for Jean Varon were extremely influential in mid-1960s London.

Daniel Hechter: Began his women's line of fresh, playful fashions in 1963, and introduced an innovative line for children in 1965, then a menswear line in 1968.

Barbara Hulanicki: Designer, and owner of Biba, a very fashionable boutique of the 1960s.

Betsey Johnson: A designer for Paraphernalia in the latter half of the 1960s before going on her own in 1969, Johnson was noted for outrageous combinations of pattern and style.

Emanuelle Khanh: Beginning in 1963, she produced designs that had an exaggerated, 1930s-style look.

Mary Quant: Designer of bright, youthful fashions which epitomized the 1960s.

Tuffin & Foale: London clothing designers popular during the 1960s, particularly for lace dresses.

Replacement Couturiers

During the sixties, many of the great couture houses continued under the design direction of a second generation of talent. Among the most important of these replacement couturiers were:

Marc Bohan: Head designer for the House of Dior from 1960.

Antonio del Castillo: Head designer for Lanvin, 1950–64; Castillo had his own house from 1965 to 1969.

Jules Crahay: With Nina Ricci from 1952–63, before moving to Lanvin.

Gérard Pipart: After several years of free-lancing, Pipart became chief designer at Nina Ricci in 1963.

The Coty American Fashion Critics Award

The Coty awards were begun in 1942 to recognize the finest in American fashion design, and over the years, the awards have become extremely prestigious. The "Winnie" is given for excellence in the field of women's clothing; "Special Awards" are given for accessories, lingerie, and so forth. There are also "Return Awards" for those who have already won a previous Winnie, and a "Hall of Fame" for those who have already won a "Return Award"!

Although the list of Coty Award winners contains some of the most famous names in fashion, it also contains some names which are relatively unfamiliar outside the fashion industry. From the collector's point of view, the Coty Awards could be a guide to recognizing some designers who are not well known now, but who may become much more valued in the future. So—here's the list of Winnie winners, from 1943 to 1969.

1943: Norman Norell
1944: Claire McCardell
1945: Gilbert Adrian and Tina Leser (at-home clothes); also Emily Wilkens (teenage clothes)
1946: Omar Kiam, Vincent Monte-Sano, Clare Potter
1947: Jack Horwitz, Mark Mooring, Nettie Rosenstein, Adele Simpson
1948: Hattie Carnegie
1949: Pauline Trigère
1950: Bonnie Cashin, Charles James
1951: Jane Derby
1952: Ben Sommers, Ben Zuckerman
1953: Thomas Brigance
1954: James Galanos
1955: Jeanne Campbell, Herbert Kasper, Anne Klein

1956: Luis Estevez, Sally Victor
1957: Leslie Morris, Sydney
   Wragge
1958: Arnold Scaasi
1959: No Winnie
1960: Ferdinando Sarmi,
   Jacques Tiffeau
1961: Bill Blass, Gustave Tassell
1962: Donald Brooks

1963: Rudi Gernreich
1964: Geoffrey Beene
1965: No Winnie
1966: Dominic
1967: Oscar de la Renta
1968: George Halley, Luba
1969: Stan Herman, Victor
   Joris

Winners of Coty Special Awards include the following:

For millinery: Lilly Daché (1943), John Fredericks (1943), Sally Victor (1944), Adolfo (1955, 1969), Halston (1962, 1969)

For shoes: David Evins (1949), Mabel and Charles Julianelli (1950), Beth and Herbert Levine (1967)

For lingerie: Nancy Melcher (1950), Sylvia Pedlar (1951, 1964)

For children's clothes: Helen Lee (1953)

For fabric design: Tzaims Luksus (1965), Julian Tomchin (1969)

For sportswear: Toni Owen (1949), Vera Maxwell (1951)

More Fashion Makers

The foregoing list of the "Great Designers" is made up of those couturiers who are widely regarded as having had a permanent influence on the development of fashion. But of course there were many other couture houses in Europe which were successful in their day, even though their work did not have a great impact on fashion history; there are also many important American designers and manufacturers who occupy a significant place in fashion, although they were not part of the couture. These labels are also important for reference in identifying high-quality collectibles.

The following list includes many minor (but successful) couture designers, along with high-quality dressmakers, tailors, stores, and boutiques. All of the names on this list were well known in their time, and a garment with one of these labels would almost certainly have been considered fashionable and/or very well made.

Amies, Hardy: A British designer favored by Queen Elizabeth, especially in the 1950s, whose clothes are notable for their fine tailoring and classic materials; in the 1960s, Amies began to produce menswear, which became the more important part of his design work.

Arrow: Men's shirt company, noted since the turn of the century for its fashion leadership.

Beer: Very conservative (but well-patronized) Paris design house from 1905 to World War I.

Brooks Brothers: Influential clothing company founded in New York in 1818; between 1890 and 1914, Brooks Brothers introduced from England to the United States some of the great menswear classics—

notably, the button-down shirt collar, the foulard tie, madras shirts, Harris tweed, Shetland sweaters, and the polo shirt.

Burberry: Makers of fine rainwear since 1891; Thomas Burberry designed a waterproof coat to be worn by army officers in World War I, and that classic garment is still known today as the "trench coat."

Busvine: London couture house, from the 1860s to the late 1930s (with New York and Paris branches added early this century); when the house closed, designers Richard Busvine and Violet Redfern continued to create custom-made clothes.

Calman Links: London furriers founded in 1893 and still in business.

Carnegie, Hattie: American designer and manufacturer who offered well-made, Americanized versions of Paris looks throughout the 1920s, 1930s, and 1940s; though her work was not especially innovative, it was very influential in developing American tastes.

Carven: Paris designer whose work has been popular since the 1940s with women interested in clothes that are fashionable but also wearable, scaled to the size and shape of the non-model.

Cassini, Oleg: American designer and manufacturer, especially known for glamorous ready-to-wear in the 1950s and early 1960s.

Cavanagh, John: A British designer of understated, elegant clothes in the 1950s and 1960s; Cavanagh was often patronized by members of the royal family.

Chaumont, Marcelle: Followed the style of her teacher, Vionnet, with considerable success in the 1940s; in the early 1950s, she pioneered the ready-to-wear boutique, under the label "Juliette Verneuil."

Cheruit, Madeleine: Her Paris house was open from the turn of the century til the mid-1930s, producing very nice—but unremarkable—clothing.

Connolly, Sybil: Irish designer popular in the 1950s and 1960s, noted for her Irish linen blouses and use of Irish laces and tweeds.

Countess Mara: Maker of fine ties.

Creed: A London tailoring house founded in the early eighteenth century, closed during World War II; after the war, Charles Creed opened a house under his own name and produced fine clothing until 1966.

Delaunay, Sonia: A painter who created unusual and influential designs in the 1920s; she frequently used a collage-like patchwork technique, and employed harlequin and geometric patterns to create textile designs, embroidered coats, and distinctive dresses.

de Rauch, Madeleine: Founded a Paris design house called "House of Friendship" in 1928, but changed to her own name in 1932 and continued to produce lovely clothes, especially sporty daywear.

di Camarino, Roberta ("Roberta"): Designer of fine accessories, particularly handbags, from 1945.

Doeuillet: Paris couture house founded in 1900 and popular into the early 1920s; Doeuillet fashions were not very original and depended more on detailing than on design, but they were steadily popular.

Drécoll: Paris couture house opened in 1905, closed in 1929; known particularly for elaborate tea gowns.

Fogarty, Anne: American designer who introduced the popular, petticoated teen silhouette of the 1950s.

Fontana: Italian couture house, founded in 1907, popular particularly in the 1950s, and noted for complex, glamorous evening gowns.

Galitzene, Princess Irene: Designer who introduced palazzo pants and created a high-fashion at-home look in the 1960s.

Gilbert, Irene: An Irish designer who began in the 1950s to offer sophisticated country clothes, using fine tweeds, linen, and lace.

Groult, Nicole: The sister of Paul Poiret—less talented, but more practical!—whose own fashion house did well from 1912 into the 1930s.

Hallée, Jeanne: Designer whose house was noted from the turn of the century to World War I, initially for its Watteau-inspired gowns.

Hanley-Seymour: Extremely conservative and exclusive British dressmakers in the 1920s and 1930s.

Hawes, Elizabeth: An American designer whose short career (1928–38) produced some interesting, Chanel-style designs, and a classic book (her autobiography) titled *Fashion is Spinach*.

Hayward: Respected London house of the aughts, teens, and 1920s.

Iris: Line of elegant, innovative lingerie, from the 1930s through the 1960s, designed by Sylvia Pedlar.

Jenny: Paris fashion house popular from 1911 through the mid-1930s.

Kaplan, Jacques: Fur designer, 1941–71.

Krizia: Italian fashion house, founded in 1954.

Lachasse: British house specializing in tailored fashions since the late 1920s.

Lafaurie, Jeanne: Paris couturiere whose house produced dependable though not spectacular clothes from 1925 to 1958.

Lapidus, Ted: French designer who opened a Paris boutique in the early 1950s; his designs—often unisex—were especially popular in the 1960s.

Laroche, Guy: Fashion ready-to-wear since the late 1950s.

Lecomte, Germaine: A small couture house of the 1920s and 1930s.

Lelong, Lucien: Paris designer whose couture house was fashionable particularly between the wars; Lucien Lelong was an influential leader among the Paris couturiers in business and political matters.

Leser, Tina: Designer noted for her resortwear and sportswear, especially during the 1950s.

Liberty of London: Store specializing in imported and unusual fabrics, as well as artistically designed garments; influential in both the aesthetic dress and the Art Nouveau movements.

Mad Carpentier: From 1939 to 1957, a Paris house that produced well-received clothing.

Manguin, Lucille: Creative Paris designer, from 1928 to 1960, noted for high standards of construction and detail.

Marimekko: Maker of brightly colored fabrics and Finnish-inspired clothing from 1951; especially popular in the 1960s.

Martial et Armand: A minor but reliable Paris house, from before World War I to after World War II.

Mattli, Giuseppe: Designer of both couture and ready-to-wear from the mid-1930s through the 1960s.

Missoni: Innovative knitwear line begun in 1953, though becoming widely known in the 1970s.

Morton, Digby: British designer very well regarded for graceful classic clothes, from the 1930s through the mid-1950s.

Nippon, Pearl: Designer of fashionable maternity clothes in the 1950s and 1960s.

Parnis, Mollie: Popular American designer from the 1930s to the 1960s; noted for reliably fashionable, yet understated clothes.

Partos, Emeric: One of America's foremost fur designers, from the 1950s to the early 1970s.

Paterson, Ronald: Successful London house, from 1947 to 1968.

Piguet: Paris fashion house from 1933 to 1951.

Premet: French fashion house successful from 1911 into the 1920s.

Pringle of Scotland: Makers of fine wool garments; famous for cashmeres in the 1920s and 1930s.

Rahvis, Raemonde: High-fashion London house since 1941; Rahvis is also noted for her costume work in British films.

Redfern: British fashion company, from the 1870s to the 1920s (see also Busvine).

Reville and Rossiter: London couture house, specializing in formal gowns, from 1906 to 1936.

Sant' Angelo, Giorgio: Sophisticated American designer who started his ready-to-wear line in 1966.

Scaasi, Arnold: An American designer of ready-to-wear from 1957 to 1963, Scaasi then shifted to custom couture, which he has continued to produce with distinction—especially luxurious evening dresses (Scaasi received some of his early experience with Charles James).

Schnurer, Carolyn: American sportswear designer, noted for innovative fabrics in the 1940s and 1950s.

Simpson, Adele: American ready-to-wear designer specializing in coordinated ensembles, popular especially during the 1950s and 1960s.

Stavropoulos, George: Greek designer during the 1950s, who moved to America and created popular couture lines emphasizing the use of flowing chiffons in the 1960s.

Steibel, Victor: British designer, noted for his romantic clothes from the 1930s to the 1960s; his own labels 1932–39, 1958–63.

Tassell, Gustave: Very finished California designer, from 1956 to 1972, when he took over Norell for four years.

Tiktiner: Modish beach and sportswear of the 1950s.

Tinling, Teddy: British designer best known for his tennis clothes, from the 1930s to the 1980s.

Venet, Phillipe: Former Givenchy designer, opened his own house in 1962; especially known for his beautifully tailored coats.

Weitz, John: An American designer of sporty clothes from 1954; in the 1960s, he created a combination ready-to-wear/couture system in which the customer chose style and fabric from a selection of sketches and swatches.

The labels in the preceding list could, in many instances, be found in accessories as well as in clothes. But there are also fine labels which are found principally in accessories. Here are some of the ones you may find in or on shoes, handbags, scarves, and other accessories:

A. Sulka and Company: Noted for elegant silk scarves and ties.

Capezio: U.S. shoemakers founded in 1887 to make ballet shoes; began producing ballet-style shoes for streetwear in 1944, and has since added a variety of shoe styles.

Fendi: Makers of fashionable handbags from 1918; introduced high-fashion fur line in the 1960s.

Ferragamo, Salvatore: Innovative shoe designer, from the 1920s on.

Gucci: Makers of fine leather accessories, particularly handbags and shoes, from the 1920s to the present.

Hermès: Has produced handcrafted leather goods since the mid-nineteenth century; particularly well known in the twentieth century for its saddlebag-style purse introduced in the 1930s (and named the "Kelly bag" after aficionado Grace Kelly in 1955), as well as for its equestrian-print silk scarves.

Jourdan, Charles: Maker of fine shoes since 1921; Paris boutique opened in 1957, and Jourdan has since become almost synonymous with fashion in shoes.

Mandalian: Maker of mesh bags, 1900–40.

Perugia, André: Beautifully crafted shoes, from the 1920s through the 1960s.

Vivier, Roger: Innovative shoe designer, noted for his unusual heels, from the 1930s.

Whiting Davis: Manufacturer of very popular metallic mesh evening bags, as well as jewelry.

Yantony: Legendary shoemaker of the early twentieth century who created incredibly expensive and beautiful shoes (some taking years to make) in his Paris shop.

And as for hats. . . . well-known milliners include:

Barthet, Jean: French, from 1949; considered by many the world's foremost milliner from the mid-1960s on.

Daché, Lilly: Probably America's most famous milliner, designing wonderful hats from the mid-1920s until the end of the 1960s.

Mr. John: Colorful American milliner who designed hats for many famous private customers, as well as for a huge number of films; from 1929 to 1948, he designed under the label "John Fredericks," thereafter as "Mr. John."

Legroux: Well-known Parisian milliners during the 1920s and 1930s.

Lucas, Otto: Fashionable London milliner from the 1930s through the 1960s.

Mirman, Simone: Popular French milliner of the 1950s and 1960s.

Paulette: French, 1939 through the 1970s.

Reboux, Caroline: Paris milliner from 1870; especially influential in the teens and 1920s.

Saint Cyr, Claude: Among the most famous Paris milliners of the 1940s and 1950s.

Smith, Graham: British milliner, from 1960.

Svend: Creative Parisian milliner in the 1950s.

Thaarup, Aage: Innovative Dane whose London millinery designs were famed from the 1930s into the 1960s.

Vernier, Rose: Popular British milliner, 1945–70.

Victor, Sally: American milliner, popular from the 1930s to the early 1950s.

Wedge, James: British, 1950s and 1960s.

A Fashion Glossary

Fashion has a language all its own, and the more you know about it, the more effective you'll be as a collector. This general glossary includes terms which apply to many types of garments and to broad aspects of the fashion world. Terms which apply more specifically to particular types of garments ("palazzo pants," for example, or "Norfolk jacket") are listed in the special glossaries that precede each listing category in Part Three.

In this general glossary, some large categories—such as Fabrics, Furs, Stripes, etc.—are treated together in order to provide an overview of important areas and make comparisons easier. The contents of these categorical inserts are not cross-referenced, but they are italicized within the larger listing. You will probably find it helpful to take a familiarization tour of the whole glossary before starting to use it, just to get an idea of its structure.

Aesthetic dress: A term used to describe an alternative fashion movement from the 1880s to the 1900s; it featured loose, flowing garments which didn't require corsets or other artificial underpinnings. Aesthetic dress had many adherents among feminists, artists, and individualists. Its style was related both to Art Nouveau and to the pre-Raphaelite school of painting, which was very romantic and somewhat fantastical.

American Indian (Native American): When used in connection with design, this designation usually refers to the motifs used in the art of tribal Indians living in North America. The motifs are generally geometric, featuring much use of the zig-zag pattern, as well as arrow shapes. In fashion, "American Indian" can also refer to the influence of Indian costume, which is most likely to mean the use of fringes,

Ideal of the aesthetic dresser.

silver, turquoise, and Indian-style beading (geometric patterns made with a solid beadwork of small, colorful beads).

Bakelite: The earliest form of plastic, developed in 1909 and used extensively for buttons, belt buckles, purses, and jewelry thereafter.

Beading: The practice of sewing small sparkling metal or glass ornaments in a pattern on fabric. Types of beads include: *bugle* (tiny cylinders, usually either plastic or metal); *paillette* (very small, round metal disc, pierced in the center and sewn on—also called "spangles" or "sequins"); *jet* (small, polished, usually faceted piece of black lignite).

Bespoke: British term for custom-made.

Bias: The diagonal grain of a fabric; cutting on the bias uses a great deal of fabric, but results in a garment that fits sleekly and hangs gracefully, since fabric cut on the bias has a built-in curve, whereas fabric cut on the straight of the grain does not.

Bodice: The part of a woman's dress which is above the waist; it may be separate, or sewn to the skirt.

Braid: A narrow, flat trimming, in many different materials and designs. Common types include: *military* (flat silk, woven in a diagonal design); *rick rack* (woven in a zig-zag pattern); *soutache* (very narrow flat cord); *middy* (narrow, ribbed).

Bustle: Generally, any gathering of fabric over the back of the hips; in the nineteenth century, an exaggerated bustle effect was created by the use of cushions or wire forms.

Cable: A knitted design of raised, interlocking serpentines.

Carnaby Street: Refers to a London street where the Mod look was introduced in the 1960s; may be used as a descriptive adjective for Mod fashions.

Celluloid: A forerunner of plastic, this ivory substitute was developed in America just after the Civil War, and used for buttons and jewelry.

Checks: Small squares of color woven into or printed on the fabric. Types include: *gingham* (even squares, one color alternating with white), *gun-club* (different colors on alternating rows—used for tweeds), *hound's tooth* (broken squares, usually bright colors), *shepherd's* (even squares of black and white or contrasting colors), *tattersall* (narrow lines crossing at less than one-inch intervals on a neutral background), *windowpane* (narrow lines crossing at two- or three-inch intervals, usually a bright color on a white or natural background).

Chenille: A fuzzy yarn, made to look like its French namesake, the caterpillar; used for embroidery (as on bathrobes and bedspreads) and knitted or crocheted accessories.

Chinoiserie: A term applied to Chinese-influenced designs.

Cloth: A term frequently used to denote a fabric developed for a particular use, often to simulate some other kind of material. Common types of cloth include: *Astrakhan cloth* (made to simulate caracul or Persian lamb), *beaver cloth* (simulates flat—not sheared—beaver), *burberry cloth* (waterproofed), *chamois cloth* (simulates chamois leather), *gold* or *silver cloth* (gold- or silver-colored metallic fiber warp and silk weft, used for evening wraps), *leopard cloth* (simulating leopard skin), *loden cloth* (waterproof wool mainly used for coats in the Tyrol), *melton cloth* (felted wool used especially in pea jackets and overcoats).

Collars:

    Buster Brown: Starched, round, lay-down collar, usually worn with a soft bow.

Button-down: The two collar points are fastened to the shirt with small buttons.

Choker: Very high collar, sometimes reaching to the earlobes, sometimes boned.

Dutch: A lay-down collar, with either round or pointed ends.

Eton: A lay-down collar, starched and folded, with slightly rounded corners.

Mandarin (Nehru): A standing band collar, fitted close to the neck, with a slight opening left at center front.

Medici: Stiffened or boned to stand up high in the back.

Peter/Pan: A round lay-down collar, two or three inches wide, with round ends.

Poet's: Soft, unstarched collar.

Sailor: A deep square in back, narrowing to form a V-shape in front.

Shawl: A long collar, rolled softly back from the front opening.

Wing: A stiff, fairly high standup collar with corners turned back from the opening to form points.

Colors: The primary colors (red, blue, and yellow) can be combined to create the secondary colors (purple, green, and orange); in turn, this basic family of colors can be mixed together to form various tertiary colors, and can be mixed with black or white to form even more different shades. In general, colors are named after things in nature or in everyday life—so we have sky blue, jade green, coral, coffee, rust, tobacco brown, bottle green, and so on. But in the fashion world, special color names are often invented which have no reference in nature. Definitions for some of these follow, along with some useful color terms, and a few of the most common shades created from the primary and secondary colors. However, there are a great many more names for fashion colors than are given here; designers are constantly creating new, complex colors and giving them poetic names—or even their own names, as with Poiret blue or Lanvin blue.

Apricot: Light orange midway between red-orange and yellow-orange.

Azure: A term which is used to denote any of a variety of light to medium blues.

Beige: A light, pinkish brown.

Blues: Common varieties of blue include: *periwinkle* and *hyacinth* (blue-purples), *aqua, teal,* and *peacock* (blue-greens), *sky blue* and *baby blue* (pale pastels), *cornflower* and *royal* (bright blues), *navy* and *midnight* (with black added), *powder* and *Wedgwood* (with gray added), *Delft* (a grayish-purplish blue), *indigo* (a deep blue, with a very slight hint of red).

Browns: Shades range from the darkest *chocolate* to the lightest *toast,* and include those with more red, such as *bronze* and *mahogany,* as well as those with more yellow, such as *hazelnut.*

Greens: Special shades include: *hunter* green (a rich, dark green, with a slight yellowish cast), *loden* (a dark, bluish green), and *verdigris* (bluish-green).

Mauve: A mixture of gray and light purple.

Off-whites: Any shades in which white is tinged with another color. The most common are: *bone, oyster, ivory, eggshell, alabaster,* and *cream.*

Oranges: More red produces *vermilion* (a very bright red-orange, almost red) and *coral* (a light, pinkish orange), while more yellow gives *amber* (a somewhat dark yellow-orange) and *topaz* (a clear, medium yellow-orange).

Pastels: Generally, any color mixed with enough white to produce a very pale and delicate shade.

Puce: A deep reddish-brown.

Purples: A predominance of red produces colors such as *wine* and *burgundy,* while a predominance of blue produces *violet.*

Reds: Common shades of red include: *laquer* and *cardinal* (bright, yellowish-reds), *lipstick* and *crimson* (bright, bluish-reds), *ruby* (a blue-black red), *shocking pink* (a light bluish-red), *rose* (a slightly grayed bluish-red).

Taupe: A fairly dark, brown-tinged gray.

Yellows: Light yellows include: *lemon* (with a hint of green), *straw* (pale yellow), and *primrose* (a rich yellow); dark yellows include *cadmium* (a very bright deep yellow) and *gold* (a somewhat drab deep yellow).

Cord: String or very light rope, made of multiple strands of thread either twisted or plaited together; used as drawstrings or for cording (in which cord is covered with bias fabric and used as an edging or decoration).

Crotch: The juncture of the two legs in a pair of pants.

Cubism: A movement in painting (led by Braque and Picasso) during the early twentieth century, which influenced the design of fabric, clothing, and accessories; Cubist patterns are typically bold and geometric.

Cuff: A fold or band of fabric at the end of a sleeve or trouser. Types of sleeve cuffs include: *barrel* (a band fastened with a button), *French* (a wide band folded back and fastened through both thicknesses with cuff links), *Mousquetaire* (very wide, ornamental turned-back cuffs).

Dart: A seam ending in a point, used to make a garment fitted or to improve the way the garment hangs.

Deco, Art Deco: In connection with design, this term usually refers to the streamlined, geometrical patterns which were fashionable in the

Dress with Art Deco influence, 1920s.

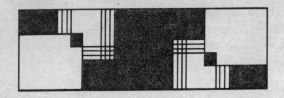

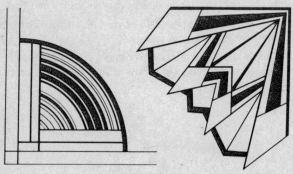

Art Deco motifs.

late 1920s and in the 1930s; the patterns are generally symmetrical and feature a combination of curved and rectilinear lines. Deco incorporated patterns from pre-Columbian and ancient Egyptian art, as well as from modern sources such as machine design.

Detail: Any specific feature of construction or finishing that gives added interest to a garment.

Directoire: Refers to a French style popular at the very end of the eighteenth century, featuring soft, high-waisted gowns with low decolleté and short, puffed sleeves; the Directoire look is a frequently revived fashion influence, and is also called Empire and Récamier.

Dot: An allover pattern of circles. Types include: *coin* dots (usually a little over half an inch in diameter), *confetti* dots (small, multicolored), and *polka* dots (evenly spaced).

Double-breasted: A front closing, in which one side of the garment overlaps the other, with a double row of buttons.

Drape: The way a fabric hangs or falls; also, loose folds or gathers of fabric used in the construction of a garment or detail.

Drawstring: Cord drawn through a casing to gather fabric at waist, wrists, or elsewhere.

Dress form: A frame simulating a woman's torso, for use in fitting or draping garments; also called a "dummy."

Dress shields: Pads worn under the arms to protect garments from perspiration.

Dyeing: The process by which fibers or fabrics are colored, either solidly or in designs. Types of dye include: *acid* (used mostly on protein-based fibers, has low resistance to washing), *alizarin* (vegetable dye, used mostly on wool), *aniline* (term used generally for synthetic dyes), *basic* (used mostly on wool and silk, poor resistance to washing or sunlight, but very strong colors), *sulphur* (good wash resistance, but poor resistance to sunlight), *vat* (highly resistant to both washing and sun). Dyeing may be done either before the fiber is woven (stock-dyed, yarn-dyed) or after the fiber is woven into fabric (piece-dyed). Types of decorative dyeing include: *batik* (in which successive applications of wax resist are used to create very complex and colorful designs) and *tie-dyeing* (in which portions of the fabric are tied off so that they will not take dye).

Egyptian: In matters of design, refers to the use of motifs from the art of ancient Egypt. These motifs are usually stylized human figures, animals, and plants. Certain colors—black and white, terra cotta, "Nile green," and faïence blue—are also associated with the Egyptian influence, which was especially prevalent during the two periods of greatest archaeological activity in Egypt, the 1890s and the 1920s.

Embroidery: Any decorative needlework. Specific types include:

Appliqué: A type of ornamentation in which cutout pieces, usually motifs of some sort, are sewn onto a background, often with decorative stitching.

Broderie anglaise: A white-on-white embroidery style in which round or oval holes, with overcast edges, make up the pattern; also called "madeira."

Chinese: Elaborate designs (usually colorful) worked in satin stitch with silk floss.

Couching: A type of raised embroidery, which is accomplished by making a design of braid or cording, fastened in place by fine stitching.

Cross-stitch: Embroidery made up of many small x's forming a design.

"weighted" silk, which has been mixed with metal salts. More than fifty percent weighting produces a very weak fabric. The many types of silk fabric include: *china,* thin, plain woven, somewhat transparent, moderately lustrous; *gazar,* a screenwire-like silk, stiff and transparent, used mainly by couture designers; *peau de soie,* twill-woven, firm and soft, with dull, satiny finish; *pongee,* a thin, soft, undyed silk, with a tan color, derived from wild silkworms; *shantung,* a heavier pongee; *shot,* shot-woven to give changeable color; *taffeta,* fine, firm-bodied silk fabric, made in a variety of types, including chiffon, faille, moiré, and paper, which is very crisp and thin; *tussah,* a term used to include both pongee and shantung.

Protein-based (animal-derived) fibers:

Alpaca: Long hair of the Peruvian alpaca; used alone or combined with wool to produce a luxurious fabric used principally for women's suits and sportswear.

Angora: The hair of the angora goat; about four to seven inches long, usually white, and quite strong; used in the late nineteenth and early twentieth centuries as a trimming, and now more frequently woven with other fibers into "mohair." Also, the fur from the angora rabbit, which is spun into a very soft and fuzzy yarn used in sweaters.

Camel's hair: Camel's hair is of three types, namely, a silky beige down, a coarser fleece, and a wiry reddish-brown outer hair; the first two types are generally used in coats for both men and women.

Cashmere: A very fine, soft wool from the undercoats of Kashmir goats; used in sweaters, suits, and coats.

Horsehair: Hairs from the mane and tail, used to produce a stiff cloth for hats and petticoats.

Merino: A soft, fine, cashmere-like wool.

Vicuña: Very soft wool from a wild relative of the llama and alpaca; its wool is used for overcoats, suits, and fine sweaters.

Wool (sheep's): Made into many different types of fabric, which are included in the "Fabrics—types" listing. Special terms associated with wool include: *virgin* (meaning that the wool fibers are newly shorn and have not been used in any other way previously), *worsted* (which refers to a woolen fabric made of smooth, compact yarn that produces a durable cloth), *tropical weight* (a lightweight wool fabric, suitable for wearing in the summer or in warm climates; also called "tropical worsted").

Synthetic fibers:

Acetate: Cellulose-based fiber made by the acetate process, which produces a lightweight, silky fabric used in lingerie, blouses, and knitwear since the 1920s; trade names include *Acele, Celanese, Seraceta,* and *Tennessee Eastman.*

Acrylic: Wool substitute introduced in 1947 and used increasingly from the 1950s on, especially for sweaters and for lining boots, gloves, and jackets; trade names include *Acrilan* and *Orlon.*

Lastex: An elastic yarn which is combined with other fibers, such as cotton or rayon, to produce a stretchy fabric.

Nylon: A sheer yarn which is stronger and more elastic than silk; production began in 1940, and nylon was in wide use in the 1950s.

Rayon: In practical usage, "rayon" is used to refer to the cellulose-based fiber made by a process different from that used to make the other two types of cellulose-based fibers, acetate and viscose. *Spun* rayon is made by a special technique which produces a softer fabric with better draping qualities; spun rayon yarns are often combined with natural fibers to produce blends. Rayon was introduced as a fashion material in the late teens.

Viscose: A cellulose-based fabric made by the viscose process.

Fabrics—types: The fabric terms listed here are ones which describe the most common types of fabric. The determining quality of a fabric "type" is not the *fiber* used, but the weight, the kind of weave, the kind of finish, and/or the kind of design. Thus, a particular type of fabric—like batiste—may be made of linen, cotton, or wool; it is "batiste" because of its very light weight and fine weave.

Batiste: A very sheer, finely woven cloth of linen, cotton, or wool.

Bengaline: Silk or wool fabrics with a corded or rep effect.

Bouclé: Soft, conspicuously nubby fabric, knitted or woven of various fibers.

Broadcloth: High-grade cotton or wool fabric of varying weights.

Brocade: Fabric woven in an allover pattern of flowers and figures in contrasting colors, often including metallic thread.

Challis: Lightweight fabric of fine wool, wool/rayon, or cotton, usually printed with a floral pattern.

Chambray: Cotton fabric made with colored warp thread and white filling thread, finished like linen.

Chiffon: Transparent and very lightweight fabric, of silk, cotton, or rayon.

Crêpe: General term for a lightweight, crinkly fabric. Specific types include: *Canton* crêpe (silk or rayon with a pebbly surface), *crêpe de chine* (very durable, lightly crinkled, made of silk or silk and cotton), *georgette* (very crinkly, very sheer; may be silk or silk blended with rayon or cotton), *plissé* (light cotton crêpe with puckered stripes).

Damask: A fabric, usually of silk or linen, with a pattern that uses both satiny and flat surfaces to create a light-and-shadow effect.

Denim: A durable, twill-woven fabric with a slightly frosted look, produced by using a colored warp and a white weft.

Felt: A fabric that is not woven; various kinds of fibers are compacted by means of moisture and pressure to form the material.

Flannel: A soft, slightly napped fabric of wool, cotton or blends, made in a variety of weights.

Foulard: A twill-woven silk or rayon; usually printed with a small, allover pattern; used in scarves and ties.

Gabardine: Durable fabric with diagonal weave, of wool, cotton, or rayon.

Gauze: A transparent fabric of silk, cotton, or rayon.

Jersey: A slightly stretchy knitted cloth of varying weights, which may be made from many different fibers.

Lamé: A flat-woven fabric made with gold or silver threads.

Madras: A gaily colored plaid or stripe fabric, made of cotton or silk, which is designed to "bleed" (that is, to let the colors run together when washed).

Matelassé: Fabric with woven-in raised designs that resemble blisters or quilting.

Moiré: A fabric of silk, blend, or synthetic, into which has been set a wavy design; the design produces a soft, rippling effect in the fabric, which is generally used for evening gowns.

Mousseline: Very fine, very soft fabric of cotton, wool, or silk; also made in heavier weights for use as a lining.

Net: Openwork fabric with meshes of various size (from very fine to very large), made from silk, cotton, linen, or cord of some sort.

Oilskin: Any fabric waterproofed with oil.

Organza: Sheer, slightly stiffened muslin, silk, or blend.

Piqué: Fabric woven in a ribbed, figured, or waffled pattern, usually of cotton, sometimes of silk or rayon.

Rep: Silk, wool, or blended fabric with a crosswise ribbed or corded surface.

Sacking: Coarsely woven, heavy linen or cotton, used for sports suits.

Sateen: Fabric made of cotton and wool, silk, or rayon, with a satiny finish.

Satin: A closely woven silk or rayon which is made in many different weights, distinguished by a glossy surface and a dull back. Specific types include: *antique* (made to look as if it has aged from white to an ivory or parchment shade, often used for wedding gowns), *charmeuse* (semi-lustrous, with a soft, draping quality), *duchesse* (highly lustrous, very heavy, yet soft, used for formal gowns), *slipper* (closely woven, fairly lightweight, semi-lustrous, often used for shoes, but also for gowns).

Seersucker: A wash-and-wear fabric made of cotton, silk, or rayon, often having a crinkled *stripe* woven in.

Serge: A fabric made of worsted cotton, wool, or blended yarns, with a diagonal twill on both sides.

Shot: Fabric with warp and weft of different colors or fibers, producing an effect of changeable color; shot silk is the most frequently used fabric of this type.

Ticking: Very closely woven, heavy fabric of cotton or linen, usually striped but sometimes figured; originally used for mattress and pillow covers, but in mid-twentieth century, introduced for sport clothing.

Toile: A linen or cotton fabric printed with a pictorial landscape design in a single color (usually red, blue, brown, purple, or green) on a natural background.

Tricot: Fabric flat-knitted from any of various fibers, such as wool, cotton, or nylon.

Tulle: A very fine silk or cotton net or gauze; silk tulle is also called "illusion."

Twill: Any fabric woven with diagonal lines running from selvage to selvage; very strong.

Velvet, velveteen: Fabric having a thick, soft pile; velvet is usually made of silk or rayon (sometimes with a cotton or linen backing), while velveteen is made of cotton. Types of velvet include: *chiffon* or *wedding ring* (a velvet fabric supposedly so fine that a width of it could be drawn through a wedding ring; this type is often called "silk velvet"), *cut* (a brocaded velvet pattern on a background of chiffon, georgette, or voile), *Lyons* (a stiff velvet with a short pile), *nacre* (the back is one color, the pile another, giving an iridescent effect), *panné* (the pile is pressed flat in one direction, which gives a very lustrous finish), *uncut* (the loops of the pile are uncut).

Viyella: Trade name of a very popular wool and cotton blend developed in 1894; very soft, warm, and durable.

Voile: Transparent fabric of cotton, silk, rayon, or wool, finely woven and very crisp.

Facing: Fabric used to provide a backing for cuffs, necklines, etc.

Faggoting: An area of straight or criss-crossed openwork connecting two edges.

Fair Isle: A knitted design which features bands of colorful geometric designs.

Fashion influences: These are the characters—both fictional and real—who become so identified with a particular fashion that their names come to stand for that type of style. For example, "Jackie Kennedy" or "Little Lord Fauntleroy" can be used as adjectives to describe a type of garment or ensemble, and it's not uncommon to see these terms used in the descriptions of vintage items. Following are some of the most familiar of these references in use.

Joan Crawford: Generally, refers to anything with extremely padded shoulders.

Isadora Duncan: Usually refers to a very long silk or chiffon scarf; may also be used for loose, flowing costumes in general.

Gibson Girl: Generally, a very crisp shirt with large sleeves and small tie, worn with a tailored long skirt.

Kate Greenaway: A style of children's dress featured in the illustrations of Kate Greenaway's books (popular from the 1870s through 1890s); these generally follow the Empire silhouette, with high waists, sashes, ruffled pantaloons, and poke bonnets.

Jean Harlow: Generally, a slinky look; specifically, a backless, bias-cut evening gown.

Katherine Hepburn: Loosely cut trousers, usually paired with a trim, simple sweater.

Jackie Kennedy: Almost always means a classic Givenchy-style suit—straight, knee-length skirt; unfitted, waist-length jacket; three-quarter-length sleeves; and a pillbox hat.

Little Lord Fauntleroy: Style for small boys (sometimes borrowed for adult feminine fashions) derived from the hero's costume in the popular book of the same title; features a soft white shirt with a rather large round collar and big, soft bow, worn with short black velvet pants, and sometimes a matching jacket.

Pierrette (and Pierot): Especially, a large flounce or ruffle at the neck, topping a full, billowing dress or one-piece pantaloon, with long, full sleeves.

Twiggy: Usually a mini-dress styled like a T-shirt or tank-top; very slender "little girl" look.

Fasteners: Any system that is used to temporarily close some opening in a garment.

Buttons: May be made in any shape, of any material; attached to one side of a closure, with a corresponding hole on the other side, through which the button is slipped; buttons may be used for decorative as well as practical purposes, and fanciful buttons were especially popular in the 1920s and 1930s.

Frog: Fastener using ball on one side, loop of braid or fabric on the other.

Hook and eye: A fastening system made of wire, involving a small, flat hook and a loop (eye); introduced in the early nineteenth century.

Lacing: Cord or ribbon drawn through a series of eyelets.

Snap: A fastening system using small metal discs, one with a ball, the other with a socket, which "snap" together; introduced in the 1900s.

Stud: Separate button inserted through two holes in the two layers of fabric to be fastened.

Toggle: A fastening system which uses loops of fabric or braid on one side, and small blocks or cylinders of wood on the other.

Velcro: Fastening system which uses strips of fabric covered in tiny nylon loops, which interlock when the strips are pressed together; first used in the early 1960s.

Zipper: A mechanical fastener, composed of two rows of metal or nylon "teeth" which are pulled together and locked by a "slide"; invented in the 1920s, but came into wide use around 1935.

Fauvism: An artistic movement of the early 1900s, featuring rather flat-looking, brightly colored patterns; Henri Matisse was the most famous of the Fauvists, and Raoul Dufy translated some of the Fauvist style into influential fabric designs.

Festoon: Trimming hung in scallops around a skirt.

Flounce: Strip of gathered material, similar to a ruffle but wider, usually attached to the bottom of a garment.

Fly front: A closure in which a concealing flap covers the fasteners.

Fringe: A border of hanging cords or tassels, or sometimes of threads raveled from the edge of the fabric.

Full-fashioned: A knit design which is shaped by increasing and reducing the number of stitches.

Furbelows: Fancy decorations, such as flounces, tassels, fringe, braid, etc.

Furs: Prior to the late nineteenth century, almost all "fur coats" had the fur on the *inside* rather than the outside. The couturier Doucet made the fur-outside coat fashionable. Fake furs, made of synthetic fur cloths, were introduced in the 1950s, and fun furs—inexpensive-to-moderate priced furs in playful styles—appeared in the 1960s. In addition to coats and jackets, popular articles made from fur include stoles and capes, tails (boa-type affairs usually made from fox tails), neckpieces (often made from the heads and paws of fur-bearing animals, especially mink), hats, and muffs. Fur is also used for trimming garments, particularly winter suits; a fad for embellishing summer evening gowns with fur bands lasted from 1910 to 1915.

The fur of the spotted cats (leopard, ocelot, and cheetah) is now protected, and it is illegal to buy or sell any item made of these furs in the last hundred years. All three furs have tawny-colored backgrounds, with black and/or white rings, dashes, and/or rosettes.

The value of a type of fur is based on a combination of factors, including beauty, scarcity, and durability; however, inexpensive furs can be manipulated (through dyeing, shearing, blending, tipping, and other techniques) to resemble more valuable furs. Vintage furs are often made from types of fur no longer popular—such as monkey or squirrel—which may be difficult to recognize, especially since labeling of fur was either non-existent or more picturesque than accurate until fairly recently.

A first step in identifying a fur is to determine whether it is short-, medium-, or long-haired. Here are the furs in each of those categories:

Short hair: Chinchilla, ermine, lamb (very short), mink, mole (very short), muskrat, otter, pony (very short), rabbit, seal, squirrel, weasel.

Medium hair: Beaver, marten, opossum, raccoon, sable, wolf.

Long hair: Fox, lynx, skunk, wolverine.

Fur generally consists of both underfur (the dense, soft layer close to the skin) and longer, coarser guard hairs. The types of the underfur and the guard hair will also aid in identifying a fur.

Chinchilla: Delicate, silky; blue-gray with white and darker stripes; very perishable and very expensive.

Ermine: A white fur, flat, silky and dense; not very durable, but rather expensive; used principally on ceremonial garments, but occasionally used in fashion as a trimming.

Fox: Lustrous, long guard hairs and deep, dense fur fiber; wide variety of colors; semi-durable. Fox types used for coats and jackets include: *silver* (also called platinum), *blue, black, cross, red, white*; fox types used primarily for scarves and trimmings include *common* and *kit*; *pointed* fox is common red fox dyed black and augmented with either silver-fox or badger hairs to emulate silver fox; "South American fox" is not true fox.

Lamb: Includes *broadtail* (flat fur with moiré design), *caracul* (tight curls with moiré pattern; also called astrakhan), and *Persian* (longer curls, lustrous texture); durable. Another type of lamb is *mouton* (Merino lamb sheared and dyed to imitate costlier furs), also called *beaver-dyed lamb*. (Lamb is not, strictly speaking, fur, but it is generally thought of in the same context.)

Lynx: Dense fur fiber with long, silky guard hair; creamy white to pale blue-gray or yellow-brown; moderately durable.

Marten: Straight, silky hair, dense fur; durable; the most desirable is from Russia and Siberia, with North America next, and Alaska the least desirable. Chinese, Japanese, and Himalayan martens vary in quality, and are often dyed or blended for improvement. *Pine* martens range from pale to dark bluish-brown, with fluffy underfur and silky guard hair; *stone* marten has a grayish or bluish-white underwool, with dark top hairs.

Mink: Silky guard hairs and soft fur fiber; wide range of natural or dyed colors; very durable. The finest—and rarest—fur comes from wild minks, especially from Labrador; the next best are mutation and ranch minks, especially European; Chinese and Japanese mink are less desirable, but among the best of these is kolinsky mink. The term "let-out" refers to a process of cutting the skins into narrower, diagonal sections, which are joined together to achieve a richer look. "Brazilian mink" is actually marmot.

Monkey: Long, lustrous black hair, with no underfur; popular in the later nineteenth century and in the 1920s, but rarely seen since then.

Muskrat: Glossy brown or black, with dense underfur and strong guard hairs; may be dyed and striped to look like mink, sheared and dyed to look like seal, or left natural; very durable.

Nutria: Similar to beaver, with shorter fur; blue-brown to yellowish-red; moderately durable.

Opossum: American opossum is light-colored, coarse, dull; Australian opossum is blue-gray or yellowish-red, with soft, smooth, dense fur.

Otter: Thick, soft, lustrous; light to dark brown; durable.

Pony: Something like leather with a flat moiré pattern of fine, lustrous fur.

Rabbit: Soft, light texture; may be left natural or dyed and sheared to resemble other furs; semi-perishable. Rabbit is found under many fancy names, which often include the words "coney" or "lapin."

Raccoon: Long- or medium-length fur, dense, with high sheen; brown-gray in color, with light, silvery highlights; very durable, moderately priced.

Sable: Russian or Siberian sable has long, silky guard hairs and soft, dense, fluffy fur fiber; naturally black-brown; looks like mink but is less durable; very expensive. Chinese, Japanese, Himalayan, and Hudson Bay "sable" are actually marten (from the same family as the sable). Mountain and rock "sable" are commercial (and illegal) terms for fur from a small relative of the raccoon.

Seal: *Fur* seals are most valuable, with Alaska or matara seal being the highest in value, cape seal somewhat less; pelts are sheared to give velvety finish, usually dyed black or brown; very durable and very expensive. *Hair* seals, which include harp, hooded, and Labrador seals, are less valuable; they have flat, sleek, bristly hair and no underfur. Imitation "seal" furs include: electric seal (sheared hare); French seal (rabbit); Hudson seal (muskrat); polar seal (rabbit); seal-dyed coney (rabbit).

Skunk: Dark brown or black, with or without white stripes; straight, thick fur, with long, lustrous guard hairs; durable.

Squirrel: Moderately silky, reasonably durable; may be natural (gray or black), bleached or dyed; best quality from Russia and Siberia.

Weasel: Brown, soft, lustrous, and dense.

Wolf: Soft, dense gray underfur, long, flowing black guard hairs; durable.

Wolverine: Dark brown center, light brown sides; coarse texture; durable.

Godet (gore, gusset): An inset of triangular-shaped fabric.

Haberdasher: A purveyor of men's clothing and furnishings; the store of such a dealer is called a "haberdashery."

Heather: A subtly mottled effect achieved in tweeds by interweaving various colors.

Hem: A fold of fabric turned back from the edge and stitched in place. Types include: *French* (the edge of the hem is pinked, strengthened with machine stitching, and then sewn in place with a delicate slip-stitch), *rolled* (held in place with stitches that alternate, one stitch taking in the garment, the next taking in the hem; used for sheer fabrics), and *soft-roll* (a hem designed not to be pressed).

Inseam: The measurement of a trouser leg from crotch to lower edge.

Inset: A piece of fabric inserted into another, either as decoration or for fitting purposes.

Intarsia: A knitted-in pattern which is designed to look as if it were inlaid.

Jabot (cascade): One or more tiers of ruffles worn on the front closing of a shirt, blouse, or dress.

Lace: The term "real lace" refers to lace that is handmade in one of two types: *bobbin lace*, which is made by working bobbins filled with thread around a pattern marked out with pins on a pillow, and *needle* or *needlepoint lace*, which is worked with a needle on a paper pattern, using buttonhole and blanket stiches. Other types of lacework made by hand include crochet lace, hairpin lace, knotted lace, and tatting. Machine-made lace may resemble any type of handmade lace, but is always less fine.

Lacemaking terms include: "brides" (the threads or bars that link parts of a design when there is no ground), "cordonnet" (fine cord or heavy thread used to outline a design), "ground" (the backing, usually net or mesh, on which the lace is worked), and "picot" (a looped edge).

Handmade laces are generally named either for the region in which they were made or for the method by which they are made. There are a *great* many different types of lace, and only some more familiar ones are listed here.

Alençon: Handmade needlepoint lace; the design (usually floral) is worked on a fine net ground and outlined with a heavier thread; often used in bridal dresses and veils.

Argentan (point de France): An Alençon-type needlepoint lace, with a bolder floral pattern and a more open mesh; used as edging.

Armenian: Very narrow edging with pointed scallops, used on small items such as infant's clothing, handkerchiefs, and lingerie.

Battenberg: Coarse lace made of linen thread or braid in varying patterns.

Binche: A Flemish bobbin lace, featuring floral scrollwork and snowflake-like dots sprinkled on the background.

Bohemian: A coarse net worked in a braid-like pattern.

Bourbon: Worked in cording on a net background.

Breton (Bretonne): Heavy, colored embroidery worked on a net background.

Brussels: Term currently used for machine-made net lace, with separately appliquéd designs.

Buckinghamshire: Fine English bobbin lace with simple design.

Carrickmacross: Irish lace made in two types: *appliqué* (designs of sheer fabric are applied to machine-made net) and *guipure* (which resembles cut work).

Chantilly: Delicate bobbin lace of silk or linen, with designs outlined in thicker threads; usually black.

Cluny: Coarse bobbin lace of heavily colored linen or cotton.

Crochet: Fairly heavy lace made of interlocking loops formed into chains, rosettes, scallops, etc.

Duchesse: Bobbin lace, with the appearance of very fine tape, usually a pattern of linked flowers and floral sprays; *Honiton* is a slightly heavier version, *princesse* a more delicate version.

Fiber: Very fragile and expensive laces, made of aloe or banana fibers.

Filet: A lace in which the pattern is formed by use of darning stitches on a square mesh.

Flat point: Lace having no raised stitches.

Crochet lace.

Gros point (Gros Point de Venise): A needlepoint lace with large, raised motifs.

Guipure: Heavy lace with no ground; the pattern is made from motifs of twisted cord, joined by bars.

Hairpin: Narrow lace with looped edges.

Irish crochet: Chain-stitched squares with medallions of shamrocks, roses, etc., and finished with scalloped or otherwise ornamented edges.

Macramé: Knotted lace, often fringed; silk types are used on shawls.

Margot: Modern lace, with cotton thread design embroidered by machine on silk net.

Milan: Picot-edged lace, frequently machine-made.

Plauen: Machine-made lace which uses a special technique for imitating complex designs; Saint Gall and Saxony are similar.

Point d'esprit: Small oval or square dots on net or tulle.

Tatting: A knotted lace, frequently made with cloverleaf or wheel motifs; most often used as an edging.

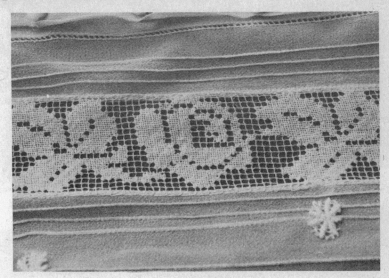

Filet lace.

Guipure lace.

Torchon (Bavarian, peasant, beggar's): Heavy cotton or linen bobbin lace.

Valenciennes (often called Val): Linen bobbin lace worked in one piece (the ground and design are made of the same thread); machine-made imitations made of cotton.

Lapel: Part of a jacket or coat that is turned back from the front closure; types include: *notched,* having a V-shaped opening on the outside edge where the lapel joins the collar; and *peaked,* coming to a point at the outer edge.

Leather: The hide of almost any mammal, reptile, or bird can be tanned to make leather. The following list includes those types of leather most commonly used in the making of clothing and accessories.

The skins of crocodile and turtle are protected, and it is illegal to buy or sell any item made of these skins in the last hundred years. Alligator is no longer protected, however.

Alligator: Water reptile skin, distinguished by its square markings.

Boarded: Leather (usually smooth calf) which has been treated to give it a closely creased finish; *boxed* leather is similar, with the creases running in both directions.

Buckskin: Originally made from deer or elk, now may be made from calf; white or cream-colored, used for shoes.

Calf: A durable, flexible, fine-grained leather, which may be made smooth and shiny or dull and sueded.

Chamois: Very soft, pliable goatskin, deep yellow; used for gloves, linings, and sometimes garments.

Cordovan: Very strong, expensive leather, generally made from horsehide butts; used principally for fine shoes.

Cowhide: Durable leather, also called *steerhide.*

Doeskin: The inner side of skins from the sheep, lamb, or doe, which is buffed and used primarily for gloves.

Kidskin: Leather from the mature goat, tanned and used principally for shoes, also for handbags; types include *French kid* and *glazed* (which really means glossy) *kid.*

Lizard: Reptile skin with a surface of fine scales.

Patent: Any leather which has been treated with coats of varnish to produce a hard, shiny finish; "real patent leather" is made with leather, but there is also "imitation patent leather" which has a similar appearance, but is much less flexible and durable.

Snakeskin: Made from various snakes, distinguished by scaly surface and, often, varicolored markings.

Suede: Leather finished on the flesh side to produce a velvety surface; originally made usually of kid (often called undressed kid), now frequently made of calf.

Line for line copy: The term for an exact copy of a Paris original made in the United States.

Marabou: Fluffy feathers of the stork, dyed and used for trimmings on clothing, especially negligées and fancy bedroom slippers, as well as for long streamers worn wrapped around the neck.

Mercerized: Denotes a type of permanent finishing used to make cotton yarn softer and stronger.

Mourning: Dark clothing worn for some period of time after the death of a relative or loved one. Victorian mourning customs were extremely elaborate, but the custom of mourning subsided rapidly after the turn of the century. "Deep" mourning clothes for women were entirely black and very plain; the fabric was not allowed to have any luster, and neither trimmings nor accessories were supposed to reflect light. A special dull-finished fabric called *crape* was frequently used in mourning clothes. "Half-mourning" (worn later) might be trimmed with gray or dark violet.

Nailhead: A trim of small metal discs which are punched into (rather than sewn onto) the fabric.

Nap: A soft surface found on some fabrics, created by hairy fibers which lie smoothly in one direction; not the same as a "pile," in which the fibers stand up.

Necklines:

Bateau neckline (boat neck): Cut straight from shoulder to shoulder, the same height front and back.

Camisole neckline: Cut straight across the chest above the bust, and held up by shoulder straps.

Cowl neck: Extra fabric cut or seamed into the neckline forms a drape.

Crew neck: Flat, round band hugs the throat.

Decolletage: Cut low (front and back); a bodice with this neckline is described as "decolleté."

Halter neckline: Cut high in front, usually to the throat, but the back and shoulders are completely bare, with the garment being fastened or tied at the back of the neck.

Jewel   Scoop   U-Neck

V-Neck   Square   Bateau

Cowl   Halter   Sweetheart

Necklines.

Jewel neckline: Cut high around the throat, with no collar; designed to provide a simple background for jewelry.

Sweetheart neckline: Cut in two semi-circular curves which look like the top of a heart.

Nouveau, Art Nouveau: In connection with design, this term usually refers to the fluid, curving patterns, often based on floral motifs, which were fashionable from the turn of the century through the teens; artist Alphonse Mucha was the leading Nouveau designer.

Novelty: Term applied to a fabric, yarn, design, or decoration which is obviously unusual.

Off-the-rack: British term for the American designation "ready-made" or "ready-to-wear"; in French, "prêt-à-porter."

Art Nouveau motifs.

Shoes with Art Nouveau influence, 1890s.

Op Art patterns.

Ombré: A type of fabric coloration, accomplished by weaving, dyeing, or painting, in which a series of hues graduate into one another very subtly.

Op, Op Art: Style based on the use of repeating geometric designs which give the illusion of movement; adapted for fabrics in the 1960s. Artist Bridget Riley's work was a leading source of Op inspiration.

Paisley: Colorful, swirled pattern of abstract, curved shapes.

Typical paisley motif.

Panel: A rectangular-shaped piece of fabric which may be sewn into a garment, as in panel sides on a dress, or sewn onto a garment (for example, at the hips in flapper-style garments, or at the shoulders to form a train).

Pannier: A term used for hoops in the seventeenth and eighteenth centuries, it is now sometimes applied to describe stiffened drapes at the sides or the back of evening gowns.

Passementerie: Elaborate decorative embroidery, generally including cording, beading, fringe, and/or tassels.

Patchwork: Pieces of different material sewn together in some sort of pattern, then made into a garment or an item such as a quilt.

Peasant costume: A term applied to almost any kind of ethnic clothing, denoting styles which have been preserved over a long period of time; these costumes are occasionally imitated for fashionable dress, but more often used as inspiration for new designs.

Picot: An edging formed of very tiny loops, which may be found on cloth, ribbon, lace, or braid.

Pile: A thick surface of standing threads (distinct from nap, which lies flat).

Placket: Opening at neckline, waistline, or sleeve, to allow garment to be put on; constructed with a concealing flap or with finished edges.

Plaid: A pattern in which bars of varying colors and widths cross each other at right angles; in Scotland, each clan (group of families) has its own design of plaid (also called a "tartan"), so some plaids are identified by a clan name. Types include: *Argyle,* a pattern of different-colored diamond shapes, often used in sweaters and socks; *blanket,* large plaid, usually in dark colors with lighter overstripe; *Glen,* alternating squares of large and small checks; *harlequin,* usually, multicolored diamond-shaped blocks; *Tattersall,* usually, two different-colored sets of regularly intersecting lines, on a lighter background.

Plastic: Material made from resin-like substances, and molded by heat and pressure into various forms; manufacture of the first plastic, Bakelite, began in 1909, and plastic became increasingly used in the production of fashion items such as buttons, jewelry, purses, belt buckles, etc.

Pleats: Repeated folds of fabric. Types of pleats include: *accordion,* equal creases alternating inward and outward; *box,* fabric creased toward the back of the fold, so that each fold shows two edges, one pointing right, the other left; *knife,* each fold overlapping the next, so that only one creased edge shows, and all edges point in the same direction; *inverted,* box pleats in reverse; *sunburst,* folds gradually increasing in depth, so that they are narrow at the top and wider at the bottom.

Pocket: A pouch of fabric, which may be seamed into the garment or sewn onto it. Types include: *bellows*, an outside pocket with pleats to make it expandable—also called *saddle bag*; *patch*, a simple pocket stitched onto the outside of the garment; *slashed*, pocket reached by means of a finished slash in the outer side of the garment.

Pre-Columbian: Usually used to refer to the motifs used in South American Indian art before the coming of Columbus. These motifs generally feature rounded shapes, often intricately fitted together.

Prêt-à-porter: French term for "ready-to-wear."

Print: Specifically, fabric having a design which is printed on, rather than woven in. Principal methods of fabric printing are *roller printing*, in which the design is applied to the fabric with inked rollers; and *screen printing*, in which color is applied to fabric through wire or cloth screens. Each color in the design requires a different screen, and the process is more costly than roller printing, but produces a high quality print and can achieve unusual color effects. Other types of printing techniques and types of printing include: *blotch*, colored background printed on, leaving design in natural color of fabric; *duplex*, printed on both sides of fabric; *hand-blocked*, hand-printed with wood blocks or linoleum blocks, most frequently seen in Japanese, Chinese, and Indonesian fabrics; and *photographic*, photographs transferred to fabric by screen or roller printing. Types of prints include: *border* prints, with a running design printed along the selvage of the fabric; *conversation*, unusual or amusing designs intended to cause remarks; *geometric* or *abstract*, non-representational designs; *Jouy*, French landscape or figure prints reproduced in one color on a light background; and *Wedgwood*, white design on a colored ground.

Quilting: Two layers of fabric, with a layer of padding in between, are stitched together, either with simple parallel lines forming squares or triangles, or in more complex designs. Types of decorative quilting include *Italian*, in which the designs have raised outlines; and *trapunto*, in which the designs themselves are raised.

Revers: Wide, shaped lapels.

Ruching: An edging made of finely pleated lace or other material.

Ruffle: Gathered or pleated material, used as an edging or other type of detail; *tiered ruffles* are layered one above another.

Savile Row: London street famous for its custom tailors.

Scalloped: Refers to an edge cut into semi-circular curves.

Seam: The line of stitching which sews two pieces of fabric together, with the raw edges usually being turned to the inside of the garment and the smooth juncture showing on the outside; special types include: *French*, the seam is stitched first with the raw edges to the outside, then the fabric is seamed again, enclosing the raw edges; *piped*, a narrow piece of fabric, sometimes encasing a very fine cording, is stitched into the seam so that it shows on the right side; and *welt*, a seam doubled over on itself and topstitched for decorative purposes.

Self: Refers to use of the same fabric as the garment to create or cover a trimming—for example, "self-buttons," "self-belt."

Selvage: The finished edge of a woven fabric, which runs the length of the goods on both sides and prevents unraveling.

Separates: Parts of a set of garments, each one of which is designed to be worn with various other coordinated, interchangeable parts; that is, one blouse might be worn with a skirt at one time, with pants at another, with a jacket or a sweater, and so on.

Shirring: Parallel lines of stitching set close together and drawn up, causing the material to gather.

Sizing: A fabric finish of starch or some synthetic substitute, used to give body and smoothness to the fabric.

Sleeves:

Angel (Dalmatian): Very long, loose, flowing.

Balloon: Fitted to the elbow, with a full, rounded puff (often with a stiffened lining) from elbow to shoulder.

Batwing: The sleeve fits an armhole which reaches from shoulder to waist, with the fullness of the sleeve gathered into a band at the wrist.

Bishop's: Long, soft sleeve which is moderately fitted through the upper arm, gently flared in the forearm, and gathered into a band at the wrist.

Bracelet (three-quarter): Ends in mid-forearm.

Cap: A circular sleeve, usually very short; something like a cape flaring over the shoulder.

Dolman: The sleeve fits a very deep armhole, which may reach from shoulder to waist, with the fullness of the sleeve tapering along the forearm to a fitted wrist.

Kimono: Cut in one piece with the body, usually extending from shoulder to waist.

Melon

Drape

Cape

Shirred

Puff

Leg-o'-
mutton

Kimono

Dolman
Sleeves.

Cap

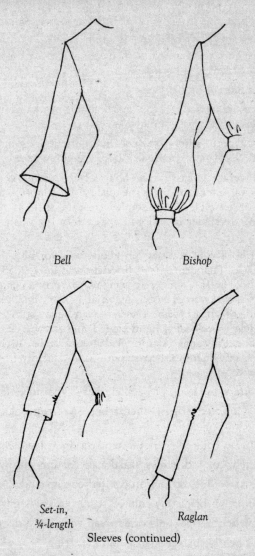

Bell

Bishop

Set-in,
¾-length

Raglan

Sleeves (continued)

Leg-o'-mutton (gigot): Fitted at the forearm, flared from elbow to shoulder.

Magyar: Very full, usually gathered at the wrist.

Peasant: Long, full sleeve which is gathered or shirred onto a drop shoulder, and usually gathered or shirred at the wrist.

Puffed: Full at the shoulder and gathered into a band or elastic opening just a few inches down the upper arm.

Raglan: Set into the garment with diagonal seams from underarm to neckline, front and back.

Set-in: A tailored long sleeve.

Slub: Irregularities in wool, cotton, or silk fabric, produced by weaving in slightly twisted or thickened fibers.

Smocking: A type of stitching which intermittently fastens together bunches of tiny pleats to produce a honeycomb pattern.

Staple: The average length of the fibers of any particular type: the length of the staple may influence the quality of the fabric woven from the fibers—for example, "long-staple" cottons, such as Sea Island and Egyptian, are silkier in feel and appearance than "short-staple" cottons.

Straw: Material of plaited or woven fibers, used for hats, handbags, and shoes. Types include: *baku*, lightweight and finely made of palm fibers, with dull finish—similar to *bangkok*, expensive; *chip*, coarse, inexpensive straw woven of woody material; *leghorn*, fine, plaited Italian straw made of wheat; *Milan*, closely woven Italian straw, very high quality; *Panama*, specifically, hand-plaited fine straw from Ecuador; *raffia*, from fibers of raffia palm in Madagascar; *ramie*, usually called China grass; *sisal*, linen-finished smooth straw, mainly from Philippines, expensive.

Stripes: A pattern made up of parallel lines. Types include:

Algerian: Colored stripes, alternating on cream-colored background.

Bengal: Woven colored stripes (often seen in striped silk ties).

Candy: Bright-colored stripes, usually alternating with white.

Chalk: Narrow white stripes on colored background.

Gypsy (Romany): Brilliantly colored stripes of varying widths.

Hairline: A light stripe, only one thread wide, on a dark ground.

Pinstripe: Slightly thicker than a hairline stripe.

Regimental: Diagonal stripes, normally used on neckties; the term is properly used in Britain to refer to the striped patterns on ties worn by British officers, the colors of the stripes corresponding to the colors of the military regiment; in America, the term is used to refer to any diagonal stripe.

Roman: Stripes of differing widths in vivid colors, running in the weft direction of the fabric.

Satin: Stripe of satin weave in a fabric of another weave.

Shadow: Woven-in stripe, barely noticeable.

Surplice: A bodice which closes by overlapping at the waist from side to side.

Surrealism: A movement in the arts during the late 1920s and early 1930s, emphasizing fantasy and dream-like images; Salvador Dali is the best-known of the surrealists, and the surrealistic influence on fashion is seen especially in the work of Schiaparelli.

Tabard: A garment made of two rectangular panels, joined at shoulders, with sides left open or sometimes joined loosely by cords or tabs of some sort.

Tassel: An ornament formed by a bunch of fringe hanging from a decorative, knob-type top.

Tortoise-shell: The distinctively mottled, semi-transparent shell of the hawk's-bill tortoise, once used widely for accessories. It is now illegal to buy or sell tortoise shell made in the last hundred years in any form. However, the use of tortoise shell declined sharply after World War II, and most tortoise-appearing items made since then are "mock tortoise," made of plastic.

Train: The long back-section of a dress, meant to trail along the floor; also, a separate piece of fabric, attached at the shoulders or at the waist, for the same purpose.

Trompe l'oeil: French for "fool the eye"; in fashion, a knitted-in or pieced-in design which creates an illusion (as of lapels, ties, or pockets that are not really there).

Trousseau: A complete wardrobe for the bride, to be worn during the wedding festivities and on the honeymoon; the term may also include other items for setting up the bride's household, such as linens, stationery, etc.

Tuck: A fold of fabric which is stitched down its length; generally used in a series for decorative purposes; *pintucks* are very narrow and delicate.

Unisex: A term introduced in the 1960s to describe clothes which could be worn by both men and women.

Utility clothes: Designation of clothes conforming to the rules governing yardage of materials and use of trimmings in England during World War II, prescribed by the Board of Trade for rationing purposes.

Weaving: The process by which fabric is made. Lengthwise threads, called the "warp," are crossed by threads called the "weft" or "filling." By varying this process, different "weaves" may be produced. The simplest weave is *plain weave*, in which each weft thread goes under one weft thread, over the next, under the next, and so on; plain weave produces an even surface, such as that of muslin or taffeta. A much stronger fabric is produced by *twill weave*, in which a diagonal rib pattern is created by passing weft threads over one warp thread, then under two or more threads. Other commonly used weaves include: *basket*, using two or more threads together to achieve a plaited effect; *broken twill*, an irregular, zig-zag-patterned twill weave, also called *chevron* or *herringbone*; *figured*, which produces a pattern—small or simple-figured weaves are called "dobby" after the loom on which they are woven, while more complex patterns are named "Jacquard," for their loom; *pile*, in which loops are formed; *satin*, in which one set of threads passes over several of the other set, to produce a very smooth and lustrous surface.

Wedding apparel: Anything worn for a wedding. Just about any kind of garment can be—and has been—worn for wedding purposes; there are no aspects of style or construction which are unique to wedding gowns. However, formal wedding clothes, for both men and women, very often borrow styles from the past, and formal bridal gowns use fine fabrics and expensive trimmings (silks, satins, lace, beadwork, etc.). Apparel for less formal weddings is likely to follow whatever styles are current, with the gowns usually in white, off-white, or a pale color.

Yoke: A section of a garment which fits over the shoulders and is joined to the lower part of the garment by a horizontal seam.

P A R T
T H R E E

A Field Guide to
Vintage Clothing and
Accessories

The game's afoot, Watson!
SHERLOCK HOLMES

Identifying Collectibles by Quality and Period

There are a great many old clothes out there, somewhere. But just being old does not necessarily make a garment collectible. Unless you are collecting from a strictly social/historical perspective—in which case, any garment that was ever worn is of interest!—every item you choose to acquire should have *something* about it that is special, even if that something is just an unusual print or a whimsical detail that appeals to you.

Acquiring garments because you like them, or because they are very typical of their times, can be a perfectly enjoyable approach to collecting. After a while, however, collectors frequently want to become more serious, more selective about collecting. And very often that means looking for clothes that represent the best, most interesting aspects of the times in which they were created.

In looking for these high-quality collectibles, it becomes important to recognize the elements that distinguish hand-finished garments from mass-produced ones, fashion garments from ordinary clothes, and so on. The serious collector needs to know something about construction, fabrics, detailing, etc., as well as learning to recognize the labels that denoted fashion leadership or traditional excellence in their own day.

The first step in determining whether a garment is *really good* and worth collecting is to give the garment a detailed examination (if at all possible). First, see how it hangs; if you can't put it on yourself, or some other person, or a dummy, use a hanger and tissue paper or some kind of stuffing to approximate the way it would look when worn. Then turn the item inside out and look carefully at the way it is made; search carefully for labels (they're not always where you expect them to be); examine the fabric closely; and note how much detailing there is and how well it has been done.

Among the things you might keep in mind when trying to establish the collectibility of a garment are the following.

Clues to Quality

Construction

Fine construction is a guide to quality in any period, but the differences in construction between very good and merely mediocre garments become much more pronounced after World War I. Before that time, when labor was cheaper and mass production was not yet in full swing, handfinished garments were plentiful. After World War I, however, the design of clothing was increasingly fitted to the requirements of manufacturing, and cheaply made clothes proliferated.

In evaluating clothing (especially garments made after World War I), look for the following characteristics that usually mark the construction of fine garments:

- Techniques used to make the garment hang or fit properly; these might involve extra sewing by using several separate pieces instead of one, or they might utilize large, shaped pieces that are more difficult and expensive to cut.

- Seams that are finished on the inside by frenching or some other method.

- Labor-intensive detailing (such as pintucks, covered buttons, faggoting, insets, beaded seams, and so forth).

- Print or plaid fabrics carefully matched at seams and closures.

Fabric

In assessing the quality of a fabric, consider the following. If the fabric is a print, is the printing well done? And is the print design distinctive, with a pleasing or arresting composition—or is it just a hodge-podge, or a cliché? There are quite a few fabrics, especially from the early teens and the twenties, which were designed by noted artists or by well-known fabric workshops; these are especially worth looking for.

Whether the fabric is a print, a woven design, or a solid color, are the dyes strong, with little fading and no bleeding of one color into another? Are the pale colors subtle and delicate, as opposed to weak, muddy, and/or nondescript? And are the bright colors vivid and rich, rather than harsh and flat?

Although it is usually not possible to tell who manufactured the fabric in a garment, there are some exceptions. There may be a selvage somewhere in the garment with the manufacturer's (or even the designer's) name woven in; very occasionally, there will be information about the fabric on the label. In the case of custom- or tailor-made garments, accompanying paperwork may identify the type and source of the fabric.

In any event, it is worthwhile to know that there are some quite famous makers and/or importers of textiles, including:

Courtauld: British fabric company, famous for its silks in the nineteenth century, and for its production of rayon and other synthetic fabrics in the twentieth century.

Bernat Klein: Textile designer and manufacturer, noted for innovative work with color since the early 1950s.

Liberty: For many decades, an important source of fine and unusual fabrics.

Linton Tweeds: Manufacturer of fine-quality tweeds from 1919; supplier to numerous couturiers.

Whether or not you know the source of the fabric, though, your fingers can be a guide to fabric quality. Fine woolens are never scratchy; high-quality fabrics should be soft without being limp—or crisp without being stiff; heavy fabrics should drape well, and should not seem bulky.

Trimmings

Trimmings include a huge variety of items, from buttons to braid, lace to flowers. On fine clothing, the trimmings should be well made, and carefully attached to the garment.

Since beautiful trimmings often outlast the garments they originally adorned, many collectors buy irreparable clothing items just for the trimmings. If the price is right, you should as a rule buy just about anything that has handmade lace, intact beading, unusual buttons, or fine embroidery—no matter what the condition of the rest of the item. The salvaged trimmings can be used in a variety of imaginative and practical ways, such as on pillows or boxes or your own modern clothes, or they can be displayed in the same way as your other collectibles.

Labels

The absence of a maker's label does not mean much in a vintage garment; the label, if there ever was one, may have been cut out or fallen out long since. But when there is a label, what it says can be very important. See Part Two for listings of the great designers, and notes on other fashionable labels.

There may be labels other than that of the maker in a garment or on an accessory. In 1952, the Fur Products Labeling Act was passed, requiring all fur products to be labeled with a correct description of the fur—that is, "sheared black-dyed muskrat" rather than "Hudson seal"! The Textile Fiber Products Identification Act became law in 1960, requiring that garments have an explanation of their fiber content firmly attached. Although there was some voluntary labeling before these laws came into effect, it is likely that if a garment contains a label of this type, it was made after the dates of the laws.

Period: An Outline by Decade

One more thing that is very important in deciding about the collectibility of a garment is its age. Although age isn't the *only* factor which makes a garment valuable, it is certainly one of them; while it's true that a Charles James ballgown from the fifties may be more valuable than the great majority of garments a hundred years older, nevertheless, a nice-but-ordinary day dress worn in 1880 is likely to be worth significantly more than a nice-but-ordinary dress from 1948.

So it is important for the collector to recognize approximately how old a garment actually is. Remember, however, that it is rarely possible to date a garment exactly. Style by itself is not a very precise guide, since styles are made and worn for some time before, and for a good while after, their period of greatest popularity; older styles are revived in later years; and some styles are "classics" that never really go in or out of fashion.

Construction will frequently offer clues, and the best way to learn about construction is to go to a *good* vintage clothing store (i.e., one where the dealer has enough expertise to date the clothes accurately) and look at clothing of different periods to see how seams and hems are made, what type of thread is used, and so on; also, look through some of the sewing books, magazines, and patterns of various periods. These can sometimes be found in second-hand book stores or at estate sales. A little bit of time spent in these pursuits will give you a better understanding of construction techniques and how they've changed.

Fabrics and fasteners are also sources of information about a period which can be very useful in some cases; if a garment has a zipper, for example, it wasn't made before the mid-thirties, and if the fabric contains acrylic, it was made after 1947. So knowing something about the history of clothing materials and manufacture can be a real help. There's a good deal of information on these subjects contained in Part Two of this book, and more is available in some of the references listed in Part Four.

The truth is, however, that unless you have a receipt, a datable photograph, a diary entry, or some other such positive evidence, you will probably never know exactly when a garment was made and purchased. The best you are likely to do, by combining style, fabric, and construction clues, is usually to place a twentieth-century garment accurately within one-half of a decade. With garments from the nineteenth century, when there were few new fabrics or construction techniques introduced, and styles changed less radically, you may be able only to determine a specific decade. In fact, many nineteenth-century garments are referred to simply as early and late Victorian, with early being mid-century and late being 1880s–1890s.

The following decade-by-decade look at the principal aspects of women's fashions should be useful in familiarizing yourself with the characteristics of different periods. Keep in mind, however, that a number of different styles overlapped in any given period. In the listings below, "Principal line" denotes the best-known silhouette of the period.

In most instances, the best-known silhouette is the one that reigned in the middle of a decade, which seems to be the time when fashion makes its strongest statement. Sleeves were at their largest in the mid-nineties, the S-bend reached its most sway-backed line in the mid-1900s, skirts were at their shortest in the mid-twenties, and fashions achieved the height of slinkiness in the middle of the thirties; the emphasized waist of the fifties gave way to the chemise just after mid-decade, and in the midst of the sixties, the mini-skirt appeared. Exceptions to this rule are the two war decades, when fashion evolution was suspended in deference to global conflict.

In the transition from one decade to the next, on the other hand, there is rarely any sharp change. The fashions of 1899 are not easy to distinguish from those of 1901, and the difference between 1959 and 1961 is no more apparent; the same goes for all the decades in between.

In the listings that follow, the section on "Other lines" includes those styles of the past which were still being worn in a decade, as well as those which were introduced during the period and subsequently became more widely popular; "Other lines" also mentions looks that were worn by eccentric or avant-garde fashionables.

The "Important Designers" section lists those designers who were at the height of their influence during the period; however, most of the designers listed overlapped several decades. (For further information on individual designers, see Part Two.)

The following period outlines are primarily based on what was worn in America, where clothing was generally a bit sportier and more relaxed than in Europe. Though the principal silhouettes and motifs of various periods are generally the same, there are significant differences, too. Some garments worn in America—such as prairie-style dresses—were never worn in Europe; other garments—such as the divided skirt—were accepted in America somewhat before becoming fashionable in Europe. But the most opulent and imaginative innovations were seen in Europe first.

To put it simply, changes that led to greater comfort and practicality often began in America and spread to Europe; conversely, changes that took style in radically new directions usually started in Europe and made their way back to America. And in the same vein, most American women were quick to accept fashion innovations that made their lives easier, but comparatively slow to adopt some of the more fanciful dictates of Paris.

The following notes cover women's clothing only. Information on dating accessories, and men's and children's clothing, will be found at the beginning of those sections in the Price Guide. There are also two "Concise Guides" to skirt lengths and period styles on page 139; these can be used for quick reference or as a reminder, but they are very general and won't take the place of thorough information.

1880–1889

Principal line: The "Grecian Bend"—figure corseted to provide small waist; bustle provided extreme emphasis on the derriere; shoulders and bust were fairly natural.

Home-made, two-piece dress of the 1880s. *(Clothing courtesy of Puttin' on the Ritz, Dallas, TX.)*

Other lines: Frontier dress, generally more practical, and including items for everyday wear such as the mother hubbard and the sun bonnet; "aesthetic dress," a romantic/neoclassical, uncorseted style introduced in England.

Popular styles:

Skirts: Skirt flat in front, usually draped back to a bustle projecting straight out from just below the waist; much detail was used on skirts, which were of floor-to-instep length; trains were worn mostly in the evening; early in the decade, skirts were often narrowed through the knees; bustles varied in size throughout the decade.

Bodices/Blouses: Bodices generally tightly fitted, with simple sleeves; some emphasis was added to sleeves at shoulder toward the end of the decade; most bodices long, often drawing to a point.

Jackets/Suits: Tailor-mades, with a masculine or somewhat military jacket over a tied-back skirt, were very popular.

Dresses: Usually two-piece for daytime; evening dresses often sleeveless, with low-cut decolletage.

Outerwear: Many styles of "wraps" were worn, most designed to accommodate the bustle by having a fuller or shorter portion in the back, with longer tails in front or at the sides, and cape-like or dolman sleeves; the Ulster coat was popular, along with the paletot, and long capes became very fashionable toward the end of the decade.

Sports/Play: These garments became more practical toward the end of the decade; skirts were fuller and shorter, bodices permitted somewhat more movement; bathing costumes featured pantaloons shortened to just below the knees.

Lingerie/Leisurewear: Chemises, camisoles, drawers, combinations, petticoats, generally of linen or cotton; also woolen or flannel winter petticoats; some silk undervests; corsets often elegantly made of satin or sateen; dressing gowns popular, along with short "combing" capes for boudoir wear.

Fabrics and trims: A huge variety of fine fabrics, including very delicate wools, silk, faille, taffeta; ruching and ribbons were popular, but again, a very wide variety of trims was used.

Construction and fasteners: Bodices lined and boned; hooks and eyes; many buttons.

Art influences: The pre-Raphaelite movement in art influenced the development of aesthetic dress; Impressionism influenced use of color.

Important designers: House of Worth, Doucet, Redfern.

1890–1899

Principal line: The "hourglass"—very small waist, wide, accented shoulders, fullness at the hips but skirts generally falling close to the body.

Other lines: The "Gibson Girl" (a sportier, trimmer look); aesthetic dress.

Popular styles:

Skirts: Plain skirts (no bustle or draperies), often with gores in front, some additional fullness in back; the bell-shaped skirt was very

The "hourglass" corset, 1890s.

popular, also yoke and sun-ray skirts; skirts were widest (up to nine yards around the bottom) in mid-decade; length was ankle to instep for day, floor-length in the evening; skirts often had ruffles inside the hem.

Bodices/Blouses: Sleeves grew steadily larger and more elaborate for the first two-thirds of the decade; the bosom was slightly full in front so that no separation of the breasts was seen; necklines were high; separate blouses (called shirtwaists and made with shirt tails) worn with skirts became popular in this period.

Jackets/Suits: Jackets fitted at the waist; short jackets such as the zouave and the bolero were popular, but hip-length jackets such as the blazer were also worn; the sailor influence was popular in suits.

Dresses: Emphasis on shoulders, back of skirt; the princess style was popular after 1893 for evening; a sleeveless, open-front caftan was sometimes worn over a day dress at home; the polonaise dress featured a short, draped overskirt.

Outerwear: Long, circular capes, often with one to three flared shoulder capes (which might be detachable), sometimes with a hood for traveling; also, redingote coats (short and long); cardigan sweaters.

Sports/Play: Divided skirts and bloomers were introduced for cycling and other active sports.

Lingerie/Leisurewear: Tea dresses with Watteau-style backs were often worn for afternoon entertaining; all the lingerie of the previous decade continued to be worn, with the addition of corset covers and bust improvers, but fewer petticoats were worn; fancy drawers were popular.

Fabrics and trims: Fabrics tended to be a bit softer and lighter than those of the previous decade; crêpe, batiste, lawn, and piqué were popular; velvet and silk continued to be worn a good deal, as were foulard, moiré, and serge; tweeds began to be popular for sporting outfits; trimmings were somewhat less ornate and less copious than previously, but among those in favor were embroidery, beading, and lace; contrasting and complementary colors and patterns of fabric were frequently used to achieve interest; flounces and accordion pleating were popular.

Construction and fasteners: Skirts usually gored, and made with both a lining and a stiffened interlining; bodices boned and lined, with stiffened lining in large sleeves.

Art influences: Art Nouveau.

Important designers: House of Worth, Liberty & Co., Doucet, Callot Soeurs, Paquin.

1900–1909

Principal line: The "S-bend"—small waist, emphasized derriere, flattened abdomen, low bosom.

Other lines: The Gibson Girl look continued in the early decade; toward the end of the decade, the more natural silhouette was introduced by Poiret and worn by the fashion avant-garde; beginning in 1908, the popular line became much straighter, and the waistline began to rise.

Popular styles:

Skirts: Similar to those of the previous decade, but slimmer through the hips; skirts were floor-length throughout most of the decade, ankle-length by 1909; gored skirts, often with added flounces, were common, and morning-glory and serpentine skirt styles were frequently seen.

Typical white lace-trimmed dresses of the 1900s. The one on the left was probably worn near the beginning of the century, as shown by the rather full, box-pleated skirt; the narrower skirt of the dress on the right suggests that it was worn after 1908. *(Clothing courtesy of Puttin' on the Ritz, Dallas, TX.)*

Bodices/Blouses: Waistlines were brought down to a shallow, curved V in front, allowing the bodice or blouse to puff out and droop slightly over the skirt in the "pigeon breast" effect; necklines were still predominantly high for daytime; sleeves were rather plain early in the period—most frequently bishop-style or elbow-length with a flounce of lace; there was a brief revival of the full upper sleeve at mid-decade; pleated and tucked shirtwaists were popular in mid-decade; bertha collars were worn; the peek-a-boo waist was fashionable in summer; white blouses—both very ornate and very simple styles—were especially popular.

Jackets/Suits: Tailor-mades continued in popularity; jacket styles were varied, including single- and double-breasted fronts (cutaway or straight), waist-length bolero shapes and hip-length basque styles.

Dresses: Until late in the decade, most dresses were still made in two pieces; one-piece dresses (often afternoon or tea dresses) were likely to be in the princess or the empire style; evening lines were the same as those for day, but evening dresses had lower necklines, often with a sheer fichu; shoulders were frequently exposed in the evening, but the upper arm was often covered by a puffed or ruffled sleeve.

Outerwear: Almost all types of coats and jackets continued to be worn; short, snug fur jackets popular in the first half of the decade.

Sports/Play: Fitted bathing suits appeared toward the end of the decade; tennis skirts were above the ankles, and white was now usually worn; linen dusters were introduced for motoring.

Lingerie/Leisurewear: Ruffled drawers popular; the chemise began to replace corset covers from mid-decade on; silk underwear became more widely worn; corsets straight-fronted for first half of decade, becoming lower-busted and much longer after about 1908; attached garters appeared on corsets; flannel, muslin, and taffeta petticoats; wrappers and kimonos worn; negligées high-necked through first half of decade, then low-necked and short-sleeved.

Trims and fabrics: Velvets, satins, and other heavy fabrics declined somewhat in use as the decade progressed, while use of crêpes, chiffons, and other soft fabrics increased; stripes were very popular; much lace was still used in the beginning of the decade; later, fashionable trims included tassels, pom-poms, and decorative buttons; shirring was popular, as was Irish crochet, which was sometimes used for whole blouses or even dresses.

Construction and fasteners: During most of the decade, bodices had much inner construction, usually having a fitted, boned lining that fastened independently of the dress or blouse, which was constructed with a good deal of fullness in front; skirts were usually lined, and high collars were wired or lightly boned; later in the period, the new straight skirts were generally unlined; snaps were introduced during this period, but hooks and eyes were still widely used.

Art influences: Art Nouveau influence continued; Fauvism.

Important designers: Doucet, Poiret, Lanvin, Boué Soeurs, Worth, Callot Soeurs.

Ivory silk-satin wedding gown, draped with silk chiffon and trimmed with silk chenille embroidery. This is the fashionably narrow, drape-fronted style of the early teens. *(Clothing courtesy of Puttin' on the Ritz, Dallas, TX.)*

1910–1919

Principal line: The "natural figure"—a basically tubular appearance, with loose waistline slightly above or below the natural waist; bosom and hips unaccentuated.

Other lines: Styles of the previous decade were still worn by conservative women; opulent Orient-influenced and Art Nouveau styles were worn by the very fashionable; wartime clothes were somewhat more austere and practical.

Popular styles:

 Skirts: The "hobble" skirt (slim and very narrow at the hem, often requiring slits or kick pleats to make walking possible) worn from

1910 to 1914, succeeded by the "peg-top," still narrow at the hem, but with more fullness at the hips; very full, divided "harem" skirts became briefly fashionable around 1911; by mid-decade, skirts were well above the ankle, though toward the end of the decade they dropped back down.

Bodices/Blouses: Tunics (sometimes wired at the hem for a "lamp-shade" effect) were very popular in the first half of the decade, along with lingerie blouses, tailored shirtwaist blouses, and short silk overblouses with embroidery or beading; later in the decade, pull-over-style sweaters and jerseys were in fashion; lower V or U neck-lines were worn throughout the decade, with Medici collars popular in the first half, sailor collars fashionable in the second; Magyar and kimono sleeves were very popular from early in the decade.

Jackets/Suits: Jackets long (below the hip), loose; Norfolk suits were popular, and the suit style in general was rather masculine.

Dresses: One-piece dresses became popular; the chemise style gained favor; lingerie dresses were still worn; the long-waisted, full-skirted robe de style came into fashion early in the decade; at the very end of the decade, the bias-cut dress and the handkerchief hem were introduced; evening dresses of the late decade frequently had tonneau skirts slit to the knees in front, with a panel or swath of fabric forming a trailing train in back; two-piece knit dresses were popular for day in the late decade.

Outerwear: Both fitted redingotes and full, dolman-sleeved one-button coats were worn in the early decade; the trench coat became popular during the war; evening coats were often cape-like, with large, standing collars; fur coats were worn, and fur trimming was widely used for cloth coats.

Sports/Play: The one-piece bathing suit was introduced in 1916, but the two-piece style consisting of chemise top and knee-length knickers was widely worn through the end of the decade; there were many sporting costumes composed of knickers (worn with puttees) or pleated skirts worn with jackets or cardigans.

Lingerie/Leisurewear: Petticoats shorter and slimmer; corsets straight, with little or no indentation at waist; bandeau-style bras-sieres suppressed rather than enhanced breasts; pajamas were intro-duced, usually made of silk in a tunic style with sash.

Trims and fabrics: Silk (often weighted) and soft wools; crêpes of all kinds; rayon began to be seen in mid-decade, and jersey became very popular near the end of the decade; trims very much in favor, especially tassels, ribbons, braid, and beading; late in the decade, crêpe de Chine and silk jersey began to gain popularity as lingerie fabrics, replacing batiste and handkerchief linen.

Construction and fasteners: Although appearing loose and relatively unconstructed, early-decade garments were often made of many pieces, and used a large number of hooks and eyes or snaps, in complex arrangements.

Art influences: Cubism.

Important designers: Poiret, Paquin, Boué Soeurs, Callot Soeurs, Lanvin, Fortuny, Lucile, Chanel.

1920–1929

Principal line: The "boyish" figure—no emphasis on any part of the body; bust flattened, waistline ignored.

Other lines: The "flapper"—an exaggerated version of the prevailing line—popular at mid-decade; the "Chanel" look—a more understated line.

Popular styles:

Skirts: Skirt length early in the decade was near the ankle, then ascended to near the knee in 1925, before slowly descending again thereafter; flared and uneven hems were popular 1928–29, leading the way to the near-ankle lengths of the early 1930s; skirt shapes were tubular in the early decade, and boxy at mid-decade; movement was added to narrow skirts by means of godets and pleats concealed at the sides, or by draping at the back or side; accordion-pleated skirts were popular; separate skirts were often attached to a slip-like bodice suspended from the shoulders and worn with an overblouse.

Bodices/Blouses: Blouses usually loose (no bust or waist shaping) and hip-length or longer, in the overblouse style; raglan sleeves were much used, but sleeveless tops were also popular; necklines were usually simple—round, bateau, V, or cowl; pullover sweaters were fashionable; tops were often sashed or belted at the hip.

Jackets/Suits: Jackets were hip-length or longer, and straight or slightly shaped below the derriere; cardigans were fashionable; the three-piece ensemble—a suit or two-piece dress with matching

Silk and chiffon dress, pale peach with clear beading, over taffeta slip. Early 1920s. *(Clothing courtesy of Puttin' on the Ritz, Dallas, TX.)*

coat—was very popular at mid-decade; the widely copied Chanel suit featured a cardigan jacket and slightly A-line skirt, often with a sleeveless top.

Dresses: One-piece dresses usually had a rather plain bodice, with more detailed skirt; the "little black dress" was extremely popular; the low back was frequently seen on evening dresses.

Outerwear: Coats generally loose, three-quarter or seven-eighths length; capes continued to be fashionable.

Sports/Play: Breeches worn for riding; bathing suits began to be sleeveless; beach pajamas were worn.

Lingerie/Leisurewear: Teddies; kimonos; silk pajamas; elastic girdles.

Trims and fabrics: Silk (less frequently weighted), silk velvet, jersey, voiles, georgette, organza, cashmere, metallic fabrics; acetate and rayon became accepted; fringes, beading, and embroidery were popular

Crystal beading on black chiffon. Mid-1920s. (*Clothing courtesy of Puttin' on the Ritz, Dallas, TX.*)

trims; asymmetric detailing was popular on all types of garments; bold futuristic and geometric patterns became popular around the middle of the decade.

Construction and fasteners: By the 1920s, inner construction had been significantly reduced, or eliminated altogether; very few fasteners—most clothing pulled on; few seams.

Art influences: Art Deco; Egyptian and Native American motifs.

Important designers: Chanel, Vionnet, Louiseboulanger, Augustabernard, Jean Patou, Molyneux, Lanvin.

1930–1939

Principal line: The "long, slender" figure—a natural but slim body shape; the waist was back at its normal level, bosom and hips rounded but not emphasized, shoulders somewhat emphasized.

Taffeta evening gown, with novelty shoulder detail, 1930s. Bright yellow. *(Clothing courtesy of Puttin' on the Ritz, Dallas, TX.)*

Other lines: The nipped-in waist began to reappear near the end of the decade.

Popular styles:

Skirts: Long and narrow through the hips, some straight with kick-pleats, many either bias-cut or with seamed-on bias flares at the bottom; hemlines for day between ankle and mid-calf near the beginning of the decade, rising to below-the-knee by the end; evening clothes ankle- or floor-length.

Bodices/Blouses: Separate blouses were not especially popular in the 1930s; some tailored blouses with slightly puffed sleeves, sometimes with peplums; also knit and crochet blouses; sleeves featured shoulder interest, and were frequently pleated or shirred into the armhole; some shoulder padding, especially from the middle of the decade; in the middle-to-later decade, the bust was given an effect of fullness by pleating it to either a shoulder yoke or a waist yoke—and sometimes to both.

Jackets/Suits: Many jackets featured padded shoulders and fitted waists; they were hip-length, often with lapels; also box jackets, as well as boleros; the "dinner suit"—evening gown with tailored jacket—was introduced.

Dresses: One-piece shirtwaist dresses became fashionable; detailing on dresses was mostly on the bodice, with skirts plain and straight; two-piece print rayon dresses were popular; summer evening gowns of cotton appeared; evening gowns were often backless or halter-style; the robe de style and the little black dress continued in popularity; bias-cutting was a feature of many dresses; in the latter part of the decade, a pleated or shirred bodice was attached to a raised waistline or to a curved or V-shaped yoke set in at the waist.

Outerwear: Coats generally fitted, with evening coats showing a Victorian influence.

Sports/Play: Jodhpurs; knitted maillot bathing suits and two-piece bra-and-shorts suits; shorts and playsuits; trousers with pleated godets opening down from the knees.

Lingerie/Leisurewear: Shaped brassieres; step-ins and tap pants; bias-cut nightgowns; bed jackets; full slips; all-in-ones.

Trims and fabrics: Silk velvet, satin, rayon, and other soft, drapeable fabrics; prints popular; large and/or distinctive buttons; beading found on daywear; lace regained popularity as a trim in the latter half of the decade.

Construction and fasteners: Bias construction was so popular in the 1930s that it is the hallmark of the period; dresses other than button-front fastened at side seam with snaps or buttons; zippers were used after 1935.

Art influences: Art Deco influence continued; Surrealism.

Important designers: Vionnet, Chanel, Schiaparelli, Grès (Alix), Maggie Rouff.

1940–1949

Principal line: The "broad-shouldered" figure—wide shoulders, small waist, hips rounded but narrower than shoulders.

Dress of the early 1940s, with corselet waist accentuated by a painted wooden belt buckle. The exceptional print is in muted shades of orchid, aqua, chartreuse, and orange, on a chocolate-brown background. (*From the author's collection.*)

Other lines: The "New Look"—natural shoulders, accentuated bosom and hips, nipped-in waist—introduced in 1947.

Popular styles: Due to the war, there were few new developments in fashion until 1947; in general, styles throughout the war were similar to those of the late 1930s, though skirts were shorter and there was generally less detail and trimming, due to wartime restrictions on use of materials.

Skirts: A-line or straight, hems just below the knee to 1947, then lengthening; wartime skirts had little detailing, but what there was accentuated the hips with pockets and draping; late in the decade, skirts became fuller, with gores, gathers, or circular cut; "New Look" skirts sometimes had padding through the hips; during the war, slacks—usually pleated in front, with straight, rather full legs—were worn extensively in place of skirts.

Bodices/Blouses: Simple; blouses often had darts at the waist, and the back button closure was popular; peplums were fashionable; sloppy Joe sweaters were worn by younger women; sleeves were generally simple, but shoulders were almost always padded; short sleeves were fairly full at the top, narrowing to fit the arm; necklines simple, jewel-style or with small Peter Pan or convertible collars; postwar necklines were lower, with more detail, and the shoulder lost its padding and began to slope.

Jackets/Suits: Many different jacket styles, but most were fitted at the waist or bolero-style; suits generally rather severe during the war; after the war, a popular suit design featured a longer jacket, fitted at the waist and slim over the hips, with one button or tie and wide revers, paired with a long, narrow skirt; the "New Look" suit topped a long, narrow skirt or a very full skirt with a jacket featuring a tight waist and flaring peplum.

Dresses: The wartime dress was skimpy, but some had draping at bust and/or hip; shirtwaist dresses remained popular, and there were some princess dresses; jacket and dress ensembles were fashionable; pinafores were worn, as were ruffled gingham dresses and Mexican-style dresses; later in the decade, square-dance dresses were popular; wartime evening dresses were often of cotton or some other informal fabric, and were cut much like day dresses, with the addition of floor-length skirts and perhaps ruffles; postwar afternoon and evening dresses often featured bustle and pannier effects.

Outerwear: A wide variety of coats, but generally rather boxy during wartime; both fitted coats (princess or redingote style) and very full wraps accompanied the "New Look."

Sports/Play: Pedal-pushers; dungarees; ranch-style pants and cowboy shirts.

Lingerie/Leisurewear: Similar to 1930s, but slips were shorter; the corset—often in the form of a waist cincher—and the taffeta petticoat were reintroduced to create the "New Look"; the housecoat was introduced.

Trims and fabrics: Many forms of rayon; crêpe and gabardine were popular; velvet was likely to be made of rayon or cotton rather than silk; gingham, denim, and other casual fabrics came into fashion.

Construction and fasteners: Most dresses fastened at the side with zipper, buttons or snaps; war regulations limited the amount of fabric in garments (making wartime clothing often recognizable by such details as fake pockets, shallow hems, etc.); toward the end of the decade, inner construction, such as boned bodices, began to reappear.

Art influences: Very little, due to the war.

Important designers: Adrian, Valentina, Pauline Trigère, Nina Ricci, Mainbocher, Dior, Claire McCardell, Jacques Griffe, Balenciaga, Balmain, Hardy Amies, Charles James, Jacques Fath, Marcel Rochas, Jacques Heim.

1950–1959

In the 1950s, such a variety of styles developed that it is difficult to isolate a single principal line. There were at least three silhouettes which characterized the 1950s: a watered-down version of the "New Look," with small, belted waists and full skirts; a continuation of the postwar "pencil-slim" trend, featuring very narrow skirts and fitted

Beaded knit cocktail dress, 1950s. The entire dress is slightly iridescent. (*Clothing courtesy of Puttin' on the Ritz, Dallas, TX.*)

tops; and appearing in the latter half of the decade, the semi-fitted "sheath" and the waistless styles known as "sack," "chemise," and "A-line." The underlying body shape for each of these styles was different, with the result that women either wore what fitted their natural body shape best, or (probably more often) altered their natural body shape by means of foundation garments. Dior's practice of introducing a new silhouette twice a year affected the whole couture community, and fostered a new variety in fashion.

Also during this decade, a distinct style for teenagers and young people developed. Youth fashion was divided into three types: the "bobby-soxer" look, marked by the wearing of many petticoats, poodle skirts, penny loafers, and the like; the "Ivy League" look, which was based on such "classic" garments as pleated skirts, button-down shirts and Peter Pan blouses, V-neck pullovers and cardigan sweaters; and late in the decade, the "student" look, built around the wearing of tights and leotard with a shift-style pullover dress.

There were also alternative styles worn by special groups and individualists of varying ages, including the "Beatnik" look, which was comprised mostly of black garments, including tight pants or straight skirts with oversized sweaters. This was actually a variation on the widely popular "Italian" look in sportswear, which followed the same lines, but was brightly colorful. "Peasant-style" clothing of various ethnic persuasions was also popular in the 1950s.

Popular styles:

Skirts: Skirt length generally mid-calf for day, a bit longer for cocktails, floor-length for evening—but there was a good deal of variance in skirt lengths, based on individual preference; toward the end of the decade, skirts approached the knees; the majority of skirts were either quite full (gathered or pleated) or very straight; circular skirts, often elaborately decorated, were popular.

Bodices/Blouses: A wide variety of styles, but on the whole, blouses were fitted, with a sloping shoulder line; nylon blouses with front tucking were popular items; decorated sweater sets were very fashionable.

Jackets/Suits: Suits of all sorts were worn, including the slim tailored suit, the softer dressmaker suit, and the Chanel revival.

Dresses: The shirtwaist and the princess dress were popular early in the decade; toward the end of the decade, the chemise and A-line styles gained favor; strapless, full-skirted evening gowns were fashionable; the cocktail dress became an important wardrobe item; the "bubble" dress—full, puffed skirt gathered into a band just below the knees—was introduced for evening wear late in the decade.

Outerwear: Coats of all kinds were worn, but among the classic styles of the 1950s were the topper and the clutch coat; stoles were popular; evening coats of brocade, taffeta, or some other dressy material were in fashion; the car coat was worn a good deal for suburban activities.

Sports/Play: Bermuda and Jamaica shorts; clam-diggers; Capri and toreador pants.

Lingerie/Leisurewear: A variety of brassieres, including wired, padded, long-line, and strapless; stiffened net petticoats; "pettipants"; baby-doll pajamas; brunch coats, popovers, and other "house-dresses."

Trims and fabrics: Many new synthetic fabrics introduced, including polyester, which appeared in 1953; faille was extremely popular, along with shantung and velveteen; felt was used extensively for circular skirts; nylon became popular for lingerie.

Construction and fasteners: Generally the same as previous decade.

Art influences: Abstract Expressionism.

Important designers: Dior, Givenchy, Balmain, Cardin, Roberto Capucci, Bonnie Cashin, Ricci, James, Chanel, Trigère, Jean Dessès, Griffe, Vera Maxwell, Norman Norell, Heim.

1960–1969

In the 1960s, several distinct fashion styles developed and overlapped. Furthermore, the idea of expressionistic, individualized dressing came into its own, and as a result, there were so many different types and styles of garment that it is really impossible to categorize them all. But for practical purposes, we can look at three distinct silhouettes in the 1960s: the "couture" look that began the decade; the "youth revolution" of the mid-decade; and the "romantic" and "hippie" styles of the late decade.

The couture look was basically a continuation of the late-1950s styles, with shorter skirts; the essential silhouettes were the semi-fitted sheath, the A-line, the blouson, and the empire. This style was current for the first three or four years of the decade, and was worn by the more conservative throughout the decade. By day, the typical garments were: for casual wear, a shirtwaist dress, or a straight or pleated skirt, with a tailored blouse or a sweater; for a dressier daytime look, a dress

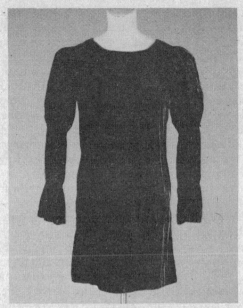

Velvet mini-dress with mameluke sleeves, 1960s. *(Clothing courtesy of Puttin' on the Ritz, Dallas, TX.)*

(sheath, blouson, princess, or A-line) or suit (usually with straight or A-line skirt, short, slightly fitted jacket). Hemlines for day were just below the knee. In the evening, the empire line was fashionable for formal occasions, as was the long princess sheath or blouson dress; at-home evening styles included two new looks—very full "palazzo" pants and the caftan.

The "youth revolution" look which began to catch hold about 1964 focused on mini-skirts and, later, pantsuits; lines were crisp and geometric, colors bold, and trim minimal. The A-line and the tube were the most frequently employed silhouettes, with skirts shortening from just above the knee in 1964 to mid-thigh by 1968. Double-knit fabrics became important for their ability to hold a stiff, sculptural line, and new, unusual materials such as vinyl and plastic were used, along with Op- and Pop-printed fabrics.

Skirts and pants were generally attached to a yoke which rested on the hips, producing the so-called "hipster" line; these were frequently worn with very snug ribbed turtlenecks or with large-collared, full-sleeved blouses. Pantlegs ranged from narrow stove-pipes to wide flares. Jackets and tunics worn over pants were usually to lower-hip or mid-thigh, with a slightly fitted A-line. Mini-dresses were severe and tailored by day, trimmed with frills or flounces at wrists and hem for evening; another evening look was glittery and quite bare at the top.

The "romantic" and "hippie" looks overlapped a great deal, since both were melanges of nostalgic styles and ethnic/tribal influences; the romantics sought a richer, more dramatic style than the prevailing fashion, while the hippies wanted to make an anti-fashion political statement, but often the result was the same. Typical garments included granny dresses, bell-bottom pants, neo-Edwardian jackets, long, gypsy-style skirts made of bandannas or neckties, and fringed leather vests. Motifs and garments of the 1920s and 1930s were adopted, either in reproductions or in original garments from thrift shops and flea markets.

Tie-dyed fabrics were popular, as was patchwork; tops were often made with different fabrics used for sleeves, collar, yoke, etc. Beads, fringe, feathers, leather, and embroidery were all popular trimmings. Halter-tops were worn, along with batik T-shirts and tops that resembled long underwear. There was no distinctive evening or formal wear associated with this style, although long dresses were often made up with velvet, lace, and other dressy fabrics. Fancy sleeves were popular, and such long-unseen sleeve styles as the mameluke and the Dalmatian reappeared on mini-skirted dresses.

Garments from the romantic/hippie category sometimes look like garments of another place or period, but they are usually identifiable as products of the 1960s by their fabrics and construction. However, these styles heavily influenced the clothes of the early seventies, and it is not easy to distinguish the two periods. In general, however, garments of this type from the seventies are more likely to show signs (such as polyester thread and department store labels) of having been mass-produced and mass-marketed; during the 1960s, when the style was more "underground," many garments were handmade and/or sold in small boutiques.

Art influences: Op; Pop.

Important designers: Rudi Gernreich, Jean Muir, Yves Saint Laurent, Betsey Johnson, Mary Quant, Cardin, André Courrèges, Oscar de la Renta, Emilio Pucci, Balenciaga, Givenchy, Norell, Valentino.

Concise Guide to Period Emphasis

PRIMARY MOTIF	SECONDARY MOTIF	DETAILING
1880–89: Bustle	Long waist	Derriere
1890–99: Big sleeve	Small waist	Shoulders
1900–09: Small waist	Mono-bosom	Bodice
1910–19: Narrow skirt	High waist	Center
1920–29: Dropped waist	No bosom	Skirt
1930–39: Bias cut	Natural figure	Bodice
1940–46: Padded shoulder	Small waist	Hipline
1947–55: Small waist	Full bosom	Bodice
1956–63: A-line	Raised waist	Little
1963–69: Long leg	Slender figure	Little

Concise Guide to Daytime Skirt Lengths

1880–99: Floor-length

1900–09: Varied, from floor-length to ankle-length

1910–19: Rising gradually from ankle-length to mid-calf

1920–29: Rising from mid-calf to knee-length in 1925–27; uneven and descending hems in 1928–29

1930–39: Rising gradually from near-ankle-length to above-mid-calf

1940–49: Below-the-knee until 1946, dropping back to mid-calf

1950–59: Rising gradually from mid-calf to below-the-knee

1960–69: Rising quickly from knee-length to above-the-knee in 1965

Concise Guide to Evening Skirt Lengths

1880–1920: Generally, the same as daytime lengths

1920–29: Usually the same as daytime length, but sometimes longer

1930–39: Usually floor-length

1940–49: Usually floor-length until late in the decade, when the ballerina-length became popular

1950–59: All lengths from below-the-knee to floor-length; generally, the more formal the occasion, the longer the skirt

1960–69: Same as previous decade until 1965, after which time mini-skirts were frequently worn for evening, though floor-length ball gowns and prom dresses continued to be worn

Pricing Vintage Clothing

Once you have decided that a garment is—in itself—worth collecting, you must then decide whether you personally should be the one to collect it! This is a decision based partly on personal taste (do you really love it?), partly on the existing shape of your collection (does it fit in?), and partly on the price. The acceptability of the price depends, in turn, on two factors: whether or not you can afford it, and whether or not it is worth it.

"Worth it" is an elastic concept. What may be worth only a little to one collector is worth a lot more to another. But factors of personal desire aside, the basic criterion for assessing a price is its relationship to the overall market. That is, you don't want to pay much more for an item than you would pay for a very similar item elsewhere. Further, you don't want to pay more for an item than you could realistically recoup if you later decided to sell the item. Ideally, of course, you want to pay *less* for the item than you could get in resale.

As discussed in Part One, *where* you buy an item is generally going to make a difference in the price; dealers are usually higher than garage sales, stores are more expensive than flea markets, and some stores are much more expensive than other stores. Geography also affects prices significantly. As a rule, prices are lower in the Midwest, where vintage clothes are relatively plentiful, than on the two coasts. Of the two coasts, vintage items are usually higher on the West coast, where everything trendy (including, ironically, "old" clothes) is more expensive.

The bottom line on all this is that there is really no such thing as a typical price for a vintage garment or accessory. To illustrate this fact, I asked mail-order dealers and store owners all across the country how they would price each of six frequently found vintage garments. I gave each dealer exactly the same description, and stipulated that they were to assume the garments were in very good condition. The results? Take a look. (Where there are both low and high figures, they come from two different dealers; some dealers from the same state may have given amounts in-between the low and the high.)

1. A 1920s silk georgette dress, flapper-style, sleeveless, with a drop waist and embroidered panels.

Mail order dealers:

California: $150–200
Idaho: $125
Indiana: $45–65
Nebraska: $75
New Jersey: $75–100
North Carolina: $75–200

Store owners:

Arizona: $150
California: $125–400
Illinois: $60–80
Indiana: $65–85
Massachusetts: $80–125
Michigan: $85
New York: $75–250

2. A Victorian cotton nightgown, long sleeves, with tucks and embroidery.

Mail order dealers:

California: $50–75
Idaho: $85
Indiana: $55–80
Nebraska: $45
New Jersey: $45–75
North Carolina: $50
Ohio: $55

Store owners:

Arizona: $75
California: $65–400
Illinois: $35–40
Indiana: $25–65
Massachusetts: $28–85
Michigan: $65
New York: $45–145

3. A circular felt skirt from the 1950s, with extensive appliqué trim.

Mail order dealers:

California: $85–100
Idaho: $50
Nebraska: $30
New Jersey: $35–40
North Carolina: $35
Ohio: $25

Store owners:

Arizona: $45
California: $36–50
Illinois: $30–45
Indiana: $25–60
Massachusetts: $30–48
New York: $200

4. A 1930s rayon print day dress, bias cut, with decorative buttons.

Mail order dealers:

California: $55
Idaho: $45
Nebraska: $60
New Jersey: $35–40
North Carolina: $25
Ohio: $35

Store owners:

Arizona: $65
California: $48–200
Illinois: $15–20
Indiana: $20–35
Massachusetts: $24–85
Michigan: $40
New York: $35–175

5. A chemise-style mini-dress, nylon lace over taffeta, long sleeves, ruffles at hem and wrists, late 1960s.

Mail order dealers:

California: $30
Idaho: $10
New Jersey: $12–20
Ohio: $10

Store owners:

Arizona: $18
California: $47–50
Illinois: $10–12
Indiana: $8–15
Massachusetts: $18

6. A man's wool tuxedo, satin lapels, date uncertain.

Mail order dealers:

California: $75
Idaho: $65–85
Indiana: $25
Nebraska: $85
New Jersey: $35–75
North Carolina: $30
Ohio: $45

Store owners:

Arizona: $40
California: $85
Illinois: $30–35
Indiana: $35–60
Massachusetts: $55–65
Michigan: $45
New York: $200

As you can see, the prices cover an enormous range. In some instances, one dealer's price is three or even four times higher than another's. Of course, in this survey, each dealer was free to imagine the garment, and if they had all actually seen the same item, their prices might have been a bit closer—but perhaps not much. The wide differences in price come from differences in location, overhead, the typical clientele of the dealer, and so on.

The moral: there is no one "right" price for any garment. And the price guidelines in this book can only be taken as examples, never as actual indicators of value.

Perhaps foremost among the variables that determine price is *condition*. No matter how wonderful a garment *once* was, if it has deteriorated badly, it has very little value. Part One covered some types of repairs you might reasonably undertake to make yourself, and a few discreet repairs will not radically lower the value of a garment. But past a certain point, repairs cannot save the integrity of a vintage piece, and most of its value is simply—sadly—gone.

Here are the conditions in which vintage garments may be found: "poor," in very deteriorated condition overall, and/or having irreparable damage; "fair," visibly worn, with some noticeable repairs; "good," some wear, no visible repairs; "excellent," very little wear, no repairs; "mint," apparently never worn, with very few signs of aging.

Most merchandise offered by dealers is in good to excellent condition. As a rule of thumb, consider that merchandise in fair condition is worth at least twenty-five percent less than that in good condition, whereas excellent condition is worth about fifteen percent more than good condition. For mint condition, add another fifteen percent for newer items (postwar) and twenty-five percent for older things. Items in poor condition should be purchased only for salvage—i.e., for special trimmings, for making patterns, etc.—and you should pay only for the value to you of the salvageable parts.

Sometimes you may also find "new-old" merchandise, which was never even sold; it has been sitting in a warehouse somewhere, perhaps for decades. New-old stock is not necessarily in "mint" condition, however; there may be signs of aging, such as fading, weakening of fabric, etc. There may also be set-in creases which are impossible to remove, water damage from improper storage, discoloration due to long exposure to dust or sunlight, and a whole host of other problems. As a rule, new-old merchandise is in the same category as good-to-excellent merchandise, and priced accordingly.

How to Use This Guide

Each division of the Price Guide begins with three introductory sections. The first section, "Contents," explains exactly what is (and is not) included in the division. Next, "Arrangement" specifies how the items are put in order—by type of garment, by skirt length, by fabric, etc. The third section, "Collecting Notes," comments on which kinds of items are relatively plentiful, and which are more difficult to find. "Collecting Notes" also includes, in some divisions, historical information which is not covered elsewhere in the book.

Next, there is a glossary of terms which apply to the particular type of garment or accessory covered in the section. The "Women's," "Men's," and "Children's" sections are each self-contained, so when a garment—like the Norfolk jacket, for example—is worn often by men, women, *and* children, it is listed in all three sections.

The third part of each section is the listing of individual items, with prices. Each item is described in as much detail as possible, based on the information available. Some dealers provided very full descriptions, while others gave virtually no useful details—so there is a wide variance in the completeness of the listings. However, I have tried to include only those items which are described well enough for the listing to be useful as a point of comparison.

Clothing items, unlike most other collectibles, do not readily fall into easily defined categories. If, for example, something is described as a "bowl," you know *exactly* what it is, at least basically. But if something is described as a "dress," it's impossible to have any idea what it might look like. Moreover, if the bowl is described as "pine" or "Majolica" or "cut crystal," then you are well on the way to knowing just what kind of bowl it is. But if a dress were described as "lace" or "beaded" or "Dior," you would still be very far away from having a useful picture of what the dress is like!

All of which goes to say that it would take about half a page to describe *each* item in this price guide well enough to give you a really good mental image—and that's obviously impractical. So I have tried to focus on the information—such as fabric and detailing—that will give you an idea of the factors that determine its value.

Each listing also includes the probable period of the item, if it can be determined. In most instances, periods are given in full decades (e.g., 1920–29), but since styles often changed in mid-decade, then lapped over into the *next* decade, there are also cases in which periods are given as either late in one decade or early in the next (e.g., 1928–34). There are some instances, too, in which a garment might have been new at any time in a twenty-year span (e.g., 1900–1919).

There are several ways to make use of the information in this guide. First, just browsing through the entries will help you get a feeling for the varieties of vintage clothing, the price ranges of particular items or periods, and so on. Second, if you have a specific *item* in mind, you can locate something similar and make comparisons. Third, if you have an amount of *money* in mind, you can focus on the dollar signs, and scan the entries to see what kinds of things might fall into that price range.

Finally, for those of you new to collecting, these lists can be a help in discovering just what sorts of things you would most like to collect— while for those of you who are old hands, some of the enticing descriptions may offer fresh inspiration to sustain you through the delightful difficulties of collecting vintage clothing!

The Prices in This Book

The majority of prices given in this book are undoubtedly for items in good-to-excellent condition. But there are higher prices which probably represent items in mint condition, or items which have been expertly restored; there are also low prices, which may be for items with some problems.

The prices come from several different sources: dealers, store owners, auction houses, collectors, and my own observations. In general, I have tried to select only those sources which are of a type available to any reader. That is—these prices come from the same stores, flea markets, auction houses, and mail-order dealers that the average reader might readily do business with.

Each price is preceded by its source, whether it be store, mail-order dealer, flea market, individual, or auction. The auction prices are actual selling prices, but prices in the other three categories are those set (optimistically!) by the dealers, and not necessarily those actually paid by buyers. Stores and mail-order dealers very rarely bargain, but of course, if an item doesn't sell, it will eventually be put on sale and sold at a price lower than the one given here. Flea-market dealers will often bargain, so flea-market prices might (or might not) be set higher—anywhere from fifteen to thirty percent—than the actual purchase price is expected to be.

It should be noted that the "flea markets" from which these prices come are not side-of-the-road affairs; they are gatherings of professional and semi-professional dealers who generally know their merchandise; the prices are sometimes the same as those of stores, other times considerably less. All of the flea-market prices come from observations made either by me or someone whose judgment I trust, so all items listed are known to be in good-to-excellent condition; in the case of dealer-supplied prices, I have only the dealer's opinion on condition.

Another warning about prices. The prices given here were all in effect during the third quarter of 1988; by the time you read this, however, two things will probably have happened. The first is inflation. You may want to add an extra five to ten percent to each price in order to offset the seemingly inevitable decrease in the value of money.

The second thing is market shifting. Prices for vintage clothing do not just keep on going steadily up; there are changing "fashions" in vintage apparel just as there are in modern clothes, so an item which is in great demand—and therefore fetching high prices—one year may be less coveted, and so less expensive, the next. (These trends are usually related to trends in current fashion, so when the up-to-the-minute look is slim and slinky, bias-cut thirties dresses enjoy a vogue, but when hemlines rise, twenties styles are more in demand.)

So, keep in mind that any particular price in this price guide will not necessarily have increased in the time that elapses before you read it; it may just as well have decreased a bit. And remember that with vintage clothing, as with stocks, it is best not to buy when the demand is high! Keep up with the fads and wait them out. If New Look suits or Victorian petticoats are "in," buy only if you find a bargain; otherwise, wait until they are "out," and prices are lower.

The various changes and adjustments which I've mentioned above probably offset one another in most cases. In practical terms, the best thing to do is put a window of about twenty-five percent on either side of a price listed in this guide, and use that range to define the probable value of a comparable garment. That is, if a fifties crêpe cocktail dress is listed at $36, and you find a similar one in good-to-excellent condition, consider that a reasonable price range for it would be from $27 to $45.

One more thing. Although there are some prices listed here which I think are very good values, I haven't included any real "bargain" prices, because every bargain is one of a kind, and represents a stroke of luck rather than the state of the market. There are certainly some bargains still out there, and just to prove it, I'll tell you that I very recently bought a wonderful Vera Maxwell jacket, in pristine condition, for $3 at a local thrift outlet. But the prices in this book are intended to reflect what vintage clothes are typically being sold for by dealers who know the market.

This book covers the American market primarily, but I have included a few prices from London auctions, and these are noted in the listings. The vintage clothing market in London is very active, and it influences the American market; also, a good many designer clothes come onto the market in London, which makes the market there interesting to follow. You can bid by mail in the London auctions if you want to (see Part Four for information on how to do this).

Once again and finally, it can't be stressed enough that the prices given here are merely and *only* meant to serve as guidelines. When using these prices to determine the value of something you want to buy or sell, please take into consideration all the variables mentioned previously, and employ liberal amounts of common sense!

Price Guide

Auction Lots

In the main price listings, individual items, including those sold at auction, are described and priced. But in addition to selling individual items, auction houses frequently sell clothing in "lots"—that is, several pieces which must be bought together. The standard practice is to include some less desirable pieces with one or two *more* desirable pieces.

Many interesting items are included in lots, and they can be good bargains. But of course, it's impossible to determine the price paid for any specific item in a lot, since it may include from three to ten or more items. So in order to give you an idea of what clothing is selling for in lots offered at auction, here is an assortment of lot prices from 1988 sales at Christie's East. (Where the sale price differs by more than $100 from the value range estimated by the auction house, I have included the estimated value as well.)

- A collection of children's costumes, including a cream piqué dress, the scalloped over-bodice collar and cuffs embroidered with self-colored acorns and foliage; a gold striped rose silk dress trimmed with fringe; and eight other items: $385.

- A cream satin damask evening dress, the empire bodice and train covered in Battenburg lace, ca. 1915; together with two cream net and lace 1920s dresses; and three others: $286.

- A collection of trimmings, including Chinese embroidery, grosgrain ribbon, crocheted trim, and batik; together with a group of silk shawls: $66.

White cotton pantaloons and corset cover. (Also see following photo.) *(Clothing courtesy of Puttin' on the Ritz, Dallas, TX.)*

Edging of the pantaloons in preceding photo, with fine schiffli embroidery. *(Clothing courtesy of Puttin' on the Ritz, Dallas, TX.)*

- A collection of Victorian dresses (mostly late nineteenth century), including one of cranberry and black silk trimmed in velvet; a deep blue velvet two-piece dress with bead-trimmed bodice; a pale green striped silk dress printed with rosebuds; and five others: $825 (est. value $200–300).

- A cream satin evening dress, the empire bodice and trained skirt trimmed with beaded lace, with a red velvet sash at the waist, ca. 1915; together with a maroon georgette evening dress trimmed in voided velvet and a silk rosette at the waist, 1920s; and three other dresses: $99.

- Ten skirts, including one of plum silk, one of brown linen, and one of pale green silk with ruched and pleated trim and bustle back, ca. 1880: $110 (est. value $200–300).

- Eight Victorian bodices, including one of blue silk velvet with cut steel buttons; and another of plum and cream silk brocade: $33 (est. value $150–250).

- Six jackets, including one of brown voided velvet; another of black wool with moiré shawl collar and toggle closures; and one of black silk-satin edged in lace: $33 (est. value $180–260).

- A robe of blue-green foliate-printed wool challis, trimmed with blue satin, 1910–15; together with five earlier dresses, including one of striped rose silk: $55 (est. value $200–300).

- A cream silk tape lace jacket, with braid button and tassel trim, lined in self-colored silk; together with a pink silk evening dress, overlaid with beaded cream net and embroidered at the bodice with faux pearls and rhinestones; and a self-embroidered cream silk dress, 1910–15: $308.

- Five 1920s dresses, including one of cream lawn with lace insertions; another of pale mauve cotton embroidered with white beads; and one of sea-green silk velvet with lace skirt: $132.

- Six 1930s evening dresses, including one of pale blue crêpe trimmed with bugle beads; and two of black lace: $55 (est. value $150–200).

- A collection of fifteen hats, including 1920s cloches and wide-brimmed hats trimmed with flowers: $110.

- A collection of fur accessories, including a white marabou cape labeled "Emily Wetherby"; a black fox collar; and a brown and white fur muff; eight in all: $55.

- A celluloid hoop, attached to woven cotton laces and waist-band, in its own celluloid box, labeled "Bell o' the Ball"; together with six knitted swimsuits, 1920s–1930s; and a bathing cap: $132.

- Two linen chemises, one trimmed with crocheted cotton lace; together with two appliqué cotton aprons, 1930s; a white cotton nightgown; and two blouses trimmed with tucking and lace: $154 (est. value $250–350).

- Five white cotton shirtwaists, including two trimmed with faggoting; and three of lace-trimmed and embroidered lawn: $110 (est. value $200–300).

- A cream net boudoir spread, appliqué and embroidered with floral motifs; together with a group of accessories including silk lingerie, crochet gloves, and beaded purses, 1920s–1930s: $275.

- A collection of paisley shawls, including one woven in multi-colored bands of foliate and boteh motifs; and another of deep crimson, turquoise, and black with black center; eight in all: $1760 (est. value $750–1000).

- A sea-green satin gilt brocade evening coat, with silk velvet collar and label "Page, Paris"; together with two gilt brocade jackets and a tunic, 1920s: $154.

- A collection of suits, including: one of black faille with peplum-waisted jacket, another of navy blue wool; together with two wool dresses, 1940s–1950s: $66.

- Three chemise-style beaded dresses, including: one of black silk embroidered with crystal-beaded floral and geometric motifs; and another of orange georgette with matching underslip, 1920s: $198.

- Four white cotton christening gowns, each worked with hand-embroidery and lace trim: $132.

- Fourteen porcelain hat pin holders, most handpainted, ca. 1910s; together with a large collection of period hat pins: $550 (est. value $300–400).

And here are a few prices for auction lots sold in the London market by Phillips:

- A 1910 dress of oyster chiffon with embroidered decoration; another of midnight-blue silk; and one of ivory silk: $117.

- A 1910 dress of café-au-lait silk, another of black lace, each bearing the maker's label "Molyneux, 14, Rue Royale"; and a coat with a Paquin label: $180.

- A 1920s dress of black velvet with looped tassel and tie skirt; and a coat of checkered design: $234.

- A 1920s skirt of ivory silk; one of beige crêpe; and a silk blouse: $144.

- A 1920s dress of dark blue chiffon printed in shades of red, having matching wrap; one of cream chiffon with button trim; one with gold brocade decoration; and one of violet velvet: $396.

- A 1930s dress of cherry crêpe, having bias-cut skirt and ribbon trim; another of ivory silk and crêpe; and one of black net: $1440 (est. value $180).

- A 1930s dress of conflower blue crêpe with pleating to the front; one of ivory silk with front button fastening; and two others: $234.

- A 1950s dress of white linen, the bodice with gold bead decoration; and another, each bearing maker's label "Paquin, Paris and London": $468 (est. value $72).

- A quantity of boudoir jackets, petticoats, and nightwear, mainly silk: $234 (est. value $90).

- A quantity of velvet and chiffon costumes, mainly 1920s: $198.

- A cape of black silk and yellow through to green-tiered chiffon; a part cape and dress similar; a robe; and three dresses of chiffon: $342.

- A quantity of costumes, mainly daywear, 1940s–1960s: $99.

Women's Clothing

Lingerie: The Foundation of Fashion

CONTENTS

The category "Lingerie" includes all items customarily worn *under* clothing (e.g., petticoats, pants, corsets, bras, and so on). Garments worn for "undress"—such as nightgowns, robes, lounging attire, etc.—are found in the "Relaxing" section.

Silk drawers (pale peach) and a pink silk georgette chemise, both probably from the teens. *(Clothing courtesy of Puttin' on the Ritz, Dallas, TX.)*

ARRANGEMENT

The price lists are organized first by type of garment, then by type of fabric.

COLLECTING NOTES

There are two categories of lingerie which are very widely available in the vintage clothing market; these are Victorian/Edwardian whites, and peach-colored silks and satins from the 1920s and 1930s. These items are often beautiful and well worth acquiring, but less common items may be more desirable from a collecting standpoint. Black lingerie seems relatively uncommon; prints are also harder to find. Foundation garments are also not frequently seen; look for them, as some are very interesting. Net petticoats of the 1950s, on the other hand, seem fairly abundant, along with nylon slips from the same period.

Princess-style full slip, turn of the century. Handkerchief linen. (Also see following photo.) *(Clothing courtesy of Puttin' on the Ritz, Dallas, TX.)*

TERMS

Foundation garments: garments worn in order to shape the body; primarily, brassieres and corsets or girdles. Types include:

Bandeau: an unshaped brassiere

Bosom improver (or amplifier): an underbodice with ruffles across the bosom to create more fullness

Contour bra: padded with foam or fiberfill

Corselette: an unboned corset

Corset: a boned or otherwise reinforced garment which controls the torso both above and below the waist

Ruffle of the slip in preceding photo, with embroidered, scalloped edge and Irish lace inserts. Note the texture of the handkerchief linen. *(Clothing courtesy of Puttin' on the Ritz, Dallas, TX.)*

Girdle: a garment which controls the torso at and below the waist

Guépiere: a waist-cincher

Long-line bra: extends to waistline

Strapless bra: no straps, usually underwired

Uplift bra: shaped with stitching of some kind on the cups

Underclothing: garments worn under clothing, whether for warmth, for modesty, or for added shaping of the outer garments. Types include:

Bloomers: very full underpants

Boxer shorts: loose, square-legged underpants

Briefs: short, body-hugging underpants

Camisole: an underbodice, ending at the hips, usually cut straight across the bosom, with narrow straps

Chemise: sleeveless, waistless one-piece undergarment, usually about mid-thigh length; the "envelope chemise" has a closed or snap crotch

Corset cover: sleeveless underbodice, usually cut with a low scoop neckline; ends at or below the waist

Crinoline: very full, stiffened petticoat

Drawers: usually knee-length underpants, often wide and frilly

Full slip: covers body from shoulder straps to any length

Half-slip: covers body from waist to any length

Knickers: underpants gathered at the knees

Pantaloons: underpants ranging from below-the-knee to ankle-length

Petticoat: full half-slip, often with decorative edge

Tap pants: wide-leg underpants, usually ending high on the thigh

Combination undergarments: serving the purpose of two or more items of underclothing or foundation. Types include:

All-in-one: combination bra and corset

Bra-slip: full slip with bra-style top

Body suit: one-piece stretch garment

Cami-knickers: combination camisole and knickers

Teddie: one-piece camisole-and-panty combination, usually with a snap crotch, ending high on the thigh

Union suit: one-piece knit garment

LINGERIE LISTED BY TYPE AND VALUE

Bra, black longline, 1950–59, source: store, *$18.00*

Bra, silk, bandeau style, silk embroidery, 1910–19, source: store, *$30.00*

Camisole, cotton (white), with crochet yoke in poinsettia pattern, 1900–09, source: store, *$45.00*

Camisole, silk, ribbon, and handmade lace, pale pink, 1900–09, source: store, *$98.00*

Chemise, silk (mint green), trimmed with lace and ribbon rosettes, 1920–29, source: store, *$38.00*

Chemise, silk (pink) with lace trim, 1920–29, source: store, *$28.00*

Chemise, silk georgette (black), straps and sash of two-sided ribbon, lace borders, trimmed with pastel silk rosettes, 1920–39, source: flea market, *$20.00*

Silk chiffon teddy, 1920s or 1930s. Black, with ecru lace and pink/apricot ribbons. (*Clothing courtesy of Puttin' on the Ritz, Dallas, TX.*)

Corset, cotton-satin, with garters; new-old, 1900–09, source: flea market, $25.00

In the late nineteenth century, corset names—such as "Primrose Path," "A La Spirite," and "The Venus"—reached a crescendo of romance. But there were noteworthy exceptions, such as the health corset reassuringly named the "Admiral Dewey."

Corset, satin with embroidery, hourglass style, 1890–99, source: store, $80.00

Corset cover, cotton (white) with lace trim, 1910–19, source: mail order, $18.00

Corset cover, cotton (white), crochet yoke, 1900–09, source: mail order, $25.00

Drawers, cotton (white), knee-length, very full, with deep eyelet ruffles, 1890–99, source: flea market, *$18.00*

Drawers, silk, mid-thigh-length, wide, with scalloped edges, 1910–19, source: store, *$45.00*

Pantaloons, cotton (white) with cotton lace, 1900–19, source: flea market, *$29.00*

Pantaloons, cotton (white) with lace trim, 1910–19, source: mail order, *$18.00*

Pantaloons, cotton, with cotton lace, 1900–19, source: store, *$69.00*

Petticoat, cotton (heavy, white), tiered ruffles top to bottom, below-the-knee-length, 1950–59, source: store, *$15.00*

Petticoat, crinoline, black, knee-length, 1950–59, source: store, *$30.00*

Petticoat, crinoline, pastel, knee-length, 1950–59, source: store, *$20.00*

Petticoat, flannel, hand-quilted, mid-calf-length, 1890–1909, source: mail order, *$75.00*

Petticoat, nylon (black) with red taffeta flounce, mid-calf-length, 1950–59, source: store, *$15.00*

Petticoat, plain, wool/cotton blend, with back pleating to accommodate bustle, 1880–89, source: flea market, *$40.00*

Petticoat, silk with heavy lace, floor-length, 1880–99, source: store, *$165.00*

Petticoat, silk, pale yellow, pintucks and scallops, long train, 1890–99, source: flea market, *$95.00*

Petticoat, taffeta with grosgrain waistband, flounced hem, deep apricot, floor-length, period ?, source: store, *$20.00*

Petticoat, taffeta (dark green), below-the-knee length, full, with velveteen trim, and jingle bells attached inside hem, 1940–59, source: individual, *$20.00*

Petticoat, velvet, with embroidered band at hem, short train; two small tears in hem, 1880–89, source: flea market, *$80.00*

Pettipants, nylon, mid-calf length, 1950–59, source: flea market, *$8.00*

Slip, black lace half-slip, 1940–49, source: store, *$5.00*

Slip, handkerchief linen with much handmade lace, princess style, deep flounce, floor-length, 1890–99, source: store, *$390.00*

Slip, nylon (red), below-the-knee, with lace and accordion-pleated trim, 1950–59, source: mail order, *$12.00*

Slip, taffeta, mid-calf length, midnight blue, with flounce, 1950–59, source: flea market, *$15.00*

Teddy, silk (peach), button crotch, lace trim, 1930–39, source: store, $32.50

Teddy, silk (pink), 1930–39, source: mail order, $20.00

Teddy, silk (yellow), lace inserts, button crotch, silk ribbon straps, 1920–29, source: mail order, $20.00

Teddy, silk with fancy lace at bodice and legs, 1920–29, source: mail order, $35.00

Teddy, voile (French, made with Egyptian cotton, buttercup yellow), with pintucks, lace edging, 1920–29, source: store, $69.00

Underpants, silk (pink), elastic back, smooth front with flat pleats and wide lace, tap style, never worn, 1930–49, source: store, $42.00

Underpants, silk jersey step-ins (pale pink), trimmed with crochet lace, 1920–29, source: store, $59.00

Underpants/bandeau, silk (pale peach), mid-thigh-length drawers and bandeau bra, small amount of embroidery, 1920–29, source: flea market, $15.00

The Basics: Everyday and Evening Wear

This section takes in all garments worn in the normal course of a day and evening, from housedresses to ballgowns. These are the clothes one puts on when "getting dressed," whether for work or for a social occasion. Things worn at home for lounging or for casual entertaining are covered in the "Relaxing" section, while clothes worn for outdoor play or for sports will be found in the "Playing" section.

The section is divided into four categories: "Tops," "Bottoms," "Suits and Jackets," and "Dresses." The first two parts of this section—"Tops" and "Bottoms"—are meant to include garments which were designed as separate items. But over the years, the tops and bottoms of many two-piece dresses and suits have become separated, so it is likely that some of the garments described were originally part of such an outfit.

Tops

CONTENTS

The category "Tops" includes all separate garments worn to cover the body above the waist.

ARRANGEMENT

Listings are organized first by type, then by fabric.

COLLECTING NOTES

The nylon blouses of the late 1940s and 1950s are frequently seen; crêpe blouses of the 1940s are also widely found. Women's tailored shirts, on the other hand, are not found so often, and neither are the casual tops of this period. Among older things, Edwardian whites and lingerie blouses of the aughts and teens are in relatively good supply, but overblouses of these periods, and of the 1920s, are less so, and tunics are hard to find. Beaded and sequined sweaters and sweater sets of the 1950s and 1960s are fairly plentiful, but bulky sweaters, and sweaters from earlier periods, are much less so.

TERMS REFERRING TO TOP GARMENTS

Basque: a long overblouse, fitted through the waist and over the hips

Camp shirt: very full cut, with breast pockets and wide sleeves that reach to the elbow

Cardigan: sweater that buttons down the front

Cowboy shirt (Western-style): fitted, front and back yoke, snap closings

Cossack: high, standup collar, side closing, full sleeves

Gibson: tailored shirtwaist, high neckline, leg-o'-mutton sleeves

Halter: backless top without sleeves

Harem: close-fitting top, ending above the midriff

Middy (sailor): overblouse with sailor collar

Overblouse: any top meant to be worn on the outside of the lower garment rather than being tucked in

Peasant: gathered at neckline (frequently with drawstring) and at sleeve edge

Peek-a-boo: shirtwaist partly made of sheer material or eyelet embroidery

Poor boy: fitted, ribbed sweater, hip-length, with boat neck and elbow-length sleeves

Pullover: sweater or other top that is put on over the head

Bustles are still the latest fashion in the 1880s.

The Big Sleeve is the hallmark of the 1890s.

The 1900s: Tea gown of ivory net, lace, and silk. Inset: A detail of the tea gown, showing silk appliqué outlined with gold braid.

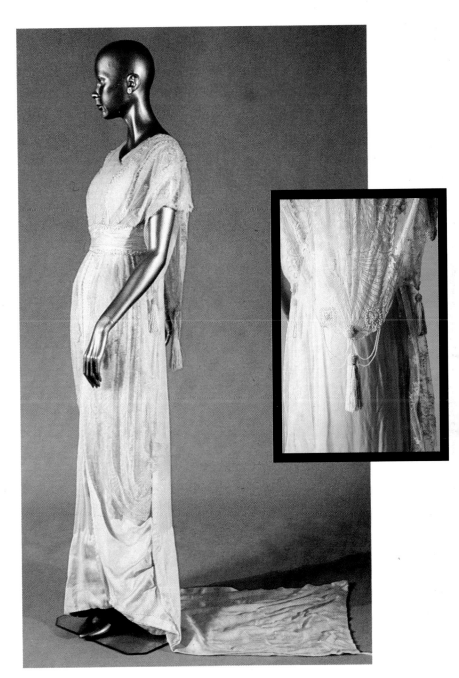

The Teens: Evening gown of ivory satin. Inset: At the back of the evening gown, the lace capelet falls to a point, trimmed with pearls and tassels.

The Twenties: Evening dress of tangerine georgette, with mink- trimmed hem and gathered side panel.

The Teens: Gray chiffon dress, with pannier draped side panels, picoted edges.

The Thirties: Taffeta evening gown, with quilting at hemline, peplum, and epaulettes.

The Forties: Ensemble by Adrian.

The Forties: Ball gown by
Charles James.

The Fifties: Cocktail dress designed by James Galanos. The
skirt of pleated chiffon measures
26 yards at the hemline!

The Sixties: Designer Coco
Chanel brings back her
classic suit.

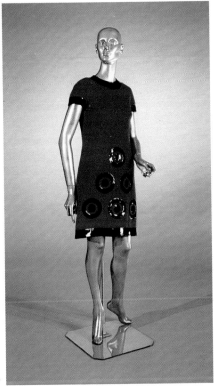

The Sixties: Designer Pierre
Cardin creates a new look for a
new generation.

Full Circle: Balenciaga returns to the bustle.

Two silk georgette blouses in shades of pink, from the teens. The one on the left is embroidered with silk thread; the one on the right has insets of filet lace. *(Clothing courtesy of Puttin' on the Ritz, Dallas, TX.)*

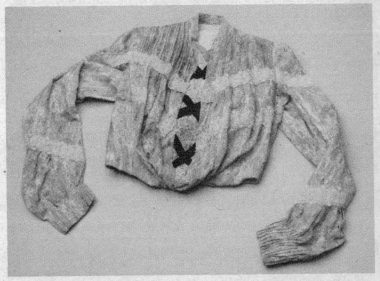

A bodice from the mid-1900s. The fabric is a paisley design, with a woven-in shadow stripe, in shades of lavender, apricot, and pale gold. Trim includes ecru lace and rosettes, and black velvet ribbon. *(From the author's collection.)*

Shell: sleeveless, plain front, with jewel neckline

Shirtwaist (waist): term used in the early twentieth century for a tailored blouse

Sloppy Joe: very loose sweater, hip-length, long sleeved, round or V neck

Step-in blouse (body shirt): top attached to panties to prevent riding-up

TOPS LISTED BY TYPE AND VALUE

Blouse, beaded all over, pigeon-breast front, ¾ sleeves with beaded fringe, 1900–09, source: store, *$185.00*

Blouse, cotton (sheer) with handmade lace, tiny pearl buttons, "suffragette" style, 1910–19, source: store, *$48.00*

Blouse, cotton (white) with much eyelet, 1890–99, source: mail order, *$50.00*

Blouse, cotton (white), "armistice" style, Irish crochet trim at collar and cuffs, 1910–19, source: store, *$50.00*

Blouse, cotton (white), "armistice" style, white with crochet trim, 1910–19, source: mail order, *$40.00*

Blouse, cotton (white), back-buttoned, with lace trim and hand embroidery, 1900–09, source: mail order, *$65.00*

Blouse, cotton (white), eyelet collar, leg-o'-mutton sleeves, 1890–1909, source: store, *$95.00*

Blouse, cotton (white), high neck, lace panel down front, 1900–09, source: store, *$65.00*

Blouse, cotton chambray (gray), high neck, white braid trim, 1910–19, source: mail order, *$25.00*

Blouse, cotton lace (black) over bright pink silk faille, hooks up the front, black ribbon-work on sleeves which end below the elbow with trim of black ribbon rosettes, 1880–99, source: store, *$150.00*

Blouse, cotton with lace trim, square neck, 1910–19, source: mail order, *$30.00*

Blouse, cotton with woven-in plaid design, short puffed sleeves with cuffs, small round collar, button front, nipped-in waist, 1940–49, source: mail order, *$5.00*

Blouse, cotton, Gibson Girl-style, lace inserts, 1900–09, source: store, *$25.00*

Blouse, cotton, high neck, back buttons, long, slim sleeve, embroidered front panel, 1880–95, source: store, $95.00

Blouse, cotton, very fine fabric with woven-in shadow stripe, allover paisley print, pigeon-breast front, novelty long sleeves, extensive trim of lace and velvet, with front panel of lace over silk, boned inner bodice, silk has deteriorated, some deterioration of fabric under arms, 1900–09, source: individual, $30.00

Blouse, crêpe (peach), deep round neckline with faggoting effect, sprinkled with rhinestones, 1940–49, source: store, $45.00

Blouse, crêpe (white) with blue trim at collar and cuffs, white embroidery and beadwork, 1910–19, source: mail order, $40.00

Blouse, fabric unknown (sheer), with ruffled front and rhinestone buttons, 1950–59, source: mail order, $8.00

Blouse, fabric unknown, blue striped floral, lace insets, high neck, long sleeves, 1890–99, source: store, $45.00

Blouse, lace, with embroidery, boned, 1880–99, source: mail order, $32.00

Blouse, lawn (white), high neck, wedding-type, with much lace and detail, 1890–1909, source: mail order, $60.00

Blouse, lawn (white), with ruffled neck, extremely large sleeves, 1890–99, source: store, $80.00

Blouse, mixed fabrics, handmade hippie/peasant style, flamingo-print rayon, sleeves of aqua silk print, black silk yoke, pink silk print collar, ties at neck closure made of plaited crewel yarn, 1960–69, source: store, $49.00

Imitation pearls were originally created by filling small, blown-glass bubbles with an iridescent substance distilled from the water used to wash whitebait fish.

Blouse, nylon (pink), ruffles and pearl buttons down front, 1950–59, source: mail order, $10.00

Blouse, nylon (white) with rhinestone buttons and lace trim, 1950–59, source: store, $12.00

Blouse, nylon lace (white), short sleeves, scoop neck, 1950–59, source: store, $8.00

Blouse, rayon (black), shallow scooped neckline, rhinestone buttons, long, cuffed sleeves, 1940–49, source: store, $12.00

Blouse, rayon (print), front buttons, small shoulder pads, 1940–49, source: mail order, $22.00

Blouse, rayon (print), peplum, long sleeves, self-bows over front snap closures, 1940–49, source: store, $15.00

Blouse, rayon crêpe (navy), long sleeves, jewel neck, back-buttoned, 1940–49, source: mail order, $15.00

Blouse, rayon crêpe (white), back-buttoned, with swirls of gold sequins around jewel neckline (new-old), 1940–49, source: store, $55.00

Blouse, silk (beige), back-buttoned, short sleeves, embroidered front, 1950–59, source: store, $17.00

Blouse, silk (burnt orange), short sleeves and round neck, with bead-work on neck, sleeves, and bottom, hip-length, 1920–29, source: mail order, $60.00

Blouse, silk (ivory), lace at neck and cuffs, front worked in Chinese embroidery, with a wisteria pattern, 1910–19, source: mail order, $45.00

Blouse, silk (pale gold), openwork collar, inset and trim of crochet lace, tucked front, ¾ sleeves, 1900–09, source: flea market, $35.00

Blouse, silk (yellow), Peter Pan collar, long sleeves, 1940–49, source: mail order, $30.00

Blouse, silk crêpe, back-buttoned, beaded neckline, 1940–49, source: mail order, $60.00

Blouse, synthetic blend, psychedelic print, full-cut with long, full sleeves and convertible collar, 1960–69, source: store, $8.00

Blouse, velvet (burgundy), fitted waist, button front, gold passementerie trim, 1880–99, source: store, $95.00

Blouse, velvet cut to chiffon, unfitted, round neckline with small tie at center, 1900–09, source: store, $40.00

Blouse, velveteen (ivory), very low neckline, diamond design of silver beads and rhinestones, 1920–29, source: mail order, $50.00

Overblouse, cotton (white), middy style, with navy trim, 1910–19, source: flea market, $15.00

Overblouse, crêpe, surplice bodice with long peplum, waistband tying to the back, long sleeves, period ?, source: store, $39.00

Overblouse, novelty fabric, perforated, trimmed with long, wide silk ties at neck, silk trim on cap sleeves, and gathered slightly to a wide silk band at the hips, trimmed at hips with two clusters of multi-colored crocheted balls, 1910–19, source: flea market, $25.00

Overblouse, silk (black), with carnival glass beads scattered at neck and hemline, short sleeves and deeply scooped neck, 1920–29, source: store, $25.00

Overblouse, silk (print), cropped, tie-sides, cape sleeves, 1930–39, source: flea market, $28.00

Overblouse, silk crêpe, deep peach, embroidery around neck, small sailor-style collar, drawstring waist, long sleeves, 1910–19, source: store, $98.00

Overblouse, silk georgette (sheer), trimmed with deep scallops of silk ribbon openwork, short sleeves, round neck with trim, ties at side, pale peach, 1920–29, source: flea market, $40.00

Overblouse, silk moiré taffeta (sea-green), short sleeves, V neck, full bust pleated to hip-length waist yoke, 1930–39, source: store, $29.00

Shirt, gabardine, Western-style, peach with brown yoke, cuffs and piping, colorful chainstitch embroidery on yoke, 1940–49, source: store, $89.00

Shirt, rayon faille with brown gabardine, two-tone, Western-style, embroidered cowgirl and bull, 1950–59, source: store, $49.00

The cardigan sweater takes its name from the woolen overvests worn by Lord Cardigan's troops in the Crimean War; Balaclava, the wintry site of Cardigan's famous "Charge of the Light Brigade," gave its name to their woolen headgear. Lord Cardigan's accomplice in the Crimean fiasco was Lord Raglan—and there's no need to explain what *he* contributed to the modern wardrobe.

Sweater, cashmere (beige) cardigan, mink collar, 1960–69, source: store, $75.00

Sweater, cashmere (navy) cardigan, allover pattern of intricate white beading, 1950–59, source: store, $210.00

Sweater, fabric unknown, lined cardigan, with extensive beading, 1960–69, source: mail order, $50.00

Sweater, lambswool (cream), hand-beaded, silk lining, 1950–59, source: store, $40.00

Sweater, wool (black) cardigan, hip-length, silk ribbon scrollwork all down the front, 1950–59, source: store, $49.00

Sweater, wool (cream), heavily beaded, 1940–59, source: store, $60.00

Beaded cardigan sweater, white on navy blue, 1950s. *(Clothing courtesy of Puttin' on the Ritz, Dallas, TX.)*

Sweater, wool (yellow) cardigan, black and gold bead trim on front, cuffs, and bottom, 1950–59, source: store, *$38.00*

Sweater, wool blend cardigan, with allover knit-in iridescent sequins, bands of large and small iridescent purple glass "jewels" and pearl beading at neck, hem, edge of long sleeves, 1950–69, source: store, *$50.00*

Top, allover sequined, multi-color, V neck with ribbed waistline, 1960–69, source: mail order, *$30.00*

Top, silk (apricot), harem style—long, full sleeves, bodice cut snugly to end above midriff, 1930–39, source: store, *$49.00*

Top, velveteen, fitted, scoop neck, cap sleeves, 1950–59, source: store, *$25.00*

Tunic, cotton (heavy, striped), with Mexican embroidery, long flared sleeves, 1960–69, source: store, *$69.00*

Tunic, cotton sailcloth with "dayglo" zodiac print, knee-length, angel sleeves and hem trimmed with black ball fringe, 1960–69, source: store, *$28.00*

Tunic, silk georgette (screen print), mid-calf length, camisole top, 1920–29, source: individual, $15.00

Tunic, vinyl faux-snake, tabard-style, knee-length, gold-tone buttons and chain trim, 1960–69, source: store, $25.00

Bottoms: Skirts, Pants

CONTENTS

The "Bottoms" category includes any separate item which covers the body below the waist.

ARRANGEMENT

Skirts are arranged according to length (because that's the easiest aspect to recognize), then by fabric. Pants are arranged first by style, then by fabric.

COLLECTING NOTES

Circular and straight skirts of the 1950s are plentiful, although the elaborately decorated circle skirts (with appliqués, sequins, etc.) are not so easy to find. Edwardian skirts seem to be in fairly good supply, but

Circle skirt of the 1950s, with brightly colored Mexican scene. The scoop-necked velveteen top is the sort of style that might have been worn with a circle skirt. (*Clothing courtesy of Puttin' on the Ritz, Dallas, TX.*)

hobble skirts of the early teens are less common. Slip-skirts from the 1920s are not seen all that often either.

Capris and pedal pushers are plentiful, as are pleated trousers. Less common are the harem pants and "bell-bottoms" (made with godet inserts opening out from the knees) of the 1930s.

SKIRT LENGTHS

Basic skirt lengths are: floor-length, instep-length, ankle-length, mid-calf, below-the-knee, knee-length, above-the-knee, and mini (four to six inches above the knee). Some specialized fashion terms used to designate length are:

Ballerina: between mid-calf and ankle

Street length (cocktail): hemline one to three inches below knee

Formal: hemline at ankle or just covering instep

Micro-mini: just covers thighs

Maxi (granny): ankle- or instep-length

TERMS REFERRING TO SKIRTS

Balloon (bubble, tulip): fitted at waistline, fullness held into fitted band at hemline

Bell (dome): gathered or pleated at waistline and stiffened to form bell shape

Bias-gored: made of multiple fabric sections cut on the diagonal

Circular: created from a full, half, or quarter circle of fabric

Dirndl: straight skirt gathered at waist

Flared: fitted at hips and full at hemline

Full (peasant): gathered, pleated, or flared, with greatest fullness at hemline

Habit-back: sporty, tailored skirt, ankle-length, fitted at the hips, flaring toward the hem, with a partially stitched-down inverted pleat at center back

Handkerchief: made of uneven lengths in such a way that the hemline ends in points

Hipster: cut to rest snugly on the hips, with the top edge well below the natural waistline, usually held in place with a wide, fitted band

Hobble: ankle-length slim skirt, slight fullness at top, very narrow at hem, usually with slit or hidden pleat

Kilt: knife-pleated, short, wraps to one side and is closed with leather straps, buckles, or decorative pins

Morning glory (trumpet): gored skirt with flare at the bottom

Overskirt: separate skirt worn over another

Pegged (peg-top, tonneau): pleated or gathered at waist and hips, very tapered at hemline

Ruffled: hemline finished with fullness greater than body of skirt

Sarong: wrapped, with gathers or soft drape at waist and hipline

Slit: very narrow, with openings at front, side, or back to allow movement

Straight (sheath): fitted, slim

Swing: flared skirt with many gores

Tunic (tiered, apron): skirt with attached overskirt

TERMS REFERRING TO PANTS

Bell-bottoms: legs flared from knee to hemline

Bermuda: short pant that ends just above the knee and fits close to the leg

Bib (overalls): pants with square or rectangular panel (with shoulder straps) attached at waist

Capri: very tapered leg, ends above the ankle

Clam digger: mid-calf length, full leg, cuffed

Culotte (gaucho, pantskirt, split skirt): skirt divided into two leg sections

Harem: very full, gathered at waist and ankle

Hipster: cut to rest snugly on the hips, with the top edge well below the natural waistline, usually held in place with a wide, fitted band

Jamaica: shorter than Bermudas, longer than short-shorts

Jeans: blue denim, pockets front and back, top-stitching, metal fasteners

Palazzo pants (lounging pants): long, very wide flare from hipline to hemline

Pedal pushers: mid-calf length, fitted

Peg-leg: pleated or gathered top, very narrow width at hem

Sailor: double-button front opening, lacing at back waist, wide flare leg

Straight (stovepipe): width of leg less than eighteen inches

Surfers: tight-fitting, ending at the knees

Toreador: tight-fitting, hemmed just below knee, wide waistband

SKIRTS LISTED BY TYPE AND VALUE

Floor-length, crêpe (black), gored, 1940–49, source: flea market, *$10.00*

Floor-length, silk velvet (black), 1930–39, source: store, *$125.00*

Floor-length, wool, very plain, 1890–99, source: flea market, *$35.00*

Instep-length, wool (gray), gored (slightly bell-shaped), many small covered buttons, stitching details, 1900–09, source: store, *$65.00*

Ankle-length, cotton (calico print), prairie-style, with self-ruffle, 1890–1909, source: mail order, *$45.00*

Ankle-length, linen (white), with embroidery, narrow, 1908–19, source: mail order, *$75.00*

Ankle-length, linen, gored, 1900–09, source: store, *$40.00*

Ankle-length, net (white), deep embroidered border, grosgrain waistband; skirt very narrow, 1910–19, source: flea market, *$17.50*

Mid-calf, cotton (black), circular, with handpainted purple and gold lilies all around, 1950–59, source: store, *$35.00*

> If you are interested in vintage clothes to wear, take all your measurements carefully, and carry a list of them, along with a tape measure; this will help out enormously at flea markets and estate sales.

Mid-calf, cotton circle skirt, with flamenco dancer and Carmen Miranda-type figures, handpainted, 1950–59, source: store, *$45.00*

Mid-calf, cotton duck, striped, novelty pocket trim, 1940–49, source: store, *$35.00*

Mid-calf, cotton-satin (lavender, quilted), circular, 1950–59, source: mail order, *$22.50*

Mid-calf, cotton (bright print), gathered, 1950–59, source: store, *$9.00*

Mid-calf, felt, circular, with allover Abstract Expressionist-style print, 1950–59, source: store, *$79.00*

Mid-calf, rayon (black), full, pleated, period ?, source: mail order, *$25.00*

Mid-calf, rayon (navy), accordion pleats, 1950–59, source: individual, *$25.00*

Mid-calf, silk faille (black), full, pockets, 1950–59, source: store, $48.00

Mid-calf, taffeta (cream), circular, with black velvet stripes, 1950–59, source: mail order, $28.00

Mid-calf, wool (gray), 6-gore, 1945–55, source: mail order, $12.00

Mid-calf, wool, straight, 1940–49, source: store, $6.00

Below-the-knee, acetate quilted circle skirt, white, with large black poodle applique, well-done decorations, 1950–59, source: store, $75.00

Below-the-knee, gabardine (plaid), wide waistband, novelty pocket details, 1940–49, source: individual, $20.00

Below-the-knee, nylon quilted circle skirt with scattered rhinestones, 1950–59, source: store, $20.00

Below-the-knee, wool (nubby, plaid), straight, kick pleat, 1950–59, source: store, $15.00

Below-the-knee, wool plaid, kilt style, 1950–59, source: store, $15.00

Knee-length, cotton (print) dirndl, side zip, 1950–59, source: mail order, $20.00

Knee-length, cotton (print), peasant-style, 3 tiers joined by bands of cotton lace, 1940–49, source: flea market, $16.00

Mini, cotton twill (gold), 1960–69, source: store, $10.00

Mini, wool (black), Ungaro label, 1960–69, source: store, $40.00

PANTS LISTED BY TYPE AND VALUE

Capri, fabric unknown, Op-art pattern of lime-green squares on white background, back zipper, new-old, 1960–69, source: store, $28.50

Capri, silk, lined, with zip front and side pockets, 1950–59, source: mail order, $8.00

Capri, velvet (red) with rhinestone-trimmed front panel, 1950–69, source: store, $15.00

Capri, wool (brown, textured), window-pane plaid, fully lined, 1960–69, source: store, $12.00

Pedal Pushers, cotton (turquoise), never worn, 1950–59, source: store, $24.00

Pedal pushers, gingham (pink and white), 1950–59, source: store, $10.00

Shorts, wool (plaid) Bermudas, 1950–59, source: store, $15.00

Slacks, gabardine (black), soft pleats, side zipper, 1940–49, source: store, $32.50

Slacks, gabardine (brown), pleated front, side pockets, 1930–39, source: store, *$10.00*

Wide-leg, cotton (blue), ankle-length full legs, side buttons, 1940–49, source: store, *$10.00*

Suits and Jackets

CONTENTS

In this category are skirt and jacket combinations, and jackets which were intended to be worn over a dress, blouse, or sweater, primarily to serve as part of an ensemble rather than as outerwear. Some of the jackets listed here were probably once part of a suit or dress-and-jacket ensemble, but since they are now solo, they have to be treated as

Suit of the late 1930s, with very wide revers and deep cuffs. Brown gabardine, with trim in two shades of rose-brown. *(Clothing courtesy of Puttin' on the Ritz, Dallas, TX.)*

Wool gabardine walking suit, turn of the century. (*Clothing courtesy of Puttin' on the Ritz, Dallas, TX.*)

separates. Jackets which have heavier material and a looser cut—and were meant, presumably, to be worn for warmth, perhaps over several layers of clothing—are included in the "Outerwear" section.

ARRANGEMENT

Suits are arranged first by length of skirt, second by type of fabric. Jackets are listed by type of fabric.

COLLECTING NOTES

Suits, especially "walking suits," are among the most available items from the Victorian and Edwardian periods—perhaps because they were generally made from sturdy materials. Suits from the 1940s and

1950s are also plentiful. But—there seem to be far fewer suits from the 1920s and 1930s.

Stranded suit jackets from the 1940s and 1950s are commonly found items, and Edwardian jackets are also accessible. Harder to find are the artfully designed stand-alone jackets of the 1920s and 1930s.

TERMS REFERRING TO SUITS

Chanel: suit with cardigan jacket, slightly A-line skirt

Dinner (theater): tailored suit of dressy fabric

Dressmaker: suit with feminine styling, such as draping

Tailleur: suit with tailored styling

Walking: a daytime suit so-called because the skirt was of a type (relatively!) easy to walk in

Jacket of tape lace, turn of the century. (Also see following photo.) (*Clothing courtesy of Puttin' on the Ritz, Dallas, TX.*)

TERMS REFERRING TO JACKETS

Bell-boy: fitted, waist-length, with standup collar, usually braid trim

Blazer: semi-fitted, hip-length, single-breasted, with patch pockets

Bolero: above-the-waist, round neckline, no collar, no buttons

Box: straight, unfitted, ending slightly below the waist

Cardigan: collarless, with front button closing, hip-length

Chanel: braid-trimmed cardigan

Edwardian: fitted, double-breasted, with deep back vents, wide lapels, length to top of thigh

Eton: fitted, waist-length, with standup or wide, notched collar

Mao: below-the-waist, unfitted, with side front closing (buttons or ties), standup collar

Norfolk: featuring box-pleat front with slot for matching belt, length to hip or mid-thigh

Back of the tape lace jacket in preceding photo. *(Clothing courtesy of Puttin' on the Ritz, Dallas, TX.)*

Peplum: features a separate pleated or gathered section between waist and hipline

SUITS LISTED BY TYPE AND VALUE

Floor-length, linen walking suit, hip-length jacket with wide collar, button trim, 1900–09, source: mail order, *$135.00*

Floor-length, silk, 3-piece, skirt of shirred silk strips alternating with net lace, floor-length with small train; pigeon-breast bodice and waist-length jacket of silk taffeta; jacket has large sleeves, embroidered buttons and trim, 1900–09, source: store, *$1,400.00*

A few drops of fine bath oil or olive oil in the rinse water will help keep wool supple after washing.

Floor-length, wool (brown), bustle, trimmed in dark brown velvet ribbon, 1880–89, source: mail order, *$175.00*

Instep-length, wool tweed, gored skirt, jacket with satin lapels and satin-covered buttons, 1900–09, source: store, *$175.00*

Ankle-length, wool (black), fur collar and cuffs, frog closures, 1910–19, source: store, *$155.00*

Ankle-length, wool (brown) walking suit, with original tan petticoat, brass and enamel buttons (small moth holes), 1900–09, source: mail order, *$150.00*

Ankle-length, wool (navy) walking suit, 1910–19, source: store, *$45.00*

Mid-calf, cotton (heavy), 11-gore skirt, jacket with ¾ sleeves, peplum, covered buttons, pointed collar, 1950–59, source: mail order, *$20.00*

Mid-calf, fabric unknown, straight skirt with kick-pleat, fitted 4-button jacket, with moderate notched lapels and long, cuffed sleeves, 1940–49, source: store, *$35.00*

Mid-calf, fabric unknown, straight skirt, long-sleeved jacket with padded shoulders, novelty collar and pocket treatment, 1950–59, source: store, *$30.00*

Mid-calf, gabardine (gray), with mouton collar and cuffs, Forstman label, 1940–49, source: mail order, *$65.00*

Mid-calf, gabardine, straight skirt, long, semi-fitted jacket, nutmeg with rose-brown trim—very wide double revers and cuffs, 1940–49, source: store, *$260.00*

Mid-calf, linen (white), straight skirt, long jacket with back belt, low patch pockets, 1930–39, source: flea market, $40.00

Mid-calf, rayon crêpe (black), pleated skirt, open, collarless jacket with lace and ribbon knit insert, ¾ cuffed sleeves, 1950–59, source: store, $28.00

Mid-calf, rayon (navy/white houndstooth check), straight skirt, fitted jacket with padded shoulders, long sleeves with turned-back cuffs, 1940–49, source: mail order, $25.00

Mid-calf, silk faille (black), fitted jacket with dolman sleeves and tailored peplum with pocket; self-belt, covered buttons, decorative buttons of carved crystal—one on lapel, one on pocket; straight skirt, 1940–49, source: store, $110.00

Mid-calf, wool (beige), tailored jacket with padded shoulders, pearl trim, 1940–49, source: mail order, $30.00

Mid-calf, wool (black), dressmaker style, 1940–49, source: mail order, $85.00

Mid-calf, wool knit (blue), slim, clinging skirt, pullover top with Peter Pan collar, short sleeves, fuzzy angora trim, period ?, source: store, $20.00

Mid-calf, wool (wine/black tweed), straight skirt, tailored jacket fitted at waist, extended shoulders and pads, 1950–59, source: store, $65.00

Below-the-knee, silk (black), tailored jacket, buttons at hip, pocket detail, shoulder pads, 1940–49, source: mail order, $45.00

Below-the-knee, wool (black) with cowl collar jacket, tailored skirt, 1950–59, source: mail order, $30.00

Below-the-knee, wool (cream), fur-trimmed jacket, fitted skirt, 1940–49, source: store, $45.00

Below-the-knee, wool (nubby, plaid), Chanel-style, 1950–59, source: store, $35.00

Below-the-knee, wool gabardine (blue), Adrian design, jacket with asymmetrical double-breasted closure, attached self-belt, straight skirt with rear pleat, label "Adrian Original," 1940–49, source: auction, $154.00

Below-the-knee, wool serge, A-line skirt with inverted front pleat, slightly fitted hip-length jacket, black, with narrow brown satin trim on jacket edges, 1935–43, source: store, $190.00

Knee-length, bouclé, two skirts (one brown, one black), brown/black tweedy bouclé knit hip-length box jacket, 1950–59, source: mail order, *$15.00*

Knee-length, silk (off-white), rhinestone buttons, 1940–49, source: mail order, *$75.00*

Knee-length, wool (black), straight skirt, fitted, belted jacket, with mink trim, 1950–59, source: store, *$80.00*

Knee-length, wool (burgundy), straight skirt, "Jackie"-style waist-length box jacket with round neck and ¾ sleeves, 3 self-buttons, 1960–69, source: flea market, *$20.00*

JACKETS LISTED BY TYPE AND VALUE

Jacket, bouclé, bolero-style, ¾ sleeves, 1950–59, source: store, *$39.00*

Jacket, crêpe (navy), bolero-style, long sleeves with Art Deco beading 2″ wide around edges, 1930–39, source: individual, *$25.00*

Jacket, leather (sueded), short vest, with calf-length leather fringe, 1960–69, source: individual, *$40.00*

Jacket, linen/cotton blend (white), box-style, ¾ sleeves, hip-length, trimmed with plaits of self-fabric, 1950–59, source: individual, *$15.00*

Jacket, rayon (black), double-breasted, mother-of-pearl buttons, ¾ sleeves, fitted waist with tailored peplum, bow in back at waist, 1940–49, source: store, *$45.00*

Jacket, satin (orchid), bolero-style with heavily draped ¾ sleeves, shirring and tie at waist, 1930–39, source: flea market, *$15.00*

Jacket, velvet (crushed, dark brown), russet silk faille lining, ¾ sleeves, peplum, Peter Pan collar of cream satin with beading, decorative buttons, 1945–55, source: individual, *$25.00*

Jacket, wool (light brown), round shoulders, ¾ sleeves, leather buttons and novelty pocket trim, tailored peplum, 1950–59, source: mail order, *$10.00*

Jacket, wool (lightweight), cuffed long sleeves, 5 fancy Deco-style buttons with tiny rhinestones, double-flapped pockets, heavily padded shoulders, period ?, source: store, *$38.00*

Jacket, wool gauze worked in a ribbed design, label "Chanel," 1920–29, source: auction (London), *$504.00*

Jacket, wool worsted (sage-green), ribbed collar and embroidered decoration, "C. Worth. No: 27901," 1920–29, source: auction (London), *$234.00*

Dresses

CONTENTS

"Dresses" are garments which have a bodice and skirt either in one piece or designed to be worn together. The majority of dresses made before the teens were of two pieces, and during the 1930s, the two-piece dress enjoyed a temporary return to popularity. Wedding dresses and ensembles are listed separately.

ARRANGEMENT

The dress lists are arranged first by length of skirt, then by fabric.

COLLECTING NOTES

Day dresses of the later 1930s and the early 1940s are in reasonably good supply; the styles of these two decades were similar, but as a general rule, dresses from the 1930s are longer and less fitted at the waist than those of the 1940s. Day dresses worn prior to the mid-1930s, however, are in rather short supply.

Dressy afternoon and evening dresses are among the most plentiful of all vintage categories; these items were worn infrequently, and because they were expensive, they were usually given careful treatment. However, the most fragile of these dresses—especially the heavily beaded ones—are now difficult to find in good condition.

TERMS REFERRING TO DRESSES

A-line (skimmer, shift): narrow shoulders, gently flaring line to hem

Baby-doll: fitted bodice and very full skirt, usually worn over petticoats

Ball gown: generally, a floor-length dress with full skirt and decolleté bodice, very sumptuous fabric, and often, elaborate trimming

Chemise: no waistline, straight-line with gentle flare at hemline

Cheongsam: the familiar "Chinese" dress—really developed in the 1920s as a compromise between Eastern and Western styles; very fitted, usually silk, fastened up the right side, with a standup collar and slit skirt

Coat dress: single- or double-breasted front opening similar to a coat

Cocktail dress: generally, dressy evening-type fabrics and styles, but in the prevailing daytime length

Dinner dress: a term used in the nineteenth and early twentieth centuries to mean roughly the same thing as an evening dress; later used to denote a dress with daytime styling, but made up in a dressier fabric

Empire evening gown of flamingo-pink silk and chiffon, with spaghetti straps and clear beading on bodice. Early 1960s. *(Clothing courtesy of Puttin' on the Ritz, Dallas, TX.)*

Drop waist: elongated bodice

Empire: dress with waistline under the bust

Evening dress: generally, a dressy dress longer than the prevailing daytime length, usually ankle-length or floor-length

Fishtail: slim body with full back, usually ruffled at the hem, and cut with a slit in front

Flapper: short chemise with fringes or hanging panels

Granny: long, full skirt, fitted bodice

Handkerchief: type of tunic dress, the overskirt formed by a series of rectangles arranged with the points falling near the hem of the under-skirt

Jumper: sleeveless, collarless, loose-fitting, generally worn with blouse or sweater underneath

Mushroom: slim dress with short, full overskirt

Pagoda: pleated, tiered dress, usually made with shoulder straps

Peasant: bodice with drawstring neck, puff sleeves, lace-up corselet-type waist; full skirt, often with gathered ruffle at hem

Peplum: slim silhouette with slightly flared, hip-length overskirt

Pinafore: bib-top apron with ruffled shoulder strap, worn over a basic dress; may also be styled as a jumper and worn over a blouse

Princess: front and back seams extend from shoulder or bustline to hemline, with no waist seam

Satin ball gown of smoke gray, the bodice beaded with jet and crystal, 1940s. *(Clothing courtesy of Puttin' on the Ritz, Dallas, TX.)*

Prom dress: a floor-length dress, usually with a very full skirt and fitted, rather bare bodice; often made of tulle, featuring many ruffles or other trimmings

Robe de style: tight-fitting bodice, the waist at or slightly below the natural line, very full skirt of mid-calf or ankle length

Sack: loose dress tapering somewhat to below-the-knee hemline

Sheath: slim dress without waistline seam, either straight or gently fitted

Shift: a very simple dress, front-opening and unstructured, of any length

Shirtwaist: tailored shirt extended to form street or evening-length dress

Strapless: bodice made without shoulders or straps, usually with a wired foundation

Sundress: dress with camisole or swimsuit-type top

Tent: very full, pyramid-shaped dress

Tiered: layers of ruffles from top edge to hem

Trapeze: full, unstructured dress with narrow shoulders, wider at hem

Tunic: two-piece dress with elongated top, narrow skirt

DRESSES LISTED BY TYPE AND VALUE

Floor-length, chiffon bodice (flesh-colored) with rhinestones, black velvet skirt with self-belt, 1930–39, source: store, *$155.00*

Floor-length, cotton (bright geometric print), sleeveless, ruffled cape collar, ruffle-hemmed skirt draping up to a slight bustle effect in back, self-sash, 1940–49, source: flea market, *$125.00*

> "When yokels pester us by following our troikas, we cut off their heads and throw them into sacks that look like *those* things," remarked Princess Bariatinsky of Russia, referring to the unwaisted dress introduced by Paul Poiret.

Floor-length, cotton (pink stripes), with lace on bodice, 1880–89, source: store, *$145.00*

Floor-length, cotton plissé (print), 2-piece, cotton lace trim, 1900–09, source: store, *$340.00*

Floor-length, cotton, white with red polka dots, large puffed sleeves, 1890–99, source: store, *$100.00*

Crêpe evening gown of the 1940s, ivory with gold sequin trim, hip-drape, dolman bodice, and self-belt. (*Clothing courtesy of Puttin' on the Ritz, Dallas, TX.*)

Floor-length, crêpe (black), bias-cut, short train, bodice fitted, cut straight across the top, with white piqué cuff at top edge, multiple piqué cording straps drawn together into a plait at top of shoulder, 1930–39, source: store, *$340.00*

Floor-length, crêpe (black), bias-cut skirt, label "Lucien Lelong, 16 Avenue Matignon, Paris," 1930–39, source: auction (London), *$270.00*

Floor-length, crêpe (burgundy), cap sleeves, shoulder pads, sequins and beading on bodice, 1940–49, source: store, *$65.00*

Floor-length, crêpe (cream), bias-cut skirt, slightly dropped waist, blouson bodice, sleeveless, scoop neck, with attached scarf draped in deep U at the front and trailing to hips at the back, accompanying slip, label "Molyneux, 48 Grosvenor Street, London," 1930–39, source: auction (London), *$504.00*

Evening gown of silk and net, black with gold-thread embroidery and trim, from the teens. (*Clothing courtesy of Puttin' on the Ritz, Dallas, TX.*)

Floor-length, crêpe (navy), draped with some beading around neck, shoulder pads, 1940–49, source: mail order, *$55.00*

Floor-length, crêpe (red) with red velvet trim at neck and on cap sleeves, 1930–39, source: store, *$65.00*

Floor-length, dotted swiss (white), "granny"-style, lots of lace, square neck, tied-back waist, deep flounce at hem, 1960–69, source: store, *$110.00*

Floor-length, fabric unknown, peplum trimmed with butterfly designs of gold sequins, 1940–49, source: mail order, *$65.00*

Floor-length, fabric unknown, rose and pink floral print, trimmed with green velvet ribbon and lace inserts, leg-o'-mutton sleeves, high neck, long train, 1890–99, source: mail order, *$175.00*

Floor-length, fabric unknown, 3-tiered skirt with bustle, basque bodice, all trimmed with broderie anglaise, 1880–89, source: mail order, *$130.00*

Floor-length, gingham (plaid), prairie-style, 2-piece, with cotton lace at neck and wrists, 1880–99, source: store, *$490.00*

Floor-length, lace (white), with bias-cut skirt, fitted waist, cap sleeves, 1930–39, source: store, *$40.00*

Floor-length, lace over acetate (black), full skirt, with off-the-shoulder boat neckline, 1930–39, source: store, *$70.00*

Floor-length, lawn (white), 2-piece, extra fancy with a great deal of lace and many frills, 1890–99, source: store, *$900.00*

Floor-length, lawn (white), long train, high neck with wide bertha collar, bodice has rows of lace insert, skirt has design of lace inserts, two flounces, 1900–09, source: mail order, *$130.00*

Floor-length, linen, with inserts of embroidery, melon sleeves, 1890–99, source: store, *$140.00*

Floor-length, Lurex (pink), wrap-style, butterfly sleeves, 1960–69, source: store, *$25.00*

Floor-length, net (black) with allover sequins, flowing skirt with train, sleeveless, fitted bodice, 1910–19, source: store, *$245.00*

Floor-length, net (gray) embroidered with blue, crystal, and jet beads and rhinestones, lined in gray charmeuse, square-cut bodice, skirt narrow and open to the knees at the center, scalloped hem, 1910–19, source: auction, *$242.00*

Floor-length, net (pink), strapless, prom-style, 1950–59, source: mail order, *$45.00*

Floor-length, net (red) over pink taffeta, with black net bow at waist, 1950–59, source: store, *$75.00*

Floor-length, net over acetate, prom-style, strapless, with big poufs of net on skirt, 1950–59, source: store, *$40.00*

Floor-length, net over taffeta (turquoise), with full skirt, wide scooped neck, waistline cut to a V in front, trimmed at neckline and on skirt with flat, rhinestone-accented velvet flowers, 1950–59, source: store, *$190.00*

Floor-length, organdy, yellow top with sailor collar and short sleeves, full bias-cut skirt in floral print, print also on sleeve cuffs, 1950–59, source: mail order, *$17.50*

Floor-length, rayon (print), with spaghetti straps, sequined panel hangs from waist to floor, 1940–59, source: store, *$135.00*

> The fabric we know today as "rayon" was originally introduced as "artificial silk" in 1910. But the word "artificial" seemed to displease some customers, so in 1924, the name "rayon" was created from the word "ray" (as in sunlight) and the ending "-on" (as in cotton)!

Floor-length, rayon crêpe (steel blue), skirt slit up front, side drapes, with rhinestone pin, V neck, flared sleeves, 1940–49, source: store, $62.00

Floor-length, silk (indigo) with gold metallic stripes, long sleeves, square neck, 1940–49, source: store, $140.00

Floor-length, silk (ivory), pleated, Fortuny design, with elbow-length sleeves and silver-printed belt affixed to make an empire waist, trimmed with amber and white Venetian glass beads, worn by Helen Hayes in a production of "Caesar and Cleopatra," period ?, source: auction, $2,200.00

Floor-length, silk (pale blue), pleated, Fortuny, sleeves and sides trimmed with striped Venetian glass beads, with printed silk belt in original Fortuny box, period ?, source: auction, $715.00

Floor-length, silk (pale rose), trimmed with dark rose satin and silver beadwork, hobble skirt, 1910–19, source: mail order, $100.00

Floor-length, silk (salmon-pink) with cream net and pearl bead decoration, ruching at waistline, train edged in ivory silk, label "By Appointment to Queen Alexandra, Jay's Limited, Regent St., London, W.," 1910–19, source: auction (London), $198.00

Floor-length, silk chiffon (apricot), bias-cut, draped sleeves, back fastened with covered buttons and loops, high neck with bodice gathered to high waist, ties to back, small train, 1930–39, source: flea market, $30.00

Floor-length, silk chiffon (beige), horizontally tucked front bodice, straight skirt with flared inset (about a 3-yard sweep) in back, 1950–59, source: store, $75.00

Floor-length, silk chiffon (flamingo-colored), empire style with spaghetti straps, beaded design of crystal and seed pearl on bodice, straight skirt with full-length chiffon drape open in front and gathering to fullness in the back, 1960–69, source: store, $290.00

Floor-length, silk chiffon velvet (black), V neck in front, back plunges to waist, blue bows down the back, 1930–39, source: store, $90.00

Floor-length, silk chiffon velvet (red) with draping, heavy beading at neckline, label reads "Registered with Fashion Originator's Guild," 1930–39, source: mail order, *$150.00*

Floor-length, silk faille (black), long sleeves, hourglass style, small bustle, very plain (probably mourning), 1880–89, source: store, *$50.00*

Floor-length, silk faille (brown), 2-piece, fitted bodice with long, slim sleeves, standup collar, 22-button front; full skirt with pleated ruffle at hem, with tied-back overskirt of contrasting fabric; entire outfit lined in brown cotton, 1880–89, source: store, *$245.00*

Floor-length, silk satin (cream), lace bodice, rhinestone detail at neckline, 1890–99, source: store, *$175.00*

Floor-length, silk velvet (burgundy), batwing sleeves shirred to wide shoulder yoke, bias-cut, band collar and sleeve edges trimmed with white and gunmetal beading, self-belt with covered buckle, 1930–39, source: store, *$1,100.00*

Floor-length, silk velvet, long sleeves, straight skirt, 1930–39, source: store, *$75.00*

Floor-length, taffeta (black) with black net overskirt, overall appliquéd white lace flowers, 1940–49, source: store, *$45.00*

Floor-length, taffeta (gray), 2-piece, basque bodice trimmed with jet beads, small bustle, 1880–89, source: auction, *$125.00*

Floor-length, taffeta (iridescent green), spaghetti straps, full skirt with big side pouf (pouf lined with pink taffeta and fastened with large pink rose), small triangular matching wrap, 1940–59, source: store, *$150.00*

Floor-length, taffeta (light blue), puffed sleeves, fitted waist, sweetheart neckline, maroon appliqués, 1940–49, source: mail order, *$25.00*

Floor-length, taffeta (taupe), skirt has back fullness gathered into a shirred panel just below waist, falling into a small train, with bodice of lace over net, off-shoulder portrait collar, 1940–49, source: store, *$390.00*

Floor-length, taffeta faille, fitted bodice with wide straps, very full skirt made of alternating black and red bands, period ?, source: store, *$130.00*

Floor-length, voile (print), puffed, shirred sleeves, very full skirt, 1940–49, source: mail order, *$45.00*

Floor-length, wool trimmed with heavy crochet lace, leg-o'-mutton sleeves, 1890–99, source: auction, *$110.00*

Two-piece dress of the 1930s, novelty-weave wool. Taupe, with natural trim, gold buckle and buttons. The skirt has a slip top. (*Clothing courtesy of Puttin' on the Ritz, Dallas, TX.*)

Instep-length, cotton (calico print), prairie-style, 2-piece, 1900–09, source: mail order, $85.00

Instep-length, cotton with net trim at neck and on front closing, 1900–09, source: flea market, $15.00

Instep-length, crêpe (black), with padded shoulders, sweetheart neckline, draping at hip gathered to one side, with ties hanging full length of skirt, 1940–49, source: store, $95.00

Instep-length, lawn (white) with broderie anglaise trim, with ¾ sleeves, handmade lace insert in bodice, 1900–09, source: store, $145.00

Instep-length, lawn (white), short train, high neck, dress elaborately worked with Irish lace insertions, 1900–09, source: auction, $264.00

Instep-length, organdy (white) over yellow underskirt, layered ruffles from shoulder to hem and on sleeves, high scoop neckline in front, cut to waist in back, 1930–39, source: store, *$50.00*

Instep-length, silk crêpe, bias-cut, sleeveless, 1930–39, source: store, *$185.00*

Instep-length, silk faille (black) with extensive beaded trim, narrow silhouette with slightly raised waist, long sleeves, high neck, skirt open at center front, 1910–19, source: flea market, *$75.00*

Instep-length, silk shantung (peach), sheath, sleeveless, with beaded arabesque pattern from shoulder to hem down one side, 1950–69, source: store, *$340.00*

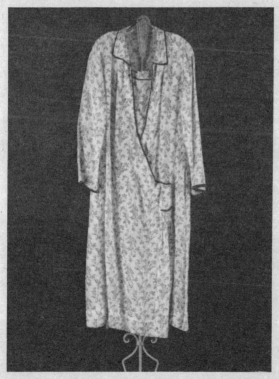

Day dress of cotton voile, 1920s, with asymmetric closing, shirring on pocket detail. (*Clothing courtesy of Puttin' on the Ritz, Dallas, TX.*)

Instep-length, taffeta (stripe of cream, yellow, taupe, and melon), bias-cut, camisole bodice with ribbon straps, low-cut back, dropped waist, one side of skirt pulled up with bow, 1930–39, source: mail order, $20.00

Instep-length, voile (yellow, with shadow stripe), 2-piece garden-party-style, with much trim of narrow ruffles and narrow black velvet ribbon, short train, long sleeves, high neck, 1900–09, source: store, $175.00

Ankle-length, chiffon (blue), bias-cut, with corded appliqué trim on sleeves and inset at waist, matching taffeta slip, 1930–39, source: store, $65.00

Ankle-length, cotton print, net lace front insert, ¾ sleeves, ruffles, 1910–19, source: store, $160.00

Ankle-length, crêpe (black), slit up the front, with net trim on bodice, 1930–39, source: store, $65.00

Ankle-length, crêpe bodice (black) with skirt of wide gray and cream crêpe bands, overlaid with deep, irregular scallops of ivory embroidery, long sleeves with trim to match skirt, slightly fitted low waist, boat neck, period ?, source: auction (London), $306.00

Ankle-length, lace (Brussels, ecru) and chiffon over satin, 1920–29, source: mail order, $200.00

Ankle-length, lawn (cream), with pin tucks and lace insertions, 1907–19, source: auction, $150.00

Ankle-length, lawn with lace inserts, slight bustle, Edwardian styling, 1900–09, source: store, $275.00

Ankle-length, net (white), with contrasting bands at hem and on sailor-style collar, trimmed extensively with cotton cutwork, filet-lace overlays, and ball fringe, 1910–19, source: auction (London), $720.00

Ankle-length, organdy (pale blue), surplice bodice, short, ruffled sleeves, bias-cut skirt, with rayon crêpe slip, 1930–39, source: flea market, $45.00

Ankle-length, organdy (pale green) with white embroidered stripe pattern and bands of white fabric trim, high neck, large, square collar, flounced side panels, 1910–19, source: flea market, $60.00

Ankle-length, satin dress with silk chiffon overdrapes, tonneau silhouette, wide satin sash with chenille embroidery, long sleeves with cutouts edged in chenille, 1910–19, source: store, $490.00

Dress of navy blue crêpe, with bolero jacket, modified Peter Pan collar and cuffs of plaid taffeta, with contrasting edging and appliqué trim; 1940s. *(Clothing courtesy of Puttin' on the Ritz, Dallas, TX.)*

Ankle-length, sequined bodice, gold-embroidered net panel, short sleeves, square neckline, 1910–19, source: auction, *$125.00*

Ankle-length, silk (cream), with bodice and overskirts striped with white beads, black silk collar and cuffs, 1910–19, source: auction (London), *$108.00*

Ankle-length, tulle (light blue) and silk brocade, gold embroidery on bodice, 1910–19, source: mail order, *$75.00*

Mid-calf, cotton (floral print), square neck, dropped waist, with pleated ribbon details, cap sleeves, 1920–29, source: mail order, *$45.00*

The first ready-made maternity dresses—simple cotton wraparound housedresses—were manufactured in the 1900s, and there were no fashionable maternity clothes until the twenties. "Designer" maternity clothes arrived in the mid-1950s, when Pearl Nippon opened her Ma Mere maternity boutique.

Mid-calf, cotton (screen print) with contrasting collar and cuffs, full skirt, 1950–59, source: store, $15.00

Mid-calf, cotton (sheer, floral print), shirtwaist, short sleeves, small shoulder pads, plastic buttons, self-belt, 1940–49, source: store, $28.00

Mid-calf, crêpe (black), allover beading in multi-colored paisley pattern, kimono sleeves, 1920–29, source: mail order, $300.00

Mid-calf, crêpe (black), fitted waist, short sleeves, side-draped skirt, gold beading around neckline, 1950–59, source: store, $42.00

Mid-calf, gabardine jumper, both bodice and skirt pleated at waistline, armholes cut almost to waist, self-buttons, 1940–49, source: store, $28.00

Mid-calf, jersey, gored skirt, separate fitted bodice with short sleeves, large buttons, bright print on black, 1940–49, source: store, $79.00

Mid-calf, lawn (print), wrapped to side, with shirred pocket and tie closure at hip, long sleeves, narrow solid-colored bands trimming all edges, 1920–29, source: store, $240.00

Mid-calf, organdy (print) over cotton underdress, square-dance-style, pale lavender with metallic gold rickrack, 1940–49, source: store, $35.00

Mid-calf, rayon (floral print), cap sleeves, V neck, 1940–49, source: store, $38.00

Mid-calf, rayon crêpe (black), flared skirt, fitted bodice with sheer inset, waist tie in back, two appliquéd flowers on bodice and skirt (rhinestone button centers), short sleeves, padded shoulders, 1940–49, source: store, $65.00

Mid-calf, rayon crêpe (blue), with needlepoint bands at neck and on short, puffed sleeves, bias-cut skirt, 1930–39, source: flea market, $20.00

Mid-calf, rayon taffeta (black) with multi-color polka dots, fitted bodice with wing collar, very full skirt, 1950–59, source: store, $45.00

Mid-calf, rayon, bias-cut skirt, puffed sleeves, navy with white flowered print, white celluloid buttons, 1930–39, source: mail order, $48.00

Mid-calf, satin (black) with bias-cut skirt, sleeveless, black beading at neckline, 1930–39, source: mail order, $75.00

Mid-calf, seersucker (ochre) housedress, short dolman sleeves, standup collar, fitted waist, full, bias-cut skirt, pocket detail, dress wrapped asymmetrically over concealed front zipper, 1946–59, source: flea market, $12.00

Mid-calf, silk (black) and gold brocade in wide stripes, bodice cut straight across, with wide straps, dress pouffed out (no waist), divided at hem in front with fabric pulled to the back and draped up to shoulders, chiffon underslip, 1920–29, source: auction (London), $990.00

Mid-calf, silk (ivory), having ivory chiffon and lace overlay of tiered design, 1910–19, source: auction (London), $990.00

Mid-calf, silk chiffon velvet skirt with taffeta slip-top, matching velvet top (mid-thigh length), shirred at waist and shoulders, short, shirred sleeves, exposed gold zipper running the length of the top in front, 1930–39, source: store, $60.00

Mid-calf, silk georgette (floral), with flounced skirt and bertha collar, 1930–39, source: mail order, $75.00

Mid-calf, silk georgette, drop waist, short sleeves, embroidered panels, 1920–29, source: flea market, $85.00

Mid-calf, silk jacquard (cream), melon sleeves, dropped waist, draped neckline, 1930–39, source: mail order, $65.00

Mid-calf, silk print, V neck with collar, shoulder pads and long fitted sleeves, skirt draped at waist, 1940–49, source: mail order, $20.00

Mid-calf, taffeta (black) with lace overlay, boned bodice with spaghetti straps, full skirt with crinoline, 1950–59, source: store, $45.00

Mid-calf, velvet (black), bowed strapless bodice and tulip skirt with draped self-ruffle at the back, "Ceil Chapman" label, 1950–59, source: auction, $55.00

Mid-calf, velvet (blue) with dolman sleeves, bias-cut, 1930–39, source: store, $45.00

Mid-calf, velvet (brown), empire-style with white satin collar and trim on cuffs and hem, many self-buttons, large white satin rose on bodice closure, "Teal Traina" label, 1960–69, source: store, $45.00

Try reviving tired velvet over a pan of steaming water, to which a little ammonia has been added.

Mid-calf, velvet (burgundy) with draped bodice, V neck, ecru lace collar extends over shoulders to form short sleeves, 1940–49, source: store, $48.00

Mid-calf, voile (floral print), puff sleeves, low scoop neckline, gored skirt, 1930–39, source: store, $18.00

Mid-calf, voile (print), shirred shoulders, white organdy standing ruffle collar, fichu, self-ties to back, 1920–29, source: store, $45.00

Mid-calf, wool (houndstooth check), ¾ sleeves and slim straight skirt, 1960–69, source: store, $12.00

Below-the-knee, camel hair, coat dress, slightly fitted at waist, narrowed at hem, ¾ sleeves, four large steerhide-covered buttons on front closure, 1960–69, source: store, $22.00

Below-the-knee, chiffon (black and ivory print, Egyptian motifs), lace trim, 1920–29, source: mail order, $65.00

Below-the-knee, chiffon (black) over black silk, sleeveless, dropped waist, with uneven chiffon streamers hanging to ankle length, label "Molyneux, 5 Rue Royale, No. 35767," 1920–29, source: auction (London), $972.00

Below-the-knee, chiffon (brown) embroidered in chain stitch of green and crimson silks, sleeveless, square neckline, dropped waist with ties at either side, matching scarf, label "Gabrielle Chanel, Paris. No: 18853," 1920–29, source: auction (London), $5,580.00

Below-the-knee, chiffon (midnight blue) over silk, sleeveless chemise, with skirt ending in tiered chiffon petals, label "Chanel. No: 42783," 1920–29, source: auction (London), $1,620.00

Below-the-knee, chiffon (print) bodice with long sleeves, dropped waist, with navy blue skirt, print flounce at hem, print tie belt, 1920–29, source: mail order, $75.00

Below-the-knee, chiffon (sea-green and blue), with trim of paprika chiffon and gold thread; sleeveless dress draped at waist, with pouffed hem; sleeveless ¾-length chiffon coat, with border of gold-thread lace, 1920–29, source: auction (London), $1,039.00

Below-the-knee, cotton (dark blue) with silver ribbon and rickrack trim, "squaw"-style, 1950–59, source: store, $140.00

Below-the-knee, cotton (gray), dolman top, self-detailing at waistline, narrow self-belt, 1940–49, source: store, $25.00

Below-the-knee, cotton (light blue) with purple rickrack, "squaw"-style, 1950–59, source: store, $79.00

Below-the-knee, cotton (print stylized map of California), full skirt, long sleeves, peasant-style bodice, girdle waistline, orange/green/rust, 1950–59, source: store, *$25.00*

Below-the-knee, crêpe (black) with draped peplum, sweetheart neckline with white beading, 1940–49, source: mail order, *$100.00*

> "Rhinestones" are so-called because they were originally made from small, crystal pebbles found on the floor of the Rhine river.

Below-the-knee, crêpe (black) with square neckline trimmed with bow and rhinestones, pleated skirt, 1950–59, source: mail order, *$25.00*

Knit dress and jacket, 1920s. *(Clothing courtesy of Puttin' on the Ritz, Dallas, TX.)*

Below-the-knee, crêpe (black), short-sleeved dress, fitted waist (side zipper), loose, sleeveless coat closing to one side with large pewter button, much foot-long silk fringe on dress and coat, 1940–49, source: flea market, $45.00

Below-the-knee, crêpe (brown) with peplum and sequin trim, 1930–39, source: store, $45.00

Below-the-knee, crêpe (navy), boat neck, raglan sleeves with bands of faggoting, 1940–49, source: store, $65.00

Below-the-knee, crêpe, drop waist with pleated skirt, no trim, sleeveless, 1920–29, source: store, $45.00

Below-the-knee, jersey (black) bodice with chiffon skirt, scoop neck, ¾ sleeves, 1950–59, source: store, $45.00

Below-the-knee, linen (blue) shirtwaist, straight skirt, ¾ sleeves, rhinestone trim on collar, 1950–59, source: store, $20.00

Below-the-knee, mohair jumper, large-scale plaid in many vivid colors, 1960–69, source: store, $22.00

Below-the-knee, novelty fabric of very fine stripe-and-openwork weave, allover print, tucked bodice with organdy ruffle edged in openwork forming collar and front trim, trumpet-style ¾ sleeves, self-belt with plastic buckle, 1935–45, source: store, $25.00

Below-the-knee, rayon (brown) with glass buttons, padded shoulders, draped skirt, 1940–49, source: mail order, $32.00

Below-the-knee, rayon (light blue, linen-textured), button front, short sleeves, round neck with yoke and bow trim, straight skirt, 1950–59, source: mail order, $8.00

Below-the-knee, rayon (sheer, navy), redingote-style, short sleeves, over taffeta slip, 1940–49, source: mail order, $35.00

Below-the-knee, rayon, screened Hawaiian print, spaghetti straps, sheath skirt, 1950–59, source: mail order, $25.00

Below-the-knee, silk (turquoise) sheath, ¾ sleeves, elaborate pattern of small handcarved wooden beads on bodice, self-fabric sash, 1960–69, source: store, $37.50

Below-the-knee, taffeta (crinkle), bias-cut, inverted fan pleats on skirt, 1950–59, source: store, $35.00

Below-the-knee, velvet (dusty pink), dropped waist, side-drape with bow, bodice wrapped around the back, label "Chanel. No: 47225," 1920–29, source: auction (London), $1,980.00

Below-the-knee, wool (black) knit sheath, scoop neck with heavy gold beading, scattered beading on dress, 1950–59, source: mail order, $65.00

Below-the-knee, wool (houndstooth), bias-cut blouson bodice, straight skirt, ¾ sleeves, 1960–69, source: store, $22.50

Knee-length, chiffon (black), clear beads and rhinestones in floral pattern, long sleeves, scoop neck, scalloped hem, 1920–29, source: store, $1,400.00

Knee-length, chiffon over silk, pink bodice, black skirt, with wide band of silver beading in geometric pattern at dropped waist, also inset of beading and panel of embroidery at side of diagonally wrapped bodice, 1920–29, source: auction (London), $828.00

Knee-length, chiffon, allover beading (Art Deco design), sleeveless, with scoop neck, 1920–29, source: mail order, $275.00

Knee-length, cotton, allover embroidery, fitted bodice with piped seams, bows at waist, straight skirt, 1950–59, source: store, $32.00

Knee-length, crêpe (black) sheath, draped bodice, scoop neck, sleeveless, 1950–59, source: store, $20.00

Knee-length, fabric unknown, chemise, embroidered with magenta sequin and crystal-beaded floral motifs, 1920–29, source: auction, $176.00

Knee-length, lace (gilt) chemise, embroidered with pink and blue abstract designs, with underslip trimmed in gilt lace, 1920–29, source: auction, $275.00

Knee-length, linen/rayon blend with both woven-in and printed patterns, sleeveless chemise trimmed with wide bands of cotton lace, new-old, 1920–29, source: store, $170.00

Knee-length, panné silk velvet, black with allover pattern of small taupe dots, long sleeves, bias fullness inset at hem, V neck with collar draped to handkerchief points at back, 1920–29, source: store, $590.00

Knee-length, satin (black) chemise, beaded in shades of blue-green and white in horizontal stripes and diamond patterns, accented with rhinestones, 1920–29, source: auction, $440.00

Knee-length, silk chiffon, Persian-print with gold metallic thread pattern, empire-style, long sleeves, jewel neck, 1960–69, source: store, $18.00

Knee-length, silk georgette (black), chemise style, embroidered with jet bugle beads in horizontal stripes and fleur-de-lis, 1920–29, source: auction, *$88.00*

Knee-length, silk print chemise, sleeveless, no trim, 1920–29, source: mail order, *$50.00*

Mini, lace (white) to mid-hip, black skirt, with bright pink sash and bow at hip, 1960–69, source: store, *$32.50*

Mini, lace (white), allover silver and pearl beaded pattern, solid beading on collars and edge of long sleeves, chemise style, 1960–69, source: flea market, *$22.00*

Mini, net over taffeta (all synthetic), allover embroidery, long sleeves, flounce at hem, ruffles at wrist and down front of dress, rhinestone buttons, 1960–69, source: flea market, *$24.00*

Mini, rayon velvet (emerald green), long, full net sleeves with velvet appliqués, 1960–69, source: flea market, *$10.00*

Mini, silk (blue) with beaded paisley design on collar and hem, Hong Kong import, 1960–69, source: store, *$30.00*

Mini, silk taffeta bouffant skirt with organza underskirt, beaded chiffon empire bodice, spaghetti straps, skirt caught in poufs at hem, 1960–69, source: flea market, *$40.00*

Uneven hem, chiffon (black) with lace trim, label "Molyneux 5, Rue Royale," 1920–29, source: auction (London), *$684.00*

Uneven hem, chiffon (black), beaded bodice, 1920–29, source: auction (London), *$468.00*

Uneven hem, chiffon (café-au-lait) and silk, with full side skirt, label "Gabrielle Chanel, Paris. No. 16769," 1920–29, source: auction (London), *$2,160.00*

Uneven hem, silk chiffon (orange) with rhinestones and silver beads, dropped waist, 1920–29, source: mail order, *$125.00*

Uneven hem, silk net (black) with woven-in dots, over satin underdress, handkerchief hem, sleeveless, 1920–29, source: store, *$75.00*

Uneven hem, silk velvet (plum) skirt, diagonal from knee to mid-calf, puffed hem, short-sleeved gold lamé bodice, pink silk velvet zig-zag inserted waist stitched with gold metallic and pink twisted silk thread, Poiret design, label with client's name, 1920–29, source: auction, *$1,980.00*

Unknown length, chiffon (black), skirt with concertina pleating and bodice of lace overlay, label "Chanel. No: 50278," 1930–39, source: auction (London), *$1,350.00*

Unknown length, chiffon (dark blue), bodice with ruching and ties falling to the side, label "Jean Dessès, 17 Avenue Matignon, Paris. No: 8369," 1950–59, source: auction (London), *$306.00*

Unknown length, chiffon (oyster) with machine blonde lace sleeves and insertion, label "C. Worth," 1920–29, source: auction (London), *$153.00*

Unknown length, chiffon (tangerine), printed mainly in green and mauve, with gold thread brocade, label "Babani 98 Bd Haussmann, Paris," 1920–29, source: auction (London), *$468.00*

Unknown length, chiffon and silk (black), label "Chanel, Cannes—31 Rue Cambon, Paris—Biarritz. No: 3035," 1920–29, source: auction (London), *$171.00*

Unknown length, chiffon and silk (cream), with diamanté decoration, tucking at waist and upper skirt, label "Doeuillet-Doucet, Paris," 1920–29, source: auction (London), *$1,170.00*

Unknown length, chiffon and silk (ivory), label "Chanel. No: 28399," 1920–29, source: auction (London), *$144.00*

Unknown length, lamé (gold) of ribbed design, with a panel of gilt net decoration, label "Jean Patou, 7 Rue Saint Florentin, Paris, No. 23449," 1920–29, source: auction (London), *$3,780.00*

Unknown length, lamé (silver) with silvered net overlay, the skirt with pink bead and ostrich feather trim, label "C. Worth. No: 039974," 1920–29, source: auction (London), *$612.00*

Unknown length, lamé (silver), the skirt and deep cuffs designed with roundels and geometric motifs in mainly crimson and pink, label "Babani 98 Bd Haussmann, Paris," 1920–29, source: auction (London), *$1,710.00*

Unknown length, lamé and net (gold), with a deep sash at the low waist, wrapped skirt, 1920–29, source: auction (London), *$234.00*

Unknown length, net and grosgrain (black), fitted bodice with fabric rose trim, label "Chanel. No: 42415," 1930–39, source: auction (London), *$1,350.00*

Unknown length, silk (black), side panels applied with chiffon roses, label "Madeleine Vionnet, No. 12061," 1920–29, source: auction (London), *$3,060.00*

Unknown length, silk (cobalt blue), tie neck, label "Jean Patou, 7 Rue St. Florentin, Paris, Cannes, No. 27350," 1920–29, source: auction (London), *$180.00*

Unknown length, silk (midnight blue), label "Callot Soeurs, Paris," 1910–19, source: auction (London), $153.00

Unknown length, silk (purple) and silver lamé, with cream lace overlay, bead and diamanté decoration, 1920–29, source: auction (London), $99.00

Unknown length, silk and net (ivory), clear and white bead decoration, the bodice and upper skirt with black net overlay, having tassel and diamanté trim, 1910–19, source: auction (London), $432.00

Unknown length, taffeta (black), chiffon collar with rhinestone detail, Hattie Carnegie, 1950–59, source: store, $325.00

Unknown length, velvet (plum), tiered skirt with tie to the back, label "Chanel. No: 67935," a belt, not matching, also included in sale, 1920–29, source: auction (London), $468.00

WEDDING DRESSES LISTED BY TYPE AND VALUE

Floor-length, dotted swiss (white) with extensive wide insets of crochet lace, high neck, ¾ sleeves, pouched bodice, tiered skirt with long train, two original petticoats of cotton with ribbon and lace trim, 1900–09, source: store, $2,400.00

Floor-length, silk satin (blush), princess-style with moderate train, low square neckline edged in same-color sequins, same-color lace appliqués with sequin trim on bodice and skirt, 1950–59, source: store, $790.00

Ankle-length, voile (white), bias-cut, with ruffled sleeves, long peach moiré ribbon sash, 1930–39, source: store, $440.00

Mid-calf, lace over taffeta (candlelight), very full skirt ("New Look"), crinoline underskirts attached; fitted, sleeveless lace-over-satin bodice, with long-sleeved bolero-style lace jacket fastened with many tiny faille-covered buttons and loops; waist-length net veil with beaded tiara, crochet shortie gloves, 1940–59, source: store, $790.00

ENSEMBLES LISTED BY TYPE AND VALUE

Dress/cape, chiffon (floral print), floor-length, sleeveless, fitted bodice with low back, matching capelet, 1930–39, source: store, $115.00

Dress/cape, silk chiffon (light blue), instep-length dress, bias-cut, low-hanging belt with rhinestone buckle, matching cape, 1930–39, source: mail order, $48.00

A wedding dress from the 1900s. It is dotted swiss, with insets of guipure lace, and has both an attached and a separate petticoat, the latter having extensive lace trim. *(Clothing courtesy of Puttin' on the Ritz, Dallas, TX.)*

Dress/cape, velveteen (dark red), floor-length gored skirt, separate high-necked bodice, back-button closure, braid-trimmed front, long, fitted sleeves with puffed shoulders, elbow-length cape with puffed hem, 1890–99, source: flea market, *$40.00*

Dress/coat, faille (beige) skirt on below-the-knee dress, with black velvet dress bodice; ¾-length coat, 1950–59, source: store, *$55.00*

Dress/coat, silk crêpe, knee-length chemise with American Indian influence, fabric fringes from bust to hem, coat with cape-style sleeves and long fringes, accents of gold sequins, 1920–29, source: store, *$1,100.00*

Dress/hat, cotton (brown), mid-calf, with Peter Pan collar, "Marshall Field" label, with matching wide-brim hat, 1940–49, source: store, $20.00

Dress/hat, velvet (burgundy), floor-length, with long, full sleeves, shirred neckline, rhinestone buttons, matching velvet turban with blue feather, 1890–99, source: mail order, $125.00

Dress/jacket, fabric unknown, mid-calf tailored dress, matching jacket, corded trim, glass buttons and velvet collar, 1940–49, source: store, $25.00

Dress/jacket, fabric unknown, sleeveless, floor-length, long-sleeved jacket (padded shoulders, gold-leather appliqué and beading on lapels), 1940–49, source: mail order, $120.00

Ralph Waldo Emerson observed that "The consciousness of being perfectly well dressed brings a tranquility that religion is powerless to possess."

Dress/jacket, knit (mint green) with white diamond pattern, mid-calf, drop-waist, with solid-color, mid-thigh-length cardigan jacket, 1920–29, source: store, $140.00

Dress/jacket, lace (Irish and other), instep-length dress, slightly trailing hemline, matching knee-length jacket, 1910–19, source: auction, $715.00

Dress/jacket, Lurex (copper), floor-length sleeveless dress, high neck, self-belt, blazer-style jacket, 1960–69, source: store, $190.00

Dress/jacket, rayon taffeta (black), strapless bodice, below-the-knee matching jacket, 1950–59, source: store, $85.00

Dress/jacket, silk (cream), dropped waist and V neck, below-the-knee, cap sleeves, self-belt, matching long-sleeved jacket, 1920–29, source: store, $38.00

Dress/jacket, silk georgette (print), long-sleeved dress, mid-calf, many-gored skirt, draped to side across front with flounce at closure and drape at low waist, hip-length jacket of same fabric with short cape sleeves, 1930–39, source: store, $390.00

Dress/jacket, silk shantung (orange), mid-calf, with cummerbund and matching jacket, 1950–59, source: store, $18.00

Dress/jacket, silk velvet, bias-cut, floor-length dress, V neck with thin straps, matching long-sleeved jacket, 1930–39, source: store, $45.00

Dress/jacket, taffeta (pink moiré), large bow in back, floor-length, strapless bodice, matching long-sleeved bolero jacket, 1940–49, source: store, *$40.00*

Skirt/tunic/scarf, rayon/cotton blend, hand-tie-dyed, ankle-length bias skirt, knee-length long-sleeved tunic, long scarf, 1960–69, source: store, *$100.00*

Playing: Sports Clothing

CONTENTS

Items included in this category are those worn for participating in sports activities or for outdoor relaxation.

ARRANGEMENT

Organized by type of garment.

COLLECTING NOTES

The most frequently found sports clothes are those for swimming and for riding. Riding pants are common, but jackets and riding skirts are not frequently seen. Neither are skating and skiing costumes. Casual play clothes—such as shorts and sunsuits—are found from the 1950s and 1960s, but much less often from the 1930s and 1940s. Beach coverups were popular from the 1920s on, and sometimes a loose garment that doesn't seem to fit into any other category can actually be identified as beachwear.

TERMS

Bathing costume: multi-piece outfit worn for swimming by most people up until the 1920s; usually composed of a short dress, knickers, stockings, and perhaps a cape

Bathing suit: one- or two-piece form-fitting suit which became the norm from the 1920s on

Duster: loose coat-like garment worn to protect clothing while motoring

Jodhpurs: "English-style" riding pants, curved out from the body above the knees, fitted snugly below

Knickers: knee-length pants, full-cut, gathered into a band

Western-style: riding pants, slim-fitting from waist to ankle, often with curved seaming and pocket openings just below the waistband

SPORTS CLOTHING LISTED BY TYPE AND PRICE

Bathing costume, cotton-satin (black) piped in pale blue, with mother-of-pearl buttons on shoulders, 1900–09, source: store, *$65.00*

Bathing costume, cotton-satin (black), tunic-style with bloomers, 1910–19, source: store, *$36.00*

Bathing costume, fabric unknown, black, knee-length top and pants, matching cap, 1900–09, source: store, *$85.00*

Bathing suit, cotton (plaid) 2-piece, pleated bottom, 1960–69, source: mail order, *$8.00*

Bathing suit, cotton-satin, with flared skirt and large back-buttons, 1930–39, source: store, *$48.00*

Bathing suit, wool (black) 1-piece, with latticework sides, 1930–39, source: store, *$35.00*

One-piece bathing suit of the 1920s.

Bathing suit, wool Jantzen, matching striped wool stockings, 1920–29, source: mail order, *$32.00*

Coat, linen (natural) duster, ¾-length, for motoring, 1900–09, source: store, *$190.00*

Coat, linen duster, large mother-of-pearl buttons, for motoring, 1900–09, source: store, *$75.00*

Coat, wool (black), ¾-length, fitted, for ice skating, 1900–09, source: mail order, *$30.00*

Jacket, cotton gabardine windbreaker, blue with snowflake print, for skiing, 1940–49, source: mail order, *$35.00*

Jacket, wool trimmed with fur, princess-style, ¾-length, for skating, 1890–99, source: mail order, *$85.00*

Jacket, wool tweed (brown herringbone), green cotton lining, tails, for riding, 1930–39, source: mail order, *$35.00*

Pants, cotton twill jodhpurs, leather insert, buttons at calves and hips, period ?, source: store, *$25.00*

Twill jodhpurs and Western-style shirt. (*Clothing courtesy of Puttin' on the Ritz, Dallas, TX.*)

Pants, gabardine jodhpurs (never worn), 1920–29, source: store, $30.00

Pants, gabardine, Western-style, "H Bar C" label, for riding, 1940–59, source: store, $39.00

Pants, khaki jodhpurs, with side-button legs, top-stitched detailing, suede knee pads, 1930–39, source: store, $65.00

Pants, linen (gray) knickers, button fly, period ?, source: store, $45.00

Pants, linen jodhpurs, period ?, source: mail order, $10.00

Pants, wool gym bloomers, a few very small moth holes, 1910–19, source: store, $20.00

Skirt, linen (cream), split, with covered buttons, for golfing, 1910–19, source: mail order, $45.00

Suit, wool (heavy), brown jacket with orange and beige horizontal stripes, zipper-bottomed pants, for skiing, 1930–49, source: store, $45.00

Suit, wool gabardine, tailored jacket, ankle-length skirt, for riding, period ?, source: store, $140.00

Relaxing: Leisure and Sleep

CONTENTS

All garments which are customarily not worn outside the home.

ARRANGEMENT

First by type of garment, then by fabric.

COLLECTING NOTES

Victorian and Edwardian nightgowns are in good supply, as are night-gowns and bedjackets of the 1930s and 1940s. Pajamas are less frequently seen, and negligées and ensembles are harder to find. Tea gowns and other forms of at-home wear popular from the 1880s through the teens are not easily found, and they may be difficult to recognize; they are frequently mistaken for maternity clothes (because of their loose waists), but in fact, special clothing for maternity wear was uncommon before the early teens.

TERMS

Hostess gown: full, flowing garment worn for relaxing and informal entertaining. Types include:

Caftan: loosely cut, gently flaring garment, with long, wide sleeves, V-shaped opening at neck

Djellabah: similar to the caftan but with a hood

Muumuu: loosely flowing from front and back yoke, ankle- or street-length, usually colorful Hawaiian print

Jumpsuit: one-piece pantlegged garment worn for lounging

Nightgown: loose, dress-like garment used for sleeping

Pajamas: loose-fitting pants and top used for sleeping or lounging. Types include:

Baby-doll: short full top with short puffy sleeves and full matching panties

Chinese: hip-length top with frog closing, mandarin collar, and side slits, straight-leg pants

Cossack: tunic top with side closing and standup collar, worn over straight-leg long pants

Harem: very wide pants gathered at ankles, with brief top or tunic top

Lounging: made in a variety of styles, but usually of more opaque or dressy fabric than sleeping pajamas

Tailored: box-shaped top with man-tailored collar and short or long straight-leg pants

Robe: loose garment worn alone or over sleepwear. Types include:

Bathrobe: any length, front-button or wrap, often made of toweling, flannel, or wool

Bedjacket: waist-length jacket worn over nightgown while in bed

Brunch coat (duster, model's coat): loose-fitting garment from knee- to ankle-length, with front zipper or button closing

Dressing gown: a tailored negligée

Happi or kabuki coat: hip-length kimono

Kimono: long, loose line, collarless, wide sleeves, tied at waist with wide fabric sash

Negligée (peignoir): dressy robe, usually trimmed with lace or ruffles

Lounging pajamas with Oriental influence, 1920s.

Tea gown: term used to describe a garment popular from the 1870s to
the 1920s; a loose dress, ranging from simple to very elaborate, which
didn't require the wearing of a corset underneath; used for relaxation
between day-dress and evening-dress, or for informal entertaining and
dining

Wrapper: a loosely fitted dress worn at home; the classic wrapper (also
called a "Mother Hubbard") is rather full, with a high neck and long
sleeves

LEISURE AND SLEEPWEAR LISTED BY TYPE AND PRICE

Bedjacket, cotton plissé, white with pale blue sprig design, shirred front
and back, long sleeves, period ?, source: flea market, $3.00

Bedjacket, rayon, handquilted, handpainted, 1940–49, source: store, $18.00

Bedjacket, rayon, pleated front, lace-edged collar, ribbon ties, period ?, source: mail order, $5.00

Bedjacket, silk crêpe (oriental print), silk tassel ties, 1930–39, source: store, $35.00

Ensemble, nylon peignoir set, below-the-knee, embroidery and lace, 1950–59, source: store, $59.00

Ensemble, rayon (blue) bias-cut nightgown, long-sleeved robe, ecru lace trim at V neck of gown, 1940–49, source: store, $30.00

Ensemble, rayon (floral print), floor-length, sleeveless gown with draped bodice, robe with shirred shoulders, short sleeves, yoke-waist, 1940–49, source: flea market, $65.00

Ensemble, silk (peach) pajamas, matching lace bedjacket, 1930–39, source: store, $75.00

Ensemble, silk crêpe de chine (peach), negligée with extensive lace inserts, gown with bodice of crêpe de chine and lace, with silk-satin skirt, all bias-cut, with train effect, 1930–39, source: store, $350.00

Ensemble, silk satin (dark peach), V-neck gown with lots of lace, tap pants, mostly lace with side button, French label, 1930–49, source: store, $145.00

Hostess gown, taffeta, ribbon stripes of gold, silver, and many colors, very full skirt, nipped waist, black velvet shawl collar, velvet cuffs on long sleeves, 1948–59, source: flea market, $48.00

Lounging pajamas, satin (dark green), wide pants and long sleeves, overblouse-type top, 1930–39, source: mail order, $25.00

Lounging pajamas, silk-satin, dark peach smoking-style jacket with burgundy pocket and sash, burgundy pants, 1930–39, source: store, $250.00

Lounging pajamas, silk, Chinese-style, 3-piece, period ?, source: mail order, $35.00

Lounging suit, cotton (multi-colored), wide legs, red buttons and red inserts in bodice, 1930–39, source: mail order, $20.00

Lounging suit, rayon velvet (black), exposed full-length gold zipper in front, shirred yoke, wide legs, thirties-revival style, 1960–69, source: store, $24.00

Negligée, fabric unknown, leg-o'-mutton sleeves, long train, broderie anglaise trim, 1890–99, source: mail order, $85.00

Double-breasted hostess gown of white silk faille with black velvet trim, portrait collar, and shirring on sleeves. Late 1940s or early 1950s. *(Clothing courtesy of Puttin' on the Ritz, Dallas, TX.)*

Negligée, net (pale blue) over pink silk, floor-length, cape sleeves, wrapped to side at waist, 1930–39, source: flea market, *$100.00*

Negligée, satin crêpe (ecru), floor-length, very full, gathered to lace yoke, long sleeves, padded shoulders, 1940–49, source: flea market, *$32.00*

Negligée, silk (dark gold), floor-length, with a deep pleat falling from each shoulder, long sleeves slightly puffed at sleeve-head, extensive trim of wide silk soutache braid, scrolls of silk cording, and tiny metallic beads, 1900–19, source: flea market, *$75.00*

Negligée, silk (white), wide bertha collar with deep lace ruffle, long full sleeves with lace ruffle, insert lace from top to bottom, long train, 1900–09, source: mail order, *$165.00*

Negligée, silk satin (pink), floor-length with closing of self-loops and pearlized plastic buttons to waist, open skirt with trim of lace and self-loops, bias-cut drape collar, batwing sleeves, self-belt, 1930–39, source: individual, *$40.00*

Nightgown, cotton (white, fine quality), very long and full, deep bertha collar, voluminous sleeves, 1890–99, source: store, *$270.00*

Nightgown, cotton knit with smocked and gathered bodice, raised waist with back ties, long sleeves with ribbed cuffs, ankle-length, 1940–49, source: store, *$18.00*

Nightgown, cotton with fine whitework, long sleeves, button yoke, completely handmade, 1890–99, source: mail order, *$75.00*

Nightgown, cotton, long sleeves, embroidered neckline, buttons, 1890–99, source: mail order, *$40.00*

Turn-of-the-century nightgown, with bertha collar and train effect. (*Clothing courtesy of Puttin' on the Ritz, Dallas, TX.*)

Nightgown, crêpe (floral print), V neck, sleeveless, full-length, bias-cut, 1940–49, source: mail order, $15.00

Nightgown, rayon (floral print), sleeveless, 1930–39, source: mail order, $30.00

Nightgown, satin (peach), bias-cut, with faggoting and French knots (never worn), 1930–39, source: mail order, $20.00

Nightgown, silk (pink), floor-length, sleeveless, lace trim on neck and pocket, 1920–29, source: store, $30.00

Nightgown, silk, pale blue with white floral print, bias-cut, 1930–39, source: flea market, $23.00

Pajamas, acetate satin, harem-style, 1940–49, source: flea market, $25.00

Pajamas, cotton print, tailored, 1950–59, source: store, $23.00

Pajamas, silk, print short-sleeved top, matching border on pants, "Made in Japan" label, period ?, source: flea market, $10.00

Pajamas, silk, tailored, 1940–49, source: store, $50.00

Pajamas, silk, with crochet edging and trim of ribbon rosettes, 1920–29, source: store, $90.00

Robe, rayon velvet, floor-length wraparound with quilted lapels and pockets, self-tie, 1940–49, source: flea market, $30.00

Robe, velvet (royal blue), floor-length, with full skirt and long sleeves, self-belt with rhinestone buckle, period ?, source: store, $40.00

Robe, velvet with fur trim, 1930–39, source: store, $275.00

Robe, wool (paisley), floor-length, gathered to small band at neck, velvet-lined collar at back, hook-and-eye closure down entire front, period ?, source: store, $490.00

Robe, wool, floor-length, allover pattern of fine wool embroidery, East Indian, some moth damage, period ?, source: individual, $75.00

Tea gown, net (cream), embroidered with dots and small flowers, trimmed with lace insertions and satin ribbon, 1910–29, source: auction, $125.00

Tea gown, net (white), instep-length, allover embroidery, ¾ sleeves with flounce, narrow ribbon sash, 1900–09, source: store, $890.00

Tea gown, organdy (black and white print), instep-length, slight train, with embroidered scalloped trim at yoke, sleeves, and down entire front, double flounce on skirt hem, loose belt, 1900–09, source: store, $290.00

Silk kimono, 1920s. (*Clothing courtesy of Puttin' on the Ritz, Dallas, TX.*)

Tea gown, silk velvet (turquoise), floor-length with train, Galenga design printed with a 17th-century-style design of birds and stylized foliate motifs, kimono sleeves edged with patterned glass and carved ivory beads, period ?, source: auction, *$1,870.00*

Tea gown, voile, extensive machine embroidery, mid-calf, scalloped hem, low neckline over net inner bodice, small square collar, 1915–29, source: mail order, *$175.00*

Wrapper, cotton (print), short sleeves, ankle-length, 1900–09, source: store, *$59.00*

Wrapper, cotton (wallpaper print), self-tie, knee-length, short sleeves, 1930–39, source: store, *$18.00*

Wrapper, cotton (calico print), ankle-length, 1890–1909, source: mail order, $75.00

Warm and Dry: Outerwear

CONTENTS

All garments intended to be worn over clothing.

ARRANGEMENT

First by type of garment, then by fabric.

COLLECTING NOTES

Evening outerwear of all periods is plentiful, but daytime outerwear is more difficult to find.

TERMS

Box coat: box-shaped body, loose-fitting, with square shoulders

Cape: flowing garment with no arms; may have slits for armholes

Car (stadium) coat: hip to three-quarter length, square, sporty

Chesterfield: semi-fitted body, single- or double-breasted, usually has black velvet collar

Chubby: hip-length, long-haired fur pelts worked in vertical direction, shoulders highly padded

Coachman: fitted to waistline, flare skirt, double-breasted opening, wide lapels, cape collar

Maxi-coat: semi-fitted, ankle-length

Parka: hooded jacket, hip-length or longer, usually quilted

Poncho: rectangular, square or circular-shaped fabric with a slit cut for the head

Princess coat: fitted coat cut in long panels from neckline to hem, with no seam at waistline, slightly flared hemline, usually single-breasted

Redingote: fitted coat

Slicker: box-style, brightly colored waterproof fabric, metal fasteners

Stole: rectangle of fabric or fur

Tent: pyramid-shaped coat

A typical coat style of the teens and 1920s.

Topper: hip-length, full-cut with slight flare from shoulders to hem, usually with one or no buttons, wide sleeves with deep cuffs

Wrap coat: straight, no buttons, fabric tie

OUTERWEAR LISTED BY TYPE AND VALUE

Cape, fabric unknown, elbow-length, with lavish lace and jet bead trim, 1900–09, source: store, *$150.00*

Cape, muskrat (bleached), hip-length, with slits for arms, small shawl collar, rayon lining, 1940–49, source: store, *$75.00*

Cape, muskrat trimmed with tails, 1930–39, source: store, *$40.00*

Cape, muskrat, hip-length, closing trimmed with 2 tails, 1930–39, source: store, *$75.00*

Velvet evening cape, with shoulder design of iridescent sequins, late 1930s. (*Clothing courtesy of Puttin' on the Ritz, Dallas, TX.*)

Cape, silk chiffon velvet (emerald green), 1910–19, source: store, $65.00

Cape, silk velvet, reversible blue and black, full-length, smocked at shoulders, 1920–29, source: auction, $132.00.

Cape, silk, floor-length, rose-colored, 1880–99, source: store, $250.00

Cape, velvet (black) and gold lamé, with a deep ruched and padded turn-back collar and extending short cape, 1920–29, source: auction (London), $2,700.00

Cape, velvet (black), excellent beading in flower design on entire cape, 1900–09, source: mail order, $100.00

Cape, wool (black), waist-length, trimmed with soutache and passementerie, 1880–99, source: store, $145.00

Cape, wool (navy), 23″ long with 1 big button at neck, 1950–59, source: mail order, $15.00

Cape, wool, above-elbow-length, with braid, 1880–99, source: mail order, *$40.00*

Coat, brocade, Impressionist print, below-the-knee, raglan ¾ sleeves, open front, 1950–59, source: store, *$35.00*

One cashmere goat produces a mere four ounces of usable fiber per year—which means that it requires the total fleece "output" of twenty-seven goats to make one topcoat. These goats have their natural habitat in the Himalayas, and although they will happily live elsewhere, they will *not* grow their valuable cashmere undercoat any place else.

Coat, cashmere, clutch style (no buttons, shawl collar), mid-calf-length, 1950–59, source: store, *$30.00*

Coat, chiffon with silvered lace trim and tasselled tie, 1920–29, source: auction (London), *$99.00*

Coat, cowhide, Western-style, knee-length, 1960–69, source: store, *$190.00*

Coat, crêpe (black) printed with multi-colored grid and dot design, with attached scarf, below-the-knee-length, hem trimmed with deep band of black fox, 1920–29, source: auction, *$220.00*

Coat, fur, full-length, chevron patterned, with monkey-fur collar, 3 large Deco-style buttons, lining replaced with brocade, 1920–29, source: store, *$195.00*

Coat, gabardine (navy), padded shoulders, tailored at waist, large Bakelite buttons, 1940–49, source: mail order, *$45.00*

Coat, gabardine (orange) topper, padded shoulders, 1940–49, source: mail order, *$50.00*

Coat, gabardine (red), fitted at waist, with flared skirt, double-caped shoulders, 2 rows of small silver buttons on front, 1940–49, source: store, *$45.00*

Coat, lace (Battenburg), mid-calf-length, long sleeves, princess line, extensively trimmed with crochet buttons, 1910–19, source: auction, *$528.00*

Coat, lace (Irish, white) in overall floral design, shawl collar, filet lace inserts at sleeves, 1920–29, source: auction, *$418.00*

Coat, lamb (curly), ankle-length, sleeveless, open front, 1960–69, source: flea market, *$40.00*

Coat, lamb (Persian, black), ¾-length, 1930–39, source: flea market, $55.00

Coat, mink (black), sleeveless, knee-length, yoke of heavy Victorian-style braid, small, unobtrusive bald spot on fur, 1920–29, source: store, $55.00

Coat, mink (ranch), full-length, 1940–49, source: mail order, $300.00

Coat, monkey fur, 1930–39, source: store, $250.00

Coat, mouton, padded shoulders, ¾-length, 1940–49, source: flea market, $65.00

Coat, muskrat, padded shoulders, very long, wide sleeves, 1940–49, source: flea market, $95.00

Coat, rayon blend, full-cut, large standup collar flowing into rolled lapels, large self-covered buttons, fully lined, below-the-knee, 1950–59, source: flea market, $30.00

Coat, satin brocade (black), mid-calf-length, open front with shawl collar, 1950–59, source: store, $25.00

Coat, seal, full-length, mink collar and cuffs, 1920–29, source: store, $175.00

Coat, sealskin, mid-calf-length, 1930–39, source: store, $100.00

Coat, silk (bitter chocolate), with shawl collar, ruching to the low waistline, sash bow fastening, label "Paquin, Paris, Londres, Buenos-Aires, Madrid," 1920–29, source: auction (London), $504.00

Coat, silk (burnt orange) with gold thread brocade, hood, knee-length, 1920–29, source: auction (London), $198.00

Coat, silk faille, asymmetric 1-button closing, deep cuffs, 1910–29, source: store, $165.00

Coat, silk velvet (black), mid-calf-length, batwing sleeves, much shirring, silk-satin lining, 1920–29, source: store, $150.00

Coat, suede (green), black fur trim at collar and hem, period ?, source: store, $32.50

Coat, taffeta (heavy, black), reverses to leopard-print taffeta, 1940–59, source: store, $58.00

Coat, velvet (black) cloak with fringed trim, label "Jay's Ltd., London," 1920–29, source: auction (London), $270.00

Coat, velvet (black) cloak, deep shawl collar and ruching at neckline, allover gold lamé decoration of flower blooms, label "Callot Soeurs, Paris. No: 3422," 1920–29, source: auction (London), $1,710.00

Coat, velvet (black), large collar, fancy buttons, floor-length, 1940–49, source: store, $60.00

Coat, velvet (black), silk lining, ermine collar, floor-length, 1940–49, source: mail order, $60.00

Coat, velvet (peach), piping and fringed trim, label "Callot Soeurs, Paris. No: 29788," 1920–29, source: auction (London), $180.00

Coat, velvet (rust), ¾-length, chinchilla trim, lining handpainted with geometric design (underarms repaired), 1920–29, source: store, $150.00

Coat, wool (black) with mink-trimmed collar and cuffs, 1-button front, 1920–29, source: mail order, $50.00

Coat, wool (black), drop-waisted blouson style, fur trim, 1920–29, source: store, $100.00

Coat, wool (blue) topper, decorative stitching, standup collar, rhinestone buttons, 1950–59, source: mail order, $45.00

Coat, wool (camel), "New Look" princess-style, mid-calf, silk lining, large self-buttons, 1940–59, source: store, $50.00

Coat, wool (gray and tan), small fur collar, parasol-shaped Bakelite buttons (small moth holes), 1920–29, source: mail order, $45.00

Coat, wool (gray and white) tweed, Jacques Fath design, cape collar trimmed with short gray fringe, below-the-knee, very narrow cut, 1950–59, source: store, $125.00

Coat, wool (green) with fur trim down both front edges, 1930–39, source: mail order, $50.00

Coat, wool (pink) topper, beaded, 1950–59, source: store, $15.00

Coat, wool with bold psychedelic print, maxi-style, front ties, pile-lined, with pile trim on outside, 1960–69, source: store, $35.00

Jacket, fox (white), "chubby" style, long sleeves unsnap to convert jacket into cape, 1940–49, source: store, $425.00

Jacket, lamb (Persian), hip-length, full-cut, satin lining, 1940–49, source: store, $69.00

Jacket, lamé with velvet trim, 1920–29, source: store, $95.00

Jacket, monkey fur, hip-length, 1930–49, source: store, $480.00

Jacket, mouton, 1950–59, source: store, $45.00

Jacket, silk satin (black), knee-length with side vents, covered buttons, silk faille lining, 1900–19, source: flea market, $40.00

Lavish cutaway jacket of embossed black velvet, 1900s. The lining
is pink satin, and the attached vest is a patterned panné velvet,
predominately pink. The many buttons are of patterned glass.
(Clothing courtesy of Puttin' on the Ritz, Dallas, TX.)

Jacket, velvet (embossed, black) with pink satin lining, cutaway, print
velvet detailing, many decorative buttons of etched glass, 1900–09,
source: store, $590.00

> According to the *New York Fashion Bazar* in 1889, "The people in this
> world who get beyond the use of patches on garments are few and
> exceedingly foolish. . . ."

Jacket, velvet (plush), fur trim, fur buttons, 1880–99, source: store,
$75.00

Jacket, velvet (purple plush), with red quilted lining, long tails-style
front, 1880–89, source: mail order, $30.00

Jacket, velveteen, blazer-style with zippered front, fitted at waist, 1960–69, source: mail order, $10.00

Jacket, wool (pink), box-style, ¾ sleeves, extensive trapunto trim, edged in metallic gold cording, 1950–59, source: store, $89.00

Jacket, wool twill (navy), fur-trimmed shawl collar, open front, 1950–59, source: store, $20.00

Raincoat, vinyl (shiny, black) with transparent vinyl circular inserts, mini-length, 1960–69, source: store, $29.00

Women's Accessories

Footwear

CONTENTS

Shoes and boots.

ARRANGEMENT

Items are arranged by type of footwear. Shoes are arranged in three categories: "Boudoir slippers," "Day," and "Evening."

COLLECTING NOTES

Leather footwear of the period 1880 to 1920 is difficult to find in good condition, but fabric shoes of these periods (usually evening wear) are more plentiful. In general, the following statements apply to the history of footwear:

1880–1910: Boots were generally worn by day, slippers for evening; shoes were narrow and toes pointed; heels were fairly high, and usually curved in the Louis or French style.

1910–1930: Shoes were worn both day and evening, though boots also continued to be worn in the teens; shoes gradually became wider and toes less pointed; oxfords were popular for day, court shoes (often with beaded buckles) for evening; T-straps were fashionable in the 1920s; curved heels (variously described as Louis, hourglass, and spool) were usual until the late 1920s, when the Cuban shape became more popular.

1930–39: Toes were rounded; heels were generally straight and a little higher than in the previous period; shoes were frequently cut high on the foot; the cutaway "peep-toe" was fashionable toward the end of the decade; wedge heels were introduced in 1936.

1940–49: Toes fairly rounded; heels generally straight and thick; platform soles fashionable; saddle oxfords worn by teenagers.

1950–59: Pointed toes returned and stiletto heels were introduced; shoes frequently cut low on the foot; ballerina shoes were popular, along with pointed "Italian" flats; penny loafers worn by teenagers.

1960–69: Blunt toes and low heels; court, bar, T-strap, and sling-back styles; boots returned to popularity.

TYPES OF HEELS

Baby Louis: low heel, hourglass shape

Boulevard: sturdy high heel, same width top and bottom

Cone: wide at top, narrow at bottom

Cuban: medium heel, straight-sided, with slight back curve

French: high heel, somewhat curved at back, wide at top, narrow at bottom

Louis: high heel, hourglass shape

Stacked: Cuban heel made of horizontal layers of leather or wood

Stiletto: very high heel, very small base

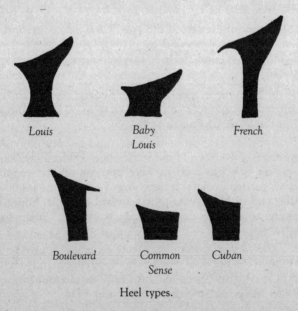

Louis   Baby   French
               Louis

Boulevard   Common   Cuban
             Sense

Heel types.

Wedge: triangular base (heel extends under the waist of the shoe to the forepart)

TERMS REFERRING TO BOOTS

Cavalier: soft, ankle-high, turned-back cuff

Cossack (Russian): knee-high, unfitted

Cowboy: mid-calf, pointed toe, stacked heel; frequently made of exotic leather, with vivid color combinations, tooled designs

Go-go: white, mid-calf

Jodhpur: ankle-high, buckled at one side

Lace-up (granny): ankle-high or calf-high, laced up the front

Riding: smooth leather, knee-high

TERMS REFERRING TO SHOES

Ballerina: fabric or soft-kid, no heel, flat sole

Clog (sabot): thick, one-piece sole and heel, usually of wood or cork, with leather uppers, usually backless

Espadrille: slip-on, canvas upper and rope-covered sole

Loafer: slip-on, low heel; variations include *penny* (leather strip added at instep to hold coin), *tassel* (tassel attached at instep)

Mary Jane: low heel, rounded toe, single strap across instep

Moccasin: slip-on formed from soft piece of leather, usually with no heel or sole

Mule (slide, scuff): open back, slide-on, open or closed toe

Oxford: low-cut, with laces at instep; variations include: *balmoral* (separate tongue stitched to the vamp), *blucher* (vamp and tongue cut as one piece), *brogue* (decorative stitching or perforations), *ghillie* (laced through loops rather than eyelets, frequently with no tongue), *saddle shoe* (sections of contrasting colors), *sneaker* (canvas lace-up)

Pump: classic women's shoe with closed toe; variations include: *bar* (having a strap across the instep), *court* (enclosed shoe with low or medium heel, frequently with a decorative flap that extends from the vamp over the top of the instep and is trimmed with beading, a rosette, a buckle, etc.), *D'Orsay* (closed heel, low-cut at vamp), *opera* (plain vamp and closed heel), *platform* (thick sole), *sling-back* (open-back, held in place with strap at back), *spectator* (sections of contrasting colors), *T-strap* (T-shaped strap holds foot at instep)

Sandal: open shoe held on foot with one or more straps; varieties include: *ankle-wrap* (straps tie around ankle), *fisherman* (closed sandal of woven leather straps), *huarache* (flat pump made of woven leather), *thong* (two straps converge between big and second toe), *T-strap* (open toe and heel, strap in form of T holds shoe on the foot, with sling-back strap)

Springalator: a backless, open-toed shoe which is held on the foot with pressure created by a tight elastic strip that lifts the foot from underneath

FOOTWEAR LISTED BY TYPE AND VALUE

Boots, brocade and fur, ribbon ties, 1890–99, source: store, $175.00

Boots, canvas (white), mint condition, French heel, 1910–19, source: store, $150.00

Boots, kid, button-up high-tops, navy and cream, 1910–19, source: store, $25.00

Boots, leather (black), ankle-length, laced, period ?, source: store, $45.00

Boots, leather (brown) high-top, laces, 1900–09, source: mail order, $40.00

Boots, leather (brown), lace-up, 1900–09, source: mail order, $45.00

Boots, material unknown, lace-up, stamped "1915 Goodyear Rubber Co." on heel; 1½" heel; never worn, 1910–19, source: store, $65.00

Boots, suede (black), Cossack-style, knee-high, side zipper and decorative lacing, 1960–69, source: store, $20.00

Boudoir slippers, mink mules, sequined heels, period ?, source: store, $18.00

Boudoir slippers, satin (quilted, pale blue), square 1" heels, braid trim with small pompoms, period ?, source: store, $22.00

Boudoir slippers, silk-satin (blue), high heels, with burgundy frog-style trim, Daniel Green, period ?, source: store, $25.00

Boudoir slippers, silk, handmade, with Chinese embroidery, 1920–29, source: store, $25.00

Day, alligator (black), spike heel, pointed toes, 1950–59, source: store, $15.00

Day, alligator (green) platform, ankle straps, 1940–49, source: mail order, $75.00

Shoes of the 1900s. Note the narrow, pointed toes and Louis heels. Left to right: a suede lace-up oxford, a silk court shoe with beading, a kid bar shoe, and a tie oxford. *(Accessories courtesy of Puttin' on the Ritz, Dallas, TX.)*

Shoes of the 1920s. Left to right: a T-strap with perforated design, a silver kid evening shoe with high vamp, a lace-up oxford, and a silk pump with French heel. *(Accessories courtesy of Puttin' on the Ritz, Dallas, TX.)*

The term "weejuns"—used to describe the loafer shoe so popular in the forties and fifties—is a corruption of the word "Norwegian." Yes, loafers came from the peasant shoes of Norway, not from the moccasins of the American Indian.

Day, alligator (red) platforms, ankle straps, 1940–49, source: store, *$115.00*

Day, embroidered uppers, high heel, stacked sole, with open toe and sling back, 1940–49, source: store, *$15.00*

Day, fabric (red and green plaid), cut-down sides, laquered bridge heel, wide black ribbon ties at ankle, Jean Rimbaud, 1960–69, source: store, *$45.00*

Day, faux-alligator (black), Italian-style flats, pointed toes, new-old, 1960–69, source: store, *$59.00*

Day, kid (taupe), high Louis heel, pointed toe, black velvet tie at instep, 1900–09, source: store, *$140.00*

Day, kid oxfords, buttons, stacked Cuban heel, 1930–39, source: flea market, *$48.00*

Day, kid-suede (brown) oxford, high Louis heel, very pointed toe, silk cord laces, 1900–09, source: store, *$140.00*

Shoes of the 1930s. On the left, two evening shoes, one of silver kid with a Cuban heel, the other having a jeweled toe and ankle-wrap strap. On the right are two high-cut pumps, one with a removable bow trim, the other with a scalloped edge and stitched design. (*Accessories courtesy of Puttin' on the Ritz, Dallas, TX.*)

Shoes of the 1940s. Left to right: a quilted silk pump, a suede pump with cut-out pattern on vamp, an ankle-wrap platform with boulevard heel, and a brocade opera pump. (*Accessories courtesy of Puttin' on the Ritz, Dallas, TX.*)

Day, kid, Louis curved heel, red and white, tied, with small beaded trim, 1920–29, source: store, $45.00

Day, leather (tan), wide T-straps with cut-out pattern, 2″ square heel, 1930–39, source: store, $30.00

Day, leather saddle oxfords, unworn, 1950–59, source: store, $35.00

Day, leather, black, baby-doll style, 1940–49, source: store, $10.00

Day, leather, spectator pumps, faux-reptile trim, high boulevard heel, 1940–49, source: store, $20.00

Day, lizard (brown), stilleto heels, bow at toe, period ?, source: store, $9.00

Day, patent leather (black) pumps, 1950–59, source: store, $9.50

Day, snakeskin sandals with platform, 1940–49, source: mail order, $25.00

Day, suede (black) pumps, boulevard heel, 1940–49, source: store, $15.00

Day, suede (black) pumps, pointed toes, high heels, 1950–59, source: mail order, $10.00

Day, suede (black), with high vamp, diagonal faille inset, high, thick heel, removable large bow clip, 1930–39, source: store, $98.00

Day, suede (brown), medium-high Cuban heel, trimmed with scroll-work stitching and metal studs, 1940–49, source: store, $69.00

Day, suede (white) pumps, peep-toe, perforated insets at front, sculptured leather bows, Andrew Geller, 1940–49, source: store, $25.00

Day, suede (white), brown leather trim, open-toed, 1930–39, source: store, $25.00

Day, suede, green with brown leather trim, two tan pearl buttons, medium heel, 1920–29, source: mail order, $45.00

Evening, gold and silver T-strap, stack heel, 1920–29, source: mail order, $35.00

Evening, gold kid, straps with rhinestone buckles, 1920–29, source: mail order, $22.00

Evening, gold lamé, 1910–19, source: store, $55.00

Evening, gold, with glitter spike heels, shocking pink inner soles, Schiaparelli, 1950–59, source: store, $350.00

Evening, leather (dark green) with gold snake design, 1920–29, source: mail order, $45.00

Evening, material unknown, ankle straps with cut-out sides, fuschia, 1930–39, source: store, $20.00

Shoes of the 1950s. Left to right: a springalator of clear plastic, with lucite trim on toe, and lucite heel with embedded rhinestones, a brocade pump with pointed toe and spike heel, a sling-back of black faille with rhinestone trim, and a suede pump with lattice side-trim. *(Accessories courtesy of Puttin' on the Ritz, Dallas, TX.)*

Evening, plastic springalators, clear, with rhinestone trim, 1950–59, source: flea market, $32.00

Evening, rhinestone-covered opera pumps, pointed toe, very thin spike heel, Andrew Geller, 1950–59, source: store, $290.00

Evening, satin (black) low-heeled slippers, 1920–29, source: store, $25.00

Evening, satin (black) T-strap, wedge heel, 1930–39, source: store, $18.00

Evening, shantung pumps, with ankle wraps, handpainted design on toes, 1950–59, source: store, $110.00

Evening, silk (black) pumps, high Louis heel, 1920–29, source: store, $98.00

Evening, silk-satin (black) pumps with large, jet-beaded flap, medium French heel, 1900–19, source: store, $95.00

Evening, silver kid sandals, 1920–29, source: store, $95.00

Evening, silver kid, medium Cuban heel, Mary Jane strap, 1920–29, source: store, $98.00

Evening, silver mesh platforms, open toe and heel, 4½" heel, 1960–69, source: store, $32.50

Evening, suede (brown) springalators with bow trim, stilt heel, 1950–59, source: store, $25.00

Evening, suede (purple) skyscraper platform, with cut-out open toe and sling-back (new-old), 1940–49, source: store, $65.00

Hats

CONTENTS

Hats.

ARRANGEMENT

By material.

COLLECTING NOTES

Hats of all sorts, from every period, are available, though of course pre–World War I hats are less easy to find in good condition. Although there are certain basic hat shapes, many hats do not fall into any typical category and must be evaluated individually, almost as if they were works of sculpture. The hats of the 1900s were certainly the most lavish of this century, but those of the 1930s were perhaps the most imaginative; both these periods produced especially collectible hats.

Here is an overview of the history of hat fashions in the vintage century:

In the 1880s, fashionable hats were generally small, and usually had a vertical line, with fairly high crowns, small brims, and vertically oriented trimmings. Bonnets were popular. Then, as the silhouette in clothing became narrower in the nineties, hats increased in size and visual importance, with the line remaining vertical. Bonnets were not fashionable. Boaters, fedoras, and tams were worn.

Early in the first decade of the twentieth century, medium-sized hats were worn, often tilted forward, with trimmings under the black brim. As the decade progressed, hats became very large and extensively decorated (often with huge flowers, whole stuffed birds, giant bows, etc.); the prevailing line tended to be horizontal.

During the next decade, hats diminished somewhat in size, and decorations became less extreme. Tam hats were very much worn early in the decade; turbans came into fashion, and veils were popular during the war. Toward the end of the decade, one-sided hats and early versions of the cloche (with a tall crown and a moderate brim) became popular.

The 1920s saw a trend toward soft, neat, and close-fitting hats. The modified cloche (no brim, close fit) was very popular; also, there were turbans, toques, berets, and boaters. The emphasis was not so much on the charms of the hat itself, but on its contribution to the general effect of the outfit. In general, hats were more ornamented in the first and last quarters of the decade, plainer in the middle of the decade.

The 1930s were very eclectic; during the first half of the decade, many 1920s looks continued to develop new twists; in the second half, there were new trends. Hats were frequently perched forward over the forehead, and there was a vogue for very small "toy" hats and quasi-hat hair ornaments such as flowers, feathers, mantillas, etc.; chou hats, harlequins, halos, profile hats, short-backs, and Peter Pans were just some of the adventurous styles popular in the 1930s. Feathers on hats were very popular at mid-decade, along with soft fabrics and brighter colors (colors had been subdued early in the decade). During the last half of the decade, black was especially fashionable, and flowers were used more extensively. Folded, twisted, pleated, and tucked hats were a particular fashion development of the 1930s.

In the early 1940s, styles continued much in the vein of the 1930s, with small hats cocked at rakish angles. The Breton was very popular. By the last two years of the war, hat materials were running short and hats became more economical in design; turbans were popular in the late-war years, as were berets. After the war, larger hats returned as part of the New Look; large brims and small crowns were the general rule. By the end of the decade, however, smaller hats were being seen, often with draped veils.

In the 1950s, hats of all types were worn, but the importance of the hat subsided sharply as the decade progressed; early in the decade, the small crown was the rule, often with a brim that tapered away in the back. Nostalgia hats came in in the mid-1950s, with large, old-fashioned designs, but there was also a strong movement toward small, rather plain hats. Toward the end of the decade, hats began to cover the brow again, with a sou'wester style gaining popularity, as well as a so-called "hairdryer hat"—a bell of organdy or stiffened tulle that was pinned to the top of a raised hairdo and resembled a dryer hood over the head. Frivolous evening hats were popular.

In the 1960s, hats became fun items rather than necessities. Some hats were made up as parts of outfits, while others were playful "costume" hats. Flower hats were very popular early in the decade, as were pillboxes. Traditionally masculine hat shapes such as the bowler and Stetson were borrowed for women's hats. Trends in the later decade included hats that resembled space helmets or swim caps, and hats of unusual materials.

Hats are sized in the number of inches around the head at the brow; women's hats are generally made in half-inches, from 21 to 23½ inches.

TERMS

Beret: round piece of fabric, folded under and attached to inner band to form soft, round hat

Boater: flat, stiff brim; low, round crown, ribbon band

Bonnet: soft, usually made of fabric, with or without a brim; bonnets generally rest on the top and/or back of the head, and tie under the chin; bonnets were extremely popular in the nineteenth century, and have occasionally been revived in the twentieth; the sunbonnet—a common style of the American frontier—has a wide, stiffened or quilted front brim, and a cape-like extension covering the back of the neck

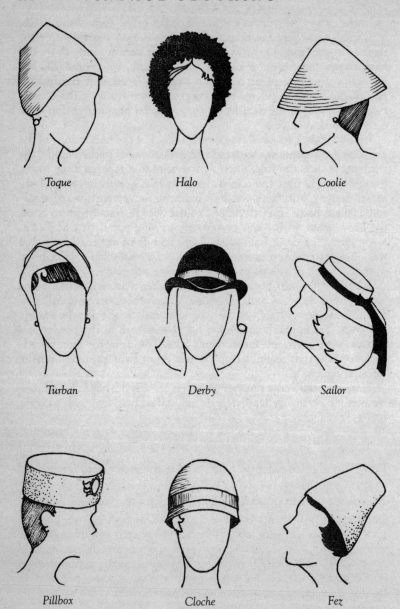

Toque   Halo   Coolie

Turban   Derby   Sailor

Pillbox   Cloche   Fez

Hats.

Fedora

Picture

Beret

Cartwheel

Breton

Watteau

Hats (continued)

Breton: rounded crown with roll-up brim

Calotte (Juliet, skull-cap, beanie): small round cap that hugs the top of the head

Cartwheel (picture hat): low crown, very large, flat brim

Chou: soft, crushed crown

Cloche: deep-crowned, little or no brim, hugs the head closely

Coolie: wide, cone-shaped

Cossack: tall, round, brimless, often made of fur

Cowboy: high crown with center crease and medium or wide brim, often curved upward at the sides, usually with a decorative band

Fedora (Homburg): felt hat with creased crown, slightly curved brim

Fez: tall, tapered, brimless, with flat top

Flower: made entirely of flowers, usually silk or organdy

Gaucho: low, circular crown, very wide flat brim

Halo: circular, low crown, turned-back brim (worn back from the forehead)

Harlequin: only the brim is seen, turned straight up and flaring out from the head

Helmet: brimless, crownless hat that covers the entire head and fastens under the chin

Jockey: small cap, with close-fitting crown, small visor-type brim

Leghorn: low crown and very large, drooping brim, made of fine leghorn straw

Matinée: picture hat with a large brim

Mob cap: a full, round fabric crown gathered to a ruffle that fits around the head

Mushroom: large brim, turned downward around the face

Panama: low, creased crown, brim turned upwards in back, made of light-colored straw

Peter Pan: small, narrow, brimless hat that runs from front to back of the head, with a lengthwise peak or soft crease along the top

Pillbox: small, round, brimless, sits on top of the head

Profile: shaped to fit well over to one side of the head, framing the face

Sailor: flat crown, with straight, stiff brim, usually made of straw

Short-back: flat, wide brim in front, but very narrow brim or none at all in back; low crown

Slouch: soft hat with flexible brim

Tam: soft, full circle of fabric gathered into a band, often with a pom-pom at center top

Tam hat: made into many different styles by draping and shaping fabric over an inner crown

Toque: round, brimless, worn close to the head

Toy (doll): tiny hat, worn perched forward on the head and held with a band around the back of the head

Turban: soft draped hat that features twists or rolls of fabric

Tyrolean (Alpine, trilby): soft felt hat with cone-shaped crown, small brim that turns up on one side

Watteau: a rather flat, oblong hat, higher at back than front, usually with trim underneath the upturned back brim

HATS LISTED BY TYPE AND VALUE

Beaver, narrow rolled brim, ostrich-feather trim, black, 1880–99, source: store, *$55.00*

Cotton, mob cap, chintz print, trimmed with deep edging of ecru handcrocheted lace, 1890–99, source: flea market, *$20.00*

Cotton, sunbonnet, 1-piece, plain fabric, stitched brim, period ?, source: flea market, *$5.00*

Cotton, sunbonnet, very large crown fastened to stitched brim with many small mother-of-pearl buttons, long ties and bavolet, 1890–1909, source: flea market, *$20.00*

Felt, chou hat, brown felt, with narrow brim of bright mint green, trim of brown silk passementerie and tassels at back, Lilly Daché, period ?, source: store, *$20.00*

Felt, cloche, purple with ornate beading, 1920–29, source: auction, *$30.00*

Felt, fez, with scalloped edges and allover design of clear sequins, period ?, source: flea market, *$8.00*

Felt, large brim of black fur felt, set on fitted headpiece; small crown topped with white sunburst effect, 1940–49, source: store, *$65.00*

Felt, low crown, narrow brim, sequin and bead band around standup edge of crown, one narrow feather, veil under chin, poison green, 1940–49, source: store, *$15.00*

Felt/feathers, "Mad Hatter"-style, very high crown, elastic back strap, huge sequins on hat, very large feathers sticking out of the top, large veil, 1940–49, source: store, $145.00

Felt/feathers, high crown, cluster of feathers, 1930–39, source: store, $19.50

Felt/feathers, turned-up brim, black, spray of small black feathers at center front, and veil over forehead area, 1940–49, source: store, $22.00

Jersey/feathers, black jersey crown, swathed in pink and black net, with large net bow at back, brim made entirely of short pink ostrich feathers, elastic holder, 1930–39, source: store, $79.00

Lace, wide brim, black with multi-colored flowers, 1920–29, source: mail, $45.00

Organdy, flower toque, net base covered with organdy flowers and velveteen leaves, 1950–59, source: flea market, $5.00

Satin, cloche, petalled crown, very narrow straw-lined brim, band of black suede leaf-shapes, 1910–19, source: flea market, $55.00

Satin, pillbox, heavily beaded, 1950–59, source: flea market, $18.00

Satin, pillbox, white, small veil, 1960–69, source: store, $5.00

A typically enormous hat of the 1900s. It is black velvet, trimmed with black net, black feathers, black ribbon, and colored velvet flowers. (*Accessories courtesy of Puttin' on the Ritz, Dallas, TX.*)

Hats. Left to right: a brightly colored brocade cloche from the teens, a black silk tam hat from the teens, and a black sailor-style with brim of pink ostrich feathers and trim of black and pink tulle, 1930s. *(Accessories courtesy of Puttin' on the Ritz, Dallas, TX.)*

Silk/velvet, tam hat, very large, draped to one side with large bow, 1910–19, source: store, *$210.00*

Straw, cloche, beige with pale green trim, flat horsehair bow on one side, 1920–29, source: store, *$38.00*

Straw, cloche, with large, sports-style brim, applied flowers, 1920–29, source: mail order, *$36.00*

Straw hats can be stiffened, if necessary, with a thin coat of clear shellac mixed half and half with rubbing alcohol.

Straw, deep crown, light blue trimmed with pale pink ribbon and large pink flowers, very large brim, 1910–19, source: mail order, *$75.00*

Straw, picture-frame, 15″ diameter, large flowers and veiling, 1930–49, source: store, *$30.00*

Hats. Left to right: a black, sequin-trimmed cloche from the 1920s, a 1940s hat with chin veil, and a toy hat of pheasant feathers and red marabou, from the 1930s. (*Accessories courtesy of Puttin' on the Ritz, Dallas, TX.*)

Straw, short-back, with cluster of large silk flowers on brim, small, fairly high crown trimmed with fabric, beading, and metallic lace; Lilly Daché, 1930–39, source: flea market, $65.00

Straw, small crown, wide horsehair brim, black, trimmed with blue and purple small flowers, 1890–1909, source: store, $45.00

Straw, white, with black bow and veil, 1930–39, source: store, $22.50

Straw, wide-brim, red, with red cloth roses, 1940–49, source: store, $28.00

Straw/feathers, toy hat, crown about 3″ across, small brim, many curly feathers, long self-ties, all aqua, 1930–39, source: store, $20.00

Straw/feathers/fabric, high crown with narrow, upturned brim; trimmed with numerous feathers, braid, and tapestry swag, shades of bronze, russet, and gold, 1880–99, source: flea market, $58.00

Suede, beret, turquoise, with self-tassel on top, period ?, source: store, $15.00

Velvet, bonnet-style, black, flat crown, narrow brim, long ties, red satin flowers, 1880–99, source: flea market, $58.00

Velvet, cap-style, covered with velvet flower petals, trimmed with large grosgrain bow with streamers, grosgrain tie-back band, shoulder-length black mesh veil, 1930–39, source: flea market, $18.00

Velvet, Peter Pan, on inner organdy cap, trimmed with satin ribbon and rhinestone detail, 1930–39, source: store, $25.00

Velvet, short-back, shocking pink, brim covered with gathered material and trimmed with small self-bows, 1950–59, source: flea market, $22.00

Velvet, tam hat, asymmetric, large, with front panel of unusual basket-weave puckered fabric, 1910–19, source: store, $180.00

Velvet, toque, black with bow at side, 1910–19, source: store, $25.00

Velvet, toque, white, with antique hat pin, 1960–69, source: flea market, $12.00

Velvet/feathers, beret, trimmed with pheasant feathers, 1940–49, source: store, $39.00

Velvet/feathers, tam hat, with silver ornament, 1910–19, source: flea market, $40.00

Wool, beret, knitted, dark red mohair, 1910–19, source: store, $30.00

Wool, pull-on cloche, knitted, alternating rows of orange yarn, gold metallic ribbon, and brown silk ribbon, all pulled into a mass of 3″ spiral-knit tassels on top, period ?, source: store, $12.00

Wool, wide, shaped bandeau, paisley fabric, bordered with twisted rolls of fabric, top covered with exceptional beading, period ?, source: flea market, $20.00

Neckwear, Gloves, Purses, Belts

CONTENTS

Scarves, collars, and other neckwear; gloves; purses, handbags, and evening bags; belts. Shawls are also included here, although heavier ones were in some periods considered outerwear.

By type of item.

Neckwear, gloves, and evening bags are plentiful; leather belts and purses are rather difficult to find in good condition, and in fact, belts of any kind are scarce. Neckwear, gloves, and bags can often be found among the miscellaneous antiques in stores and flea-market booths that don't carry other vintage clothing.

Here is an historical overview of vintage accessories:

1880–1899: Handbags were generally small; flat leather purses were carried by day, and for evening, bags styled like drawstring sacks, or attached to a metal top frame. Evening bags were usually made of tapestry or beading; from early in the nineties, metal mesh became popular. (Whiting and Davis made their first mesh bags in 1892.) In the 1890s, handbag frames frequently were hinged both in the middle and at the ends, so that they opened into a square shape. Muffs were carried, often with matching fur scarves called "tippets." Separate collars of all sorts—from narrow lace or crochet to wide berthas—were worn. Separate belts and sashes were popular in the 1890s. In general, short gloves were worn for day, long gloves for evening (¾ with short sleeves, elbow-length with sleeveless).

1900–1909: Headscarves of chiffon, lace, or silk were worn, as well as lacy woolen scarves called "fascinators." The boa was fashionable, and muffs continued in popularity. Purses and gloves were similar to those of the previous period, though purses were somewhat larger.

1910–19: Both purses and muffs grew larger; muffs might have straps so that they could hang from the neck, and purses might be suspended on very long chains hanging almost to the ground. A soft gauntlet glove was in fashion, and very long gloves were often worn in the evening, crushed all the way down the arm. Purses of embossed leather or alligator were popular. Gauze and chiffon scarves were worn.

1920–1929: "Flapper" bags of the 1920s were distinguished by a tassel of fringe or metal mesh at the bottom. Small envelope bags were popular, and enameled mesh bags came into fashion toward the end of the decade. Shawls, frequently with long fringe, were popular: long scarves were worn tied around the neck with the ends hanging down the back. The shorty glove was revived, and for longer gloves, elastic began to replace buttons at the wrist. Belts and sashes of this period are long, to fit the hip-level waistline.

Tapestry bag of the 1890s. Extra hinges under the clasp allow the top of the bag to open into a square. *(Accessories courtesy of Puttin' on the Ritz, Dallas, TX.)*

1930–39: The popularity of metal mesh bags finally declined. Clutch bags were fashionable. Matching handbags and shoes (and sometimes belts) became popular. Free-finger gloves were introduced late in the decade. Gauntlet gloves were much worn. Batik scarves were worn, along with handpainted silks.

1940–49: Styles of the 1930s continued, with modifications and additions, throughout the war. Shoulder bags became very popular, with the wrist-strap bag appearing later in the decade. String gloves were frequently worn. During the war, belts were narrow, but wider ones came into fashion later in the decade. Colorful commemorative scarves and kerchiefs were popular.

1950–59: Box bags were fashionable, and most bags had rigid double handles. Contour and cinch belts were popular, along with cummerbunds. Gloves were no longer necessary for day, but ¾ gloves, often

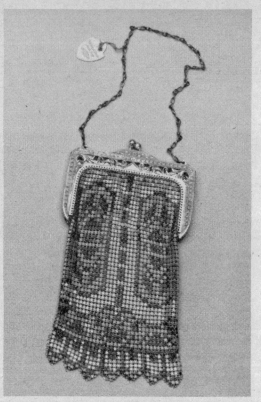

Metal mesh bag from Whiting and Davis. Enameled mesh was popular in the late 1920s. (*Accessories courtesy of Puttin' on the Ritz, Dallas, TX.*)

black, were worn early in the decade, with white shorty gloves becoming popular at the end; nylon gloves also enjoyed a vogue. Long white gloves were still worn for formal evening dress.

1960–69: The Chanel bag was revived, and gloves—short, long, and 3/4—continued to be worn, though now strictly as a fashion statement, rather than as a matter of etiquette; novelty gloves were common. Belts were not very important with the unfitted fashion of the early decade, but later, wide "hipster" belts were worn, often made of plastic or metal.

TERMS REFERRING TO NECKWEAR

Ascot: wide, soft tie held in place with stickpin

Bandanna: brightly colored traditional print cotton square

Bertha: a large, cape-like collar, usually lace

Boa: long, narrow scarf made of fur or feathers

Bolo: thin tie made of cording, usually tipped with metal on the ends, and held together by a decorative slide

Collar: a separate collar worn as an accessory with different dresses and blouses

Kerchief: small, square scarf meant to be folded in a triangle and tied on the head or around the neck

Muffler: long, narrow rectangle of fabric or knitting, to be wrapped around the neck as outerwear

Scarf: square or rectangle of fabric, usually tied at the neck or draped over the shoulders

Smoke ring: bias-cut material, usually chiffon, formed into a tube

TERMS REFERRING TO BELTS

Cinch: tight-fitting, elasticized, clasp in front

Contour: curved belt, shaped in any of various ways to conform to or accentuate the figure

Cowboy: wide, decorated with tooled designs or studs

Cummerbund: wide fabric belt, shirred or pleated

Sash: soft belt that ties in bow or knot

TERMS REFERRING TO HANDBAGS

Box: rigid frame, rigid top handle

Chanel: soft, quilted leather, adjustable shoulder chain strap

Clutch: soft handbag with no handle

Envelope: flat, rectangular bag shaped like business envelope

Minaudiere: small, rigid evening bag made of metal or covered with metallic fabric

Pocketbook: flat, compartmented style of purse

Reticule: bag with drawstring top

TERMS REFERRING TO GLOVES

Free-finger: having a separate band for the sides and tip of the fingers, for easier movement

Gauntlet: wide flare above the wrist

Mitt: fingerless glove, generally formal wear

Mitten: separate thumb

Mousquetaire: long glove with no wrist opening, or with small slit and buttons at wrist (can be worn long or crushed down)

Novelty: any glove with trimming or with unusual materials

String: crocheted or knitted

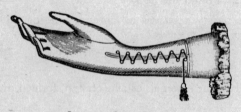

Lace-up glove, 1900s.

LENGTHS

Shorty, wrist-length (one-button)

Classic (covers the wristbone)

Mid-forearm (four- or five-button)

Elbow (eight-button)

Above elbow (twelve-button)

Shoulder (sixteen-button)

TERMS REFERRING TO SHAWLS

Egyptian silver: made of open-net linen weave, usually black, with a geometric pattern made of silver- or gold-toned staples

Paisley: woven of wool, often cashmere, in intricate Persian designs; so-called because the best quality shawls came from the looms of Paisley, Scotland

Spanish: black silk crêpe covered with brightly colored embroidery, usually of flowers and birds, edged with long silk fringe

ACCESSORIES LISTED BY TYPE AND VALUE

Belt, faux-leopard, very narrow, 1955–69, source: flea market, $10.00

Belt, leather (white), contour, with scattered trim of painted metal flowers and butterflies (3-dimensional), 1950–59, source: flea market, $24.00

Belt, leather, handtooled, with stainless steel horse buckle, period ?, source: store, $18.50

Belt, velvet, large buckle, period ?, source: store, $12.00

Collar, beading (clear bugles and seed pearls), allover pattern on silk, 1910–19, source: flea market, $15.00

Collar, eyelet and organdy, round, period ?, source: flea market, $10.00

Collar, lace, sailor-style, 1910–19, source: flea market, $12.00

Collar, linen (ecru), deep V, insets of ecru lace and faggoting, 1910–19, source: flea market, $18.00

Collar, net and organdy, three layers of petals, 1900–09, source: flea market, $28.00

Collar, seal lined with silk velvet, funnel neck, deep V front and back, covers shoulders, pulls over, period ?, source: flea market, $39.00

Gloves, cotton (double-woven), navy with piqué gauntlets, 3 decorative pearl buttons, 1930–39, source: store, $39.00

Gloves, cotton (white) with beading, ¾-length, period ?, source: flea market, $25.00

Gloves, crochet, with embroidered flares above wrist, period ?, source: store, $39.00

Gloves, kid (gray), flared above the wrist, cream leather insets with geometric design, period ?, source: store, $25.00

Gloves, kid (white), classic length, with colorful French-knot flowers, period ?, source: store, $49.00

Gloves, kid (white), opera-length, 3 buttons at wrist, period ?, source: flea market, $40.00

Gloves, kid-suede (black), classic length, with bands of gold kid at wrists and between fingers, handmade, period ?, source: store, $49.00

Gloves, nylon (light blue) shortie, with small ruffle at wrist, 1950–59, source: store, $19.00

Gloves, nylon (stretch, shiny black), wrist-length, clear plastic half-circle insets at wrist, 1960–69, source: store, $10.00

Gloves, silk-satin (black), above-the-elbow, with scalloped tops, all handsewn, period ?, source: store, $69.00

Gloves, suede (green), with beadwork on cuffs, ¾ length, 1940–59, source: store, $12.00

Muff, seal (black), lined, large, period ?, source: mail order, $35.00

Muff, silk velvet (blue), shirred, silk crêpe lining, period ?, source: store, $30.00

Muff, velvet (black), period ?, source: store, $10.00

Purse, alligator (black), box-style, period ?, source: store, $35.00

Purse, alligator (Cuban), 7″ × 9″, cordovan red with convertible strap, laced edges, period ?, source: mail order, $25.00

Purse, alligator (natural), with head, period ?, source: store, $40.00

Purse, beaded bag on Bakelite frame with Bakelite chain handle, white, period ?, source: flea market, $18.00

Purse, beaded bag, crystal on silver frame, period ?, source: flea market, $45.00

Purse, beaded, paisley design, pinks and greens on black ground, brass filagree frame, period ?, source: store, $85.00

Purse, carnival glass beads (dark blue), flapper-style, about 14″ long, with allover fringes of bugle beads, 1920–29, source: mail order, $65.00

Purse, corduroy (navy blue), large flat bag with Bakelite handles, 1940–49, source: mail order, $22.00

Purse, crochet (white cotton), drawstring-type, handmade, with satin lining, 1880–89, source: store, $25.00

Purse, faille (brown), gathered, with fabric handles, catch of clear acrylic and brass, 1940–49, source: flea market, $18.00

Purse, kid reticule, with cutout Art Nouveau design, studded with tiny green faux-gems, silk lining somewhat deteriorated, 1890–1919, source: flea market, $35.00

Two secrets for improving the appearance of leather: (1) Stains on both smooth leather and suede can sometimes be improved by the use of an artgum eraser; stained suede can also be napped up again with gentle abrasion from an emery board. (2) Scratches on black leather can be touched up with an indelible black marker, then rubbed gently with a little pure oil, such as olive oil. (Markers are available in a wide range of colors now, so you might try this with other colors of leather too, if you can make a match.)

Purse, leather (black) clutch, 1930–39, source: mail order, *$12.00*

Purse, leather, embossed and colored in elaborate East Indian design, satchel-style, triangular, with leather ring handles, period ?, source: individual, *$30.00*

Purse, leather, hippie-style shoulder bag, small, with long leather fringe, 1960–69, source: store, *$20.00*

Purse, metal and plastic strips woven together, oval, marbleized plastic top and Lucite handle, period ?, source: mail order, *$5.00*

Purse, metal mesh (with metal hangtag inside), ornate enameled floral pattern, pink/blue/black on white, Whiting and Davis, period ?, source: store, *$65.00*

Purse, metal mesh bag, enameled in geometric pattern, very small, 1920–29, source: flea market, *$120.00*

Purse, metal mesh bag, painted, Impressionist design, on gold frame, period ?, source: flea market, *$190.00*

Purse, patent (black) box, with patent belt-and-buckle closure, period ?, source: store, *$16.50*

Purses, clockwise from top: a 1930s envelope bag with stitched Deco design, "coffin" purse from the 1940s, black faille box bag from the 1930s, with sliding celluloid mock-tortoise top, lizard satchel bag. (*Accessories courtesy of Puttin' on the Ritz, Dallas, TX.*)

Evening bags, clockwise from top: an envelope bag of black velvet with pattern of metallic gold cord and trim of cabochon stones, a triangular bag covered with ropes of bugle beads, 1940s, and a 1930s bag of carnival glass beads. *(Accessories courtesy of Puttin' on the Ritz, Dallas, TX.)*

Purse, petit-point, design of spreading flowers in urn worked in colored and gold-metallic threads, yellow silk lining, frame set with 3 cabochons of smoky quartz, 1890–1909, source: mail order, *$40.00*

Purse, plastic-flex clutch, 1950–59, source: store, *$17.50*

Purse, silk, brass frame and chain, Chinese embroidery, 1900–09, source: store, *$75.00*

Purse, silvertone clutch, 1950–59, source: store, *$8.00*

Purse, silvertone suitcase, plastic sides with poodle desins of glued-on beads, moiré taffeta lining, 1950–59, source: store, *$69.00*

Purse, velvet bag on ornate silver frame, with silver mesh tassel, silk print lining, period ?, source: flea market, *$45.00*

Purse, wooden box-style, handpainted, Bakelite handle, period ?, source: store, *$39.00*

Scarf, faux-cheetah print with taffeta faille lining, long narrow rectangle, 1950–59, source: store, $29.00

Scarf, lace, period ?, source: store, $18.00

Scarf, rayon chiffon, 14″ × 30″, white with allover embroidered flowers, period ?, source: mail order, $4.00

Scarf, rayon, handpainted, souvenir of Fort Ord, California, 1940–49, source: store, $20.00

Scarf, rayon, yellow, brown, and shocking pink pattern of dancers, with border of musical instruments, 1940–49, source: store, $39.00

Scarf, silk, flowered print, Isadora Duncan-type, 1920–29, source: mail order, $20.00

Spanish shawl, 1920s. (Clothing courtesy of Puttin' on the Ritz, Dallas, TX.)

Set, high-heeled multi-color woven sandals, matching box purse, 1940–49, source: store, $55.00

Shawl, mohair, handknitted, shrug-style, with shirred acetate lining, period ?, source: flea market, $35.00

Shawl, net (black) with allover pattern of small gold sequins, period ?, source: store, $59.00

Shawl, net (black), Egyptian silver type, rectangle 8' long, 1920–29, source: store, $390.00

Shawl, silk-tape macramé, triangular, with deep fringe, medium-sized, period ?, source: flea market, $85.00

Shawl, wool, Indian, pieced paisley, woven in red, green, ivory, lavender, and blue wool, with black center and embroidered border, period ?, source: auction, $1,210.00

Men's Clothing and Accessories

CONTENTS

All clothing items and accessories worn by men.

ARRANGEMENT

First by type of garment or accessory, then by style.

COLLECTING NOTES

Men's vintage clothing is greatly in demand. Certain items are in fair supply, such as dinner jackets and tuxedos, formal shirts, suits from the 1940s and 1950s, dressing gowns, pleated trousers, gabardine shirts, ties, and outerwear. Other items are hard to find, especially the elegant sportswear of the teens, 1920s, and 1930s; collarless shirts of silk and fine, striped cotton; hats and suspenders; eccentric items such as zoot suits; and the "peacock" fashions of the 1960s.

Authentic Hawaiian shirts from the 1940s and 1950s are specially prized by collectors. The most desirable are those which have complex Hawaiian scenes, well-done floral patterns, or stylized primitive prints. There are also some very fine Hawaiian shirts made under California labels, with some of the best coming from Cisco, Art Vogue, and Duke of Hollywood.

Men's cowboy shirts of the 1940s and 1950s are another popular collecting area—especially the extensively decorated "rodeo" shirts. The best examples are usually rayon gabardine, with mother-of-pearl snaps and embroidery of Western scenes. Excellent labels include H Bar C Company and Rocky Mountain Ranch Wear.

There is a good deal less change and variation in men's clothing than in women's, but there have been definite styles associated with specific periods. Here is an overview:

1880–1899

Underthings and sleepwear: Underthings were usually woolen; vests and underpants were worn, and combinations became popular; nightshirts were worn throughout the period, but pajamas (of silk or wool) were introduced in the 1880s and quickly gained popularity.

Suits, jackets, and trousers: Shoulders were padded, and most jacket styles buttoned fairly high, with three or four buttons; trousers were generally tubular, with creases introduced in the 1890s. There were many styles of jackets for various occasions; most frequently worn were the frock coat or morning coat for formal occasions, and the sack coat for informal wear. The tuxedo was introduced. Trousers were fairly tight with cutaway coats, looser with the sack coat. The sack jacket was straight-waisted and high-buttoned. There were also male "aesthetic dressers" during this period, mostly artists and intellectuals, who wore a looser, more romantic style of clothing, made up in soft velvets and homespun tweeds.

Shirts: Separate collars—fairly high, and wing-style for formal wear, turned over for everyday—were worn with collarless shirts; white remained the norm for shirts, but stripes were increasingly accepted (though still worn with a white collar); unconventional dressers might wear colored shirts.

Sports clothes: Tight breeches and knickerbockers were worn for cycling, golf, etc.; sweaters, fairly long and crew- or polo-necked, became popular in the 1890s; bathing costumes were usually knit, composed of a short-sleeved shirt and knee-length breeches. The Norfolk jacket was popular.

Outerwear: Coats were to knee or just below. The Inverness cape was popular, along with caped overcoats. Coats frequently had velvet collars.

Accessories: Waistcoats were fairly plain, with those for day frequently of matching fabric with jacket and trousers, those for evening black or

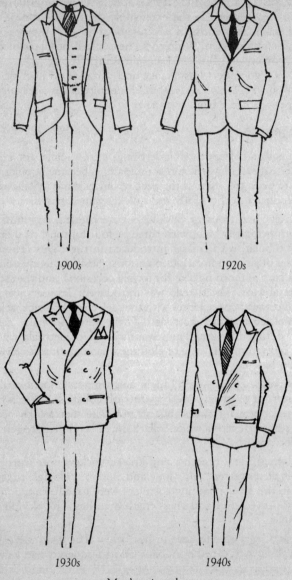

1900s

1920s

1930s

1940s

Men's suit styles.

white, and those for informal or country wear in checked or plaid wool; the four-in-hand tie, the Ascot, and the bow tie were all worn; the top hat, the bowler, the homberg, the trilby, and the boater were all worn, as well as tweed caps and deer-stalkers. High-top, laced, or buttoned shoes were customarily worn.

1900–1919

Underthings and sleepwear: Underwear became lighter weight and pajamas completely replaced nightshirts. Although union suits were still worn by some, the change to undershirts and shorts was well under way.

Suits, trousers, and jackets: Shoulders were heavily padded (especially at the sleeve-heads) in the 1900s, more natural in the teens. Trousers were shorter, showing the ankle after 1908. Peg-top trousers were popular in the early teens. Formality declined steadily throughout this period, with the frock coat worn mainly by the elderly, and by members of a few professions. The morning coat was reserved for very formal occasions, with the three-piece sack suit being worn for day and business wear by most men. The sack jacket, which might be either single- or double-breasted, was fairly short, very slightly fitted, and still buttoned rather high during this period.

Shirts: Shirts continued much the same as before, but collars were very high at the beginning of the century and gradually became lower; colored collars began to be worn toward the end of the period; unstarched collars became acceptable.

Sports clothes: Much the same as the previous period, with sweaters very popular and jodhpurs being worn. Tweed became a popular fabric for "country clothes" and casual wear.

Outerwear: Additions included the motoring duster, the Mackintosh, fur coats, and short, raglan-sleeved tweed coats. The camel-hair polo coat was also introduced in the 1900s, and World War I produced the trench coat.

Accessories: Gloves were normally worn, and mufflers were popular. Belts replaced suspenders. Hats generally had higher crowns and wider brims than in the previous period; the Panama was worn in summer, and the fedora and slouch hat became popular. Almost all of the low-cut shoe styles customarily worn today were introduced by this period: oxfords, wing-tips, rubber-soled canvas shoes, and white bucks were available by 1915.

1920–1939

Underthings and sleepwear: Undershorts became more colorful, being made up in stripes and prints. Dressing gowns were very popular.

Suits, trousers, and jackets: Trousers were full and somewhat longer in the 1920s; the enormously wide Oxford bags had a fashionable following. In the 1930s, a tapered style, pleated at the waist, became fashionable. Shoulders were natural in the 1920s and generally somewhat padded in the 1930s, though the English drape, with broad but unpadded shoulders, was popular among the very fashionable in the 1930s. Jackets were generally more closely fitted than in the previous period, and somewhat shorter in the 1920s than in the 1930s; a high waist was fashionable in the mid-1920s, while in the 1930s, jackets were buttoned somewhat lower than they had been, with two or three buttons. The double-breasted suit also gained great popularity in the 1930s. In the early 1930s, the mess jacket was introduced for semi-formal wear in summer, and later in the decade, the white dinner jacket came into fashion. The summer suit of linen, seersucker, or tropical worsted was widely worn after World War I. Suits were now made up in a wide variety of fabrics, with lighter colors and patterns of all sorts (pin stripes, herringbone, plaids, etc.) becoming acceptable. The zipper fly replaced buttons in the late 1930s.

Shirts: By the 1930s, collar and shirt were frequently attached. Print and plaid sport shirts, in silks and flannels, were worn by the late 1920s, and the 1930s introduced dark-colored (wine, brown, navy) shirts. The pin collar was popular during this period, as was the tab collar.

Sports clothes: Knickers were still worn in the 1920s, but a new variation, the "plus-four," became very popular. Colorful Fair Isle sweaters were worn, along with the V-neck pullover (both with and without sleeves) and the cardigan. The blazer became very popular, and the sports coat appeared in the mid-1920s. Polo shirts came in in the 1930s.

Outerwear: Continued much the same as in the previous period. Raccoon coats were a feature of the 1920s. Windbreakers and bush jackets appeared.

Accessories: Most hats of the previous period were still worn; caps were popular, and the Tyrolean and the snap-brim appeared. Cotton ties, foulard scarves (tied like ascots), and bow ties were all popular. Loafers (also called "slip-ons") were introduced in the 1930s.

1940–1959

Underthings and sleepwear: Much the same, except for the introduction of cotton knit briefs.

Suits, trousers, and jackets: Civilian men's clothing during wartime was subdued, and there was little emphasis on fashion; early in the 1940s, however, the "zoot suit" enjoyed a brief popularity among non-conformists. As the war progressed, restrictions affected men's clothing, so that suits were usually made with less and cheaper fabric. In 1947, the menswear version of the "New Look" (called the "Bold New Look") appeared, stressing brighter colors, bolder ties, and a generally more fashion-conscious look for men. Throughout the 1940s, shoulders were well padded, and the "American shoulder" became the prevailing fashion. This trend reached its peak in the early 1950s, with suits that featured a low, two- or three-button closing, wide, peaked lapels, and wide trousers. But a reaction also began, in the form of the Ivy League or "natural shoulder" look, which featured narrow shoulders and lapels, unfitted jackets and unpleated trousers with narrow cuffs. A "conservative" look was also established in the 1950s, mostly by older men; this look—which is basically similar to the business suit of today—was essentially a return to English tailoring, with a moderately padded shoulder and moderation in fitting and detail throughout the suit. Finally, the Italian influence was introduced to men's clothing in the late 1950s, with the advent of the "Continental style." The Continental silhouette was quite fitted, with a somewhat shortened jacket, usually two buttons, and narrow lapels; Continental trousers were slim, cuffless, low-rise, and sometimes beltless. These suits effected a sleek appearance through the use of hard-finish (rather than nappy or tweedy) fabrics.

Shirts: Dress shirts continued much the same, with the addition in the 1950s of the button-down oxford-cloth shirt favored with the Ivy League look; the casual madras shirt was also much worn by the Ivy Leaguers. Shirt collars varied widely, according to the style of the suit. Sports shirts were now very popular, and throughout the 1940s, gabardine sport shirts with patch pockets were worn, as were lumberjack shirts. Hawaiian shirts were a colorful feature of this period.

Sports clothes: Sportswear in the postwar 1940s and 1950s was a substantial change from the previous period. Knickers were worn mainly for golf and jodhpurs mainly for riding, while casual pants of khaki or corduroy became the norm for most outdoor activities. Levis became acceptable for very casual wear. Stretch-knit pullovers were popular for golf. Long khaki shorts appeared in the late 1940s, with Bermuda shorts (often plaid) widely worn in the 1950s.

Outerwear: The topcoat and the overcoat were worn. Coats with mouton collars were popular in the 1950s, as were pile-lined coats and coats with detachable linings. Bomber jackets were introduced in World War II, and were worn, along with Eisenhower jackets, throughout this period. The car-coat and benchwarmer were much worn in the 1950s.

Accessories: Wide, boldly figured ties and wide-brimmed hats were generally worn with the broad-shouldered suits of the late 1940s and early 1950s, while the Ivy League look featured a narrow tie, frequently cotton or knit, and a proportionately smaller hat. Madras bow ties and cummerbunds were worn by proponents of the Ivy League style to update formal dress. A wide variety of casual shoes were introduced, and dressy slip-on shoes became popular.

1960–1969

As with women's clothing, men's clothing of the 1960s broke up into several very different categories. In the first third of the decade, the conservative look and the Ivy League look of the previous period were dominant themes, along with the Continental style.

By the mid 1960s, the Mod and Carnaby styles of Britain were influencing the clothing of younger men. These clothes covered a wide range of styles, but they all had in common some form of exaggeration; the classic Beatle jacket, for example, buttoned very high and had no lapels, while the neo-Edwardian coat had long skirts and velvet trimming. Bright colors, "psychedelic" patterns, huge collars and full sleeves marked shirts of this style, worn along with bell-bottom hipster pants. Unisex clothing became popular, with men wearing the same skinny-ribbed turtlenecks, velvet pants, boots, blue jeans, fringed vests, etc., as women.

Even business dress was influenced by the youth revolution as the decade drew to an end. Suit styles became more exaggerated (wider lapels, slightly flared trousers); print and colored dress shirts became popular; half-boots were worn with suits. Ties were wider and more colorful. Men began to wear more accessories, such as decorative belt buckles and chunky bracelets. Trousers tended to have cross-pockets rather than side-seam pockets.

In formal wear, a wide variety of innovations appeared—turtleneck silk evening shirts, for example, and shirts with heavily frilled fronts and cuffs. Brocade and velvet dinner jackets were popular.

TERMS REFERRING TO SHIRTS

Button-down collar: the collar points button to the shirt

Club collar: rounded (instead of pointed!) points

Convertible collar: constructed so that it may be worn either open or closed

Dashiki: collarless, full body; full-, elbow-length sleeves; usually African print or motif

Dress shirt: term generally used for a formal evening shirt; since the 1960s, the term has been increasingly used to refer to an everyday business shirt (as opposed to a sports shirt), while an evening shirt is often called a "formal" shirt

Hawaiian (aloha) shirt: boxy overshirt, slightly shorter than the usual men's shirt; bright colors, vivid floral, scenic or graphic pattern; convertible collar

Henley: collarless, short-sleeved, knitted pullover with placket front

Ivy League shirt: button-down collar, back yoke with pleat, usually made of Oxford cloth

Neckband shirt: shirt with a narrow band at neck; the band has buttonholes, so that a separate collar can be attached

The classic men's gabardine shirt, 1940s and 1950s.

Pin collar: collar designed so that a collar pin may be inserted to hold the points together

Point collar: plain fold-over collar, either long ("long point") or short ("short point")

Polo shirt: knitted stripe or solid pullover with crew neck or square collar

Ruffle shirt: dress shirt with ruffle front, for evening formal wear

Sports shirt: colorful shirt of solid, print, or plaid fabric, usually with convertible collar worn open

Spread collar: collar which has a relatively large amount of space between the points

Starched collar: high, stiff detachable collar

Tab collar: collar with button-across tab to hold collar points together

Tank top (athletic shirt): pullover with scooped neckline and large sleeveless openings

Wing collar: a stiff, fairly high standup collar with tips turned back to form points

TERMS REFERRING TO SUITS, JACKETS, AND TROUSERS

American shoulder (American blade): jacket style featuring broad, heavily padded shoulders, with fullness at upper arm and across the back

Battle (Eisenhower) jacket: waist-length jacket, with fitted waistband, breast pockets, and notched collar

Bell-bottom pants: trousers with extreme flare from knee to ankle

Blazer: semi-fitted, hip-length, single-breasted or double-breasted, usually with metal buttons

Cutaway: fitted coat cut so that the skirt portion tapers away from front center to back, forming a half-skirt or tails at the back

Dinner jacket (tuxedo): semi-fitted jacket with shawl collar, length to hip or top of thigh

English drape (English blade): suit style featuring broad but unpadded shoulders, moderate lapels, tapered sleeves, and a nipped waist, worn with high-waisted, double-pleated trousers

Frock coat (Prince Albert): double-breasted coat with knee-length skirt

Hipsters: trousers cut with a very low rise, so that the waistband rides on the hips

Ivy League (Brooks Brothers): natural shoulder, single-breasted jacket with narrow lapels, worn with clean-fitting trousers

Mess jacket: essentially, a tail coat without tails; usually white

Morning coat: cutaway coat, single-breasted, with skirt falling to knees in back; black or oxford gray, usually worn with pin-striped trousers

Nehru jacket: slim, hip-length or longer, slightly fitted, with standup collar

Norfolk: jacket featuring box-pleat front with slot for matching belt, length to hip or mid-thigh; the Norfolk suit included knickers

Oxford bags: very wide (up to 24 inches at the hem) trousers

Peg-top trousers: pants having fullness at the top, tapering to a close fit at the ankle

Sack: jacket or suit style which was originally introduced as a more comfortable alternative to the cutaway or frock coat for informal occasions; the sack (called the "lounge" in England) is the style we are now familiar with as the "business suit"; it may be two- or three-piece, single- or double-breasted

Safari jacket (bush jacket): single-breasted, hip-length, with bellows pockets, fabric belt, usually made of khaki

Smoking jacket: a velvet or brocade jacket worn for semi-formal at-home entertainment; originally cut in the lounge style and fastened with frogs, older versions are frequently of deep rich colors, and sometimes are quilted; the term "smoking jacket" is now often used to mean a short dressing gown, using the same types of fabric in a wraparound, shawl-colored style, with a fabric tie

Sports jacket: a sack-style jacket, worn with unmatched trousers

Tail coat (swallow-tail coat, claw-hammer coat): formal evening coat, cut straight across at the waist in front, with a long divided skirt in back

Zoot suit: exaggerated suit, with very full trousers, very long jacket, very wide lapels and shoulders

TERMS REFERRING TO SPORTS CLOTHING

Bermuda shorts: pants cut just above the knee

Jodhpurs: pants with wide, outwardly curved seam along thigh, with leg closely fitted at the knee and calf

Knickers: full, baggy pants gathered to a band just below the knee

Plus-fours: similar to knickers, but longer, falling four inches below the knee; the band is not seen

Riding pants (Western-style): snug-fitting pants, frequently having cross-pockets that close with mother-of-pearl snaps

TERMS REFERRING TO OUTERWEAR

Balmacaan: loose-fitting body, with raglan sleeves, small convertible collar, usually made of water-repellent fabric

Battle jacket (Eisenhower): waist-length jacket, single-breasted, usually with slight fullness fitted into waistband, and two large, flapped patch pockets on chest

This trench coat was the latest fashion in 1919, and it's been a classic ever since.

Bomber jacket: waist-length jacket, usually leather, with sheepskin or pile lining

Car (stadium) coat: hip- to three-quarter-length, square, sporty

Chesterfield: semi-fitted body, single- or double-breasted, usually has black velvet collar

Inverness: may refer to a long, full cape, fitted at the neck, or to a sleeveless, belted coat with an attached short cape

Lumber jacket: hip- or waist-length jacket, usually made of plaid wool

Mackinaw: double-breasted jacket, belted, usually made of blanket-like wool in plaid or stripe

Mackintosh: waterproof coat

Overcoat: heavy, long (below-the-knee) coat; varying designs

Parka: hooded jacket, hip-length or longer, usually quilted

Pea jacket (reefer): hip-length or longer, double-breasted, with large buttons, vertical slash pockets, usually made of navy blue blanket wool

Polo coat: straight-line, three-quarter-length, usually made of camel hair or camel-colored wool

Topcoat: lighter weight, knee-length coat

Trench coat: double-breasted, epaulets, loose shoulder yoke, slotted pockets, buckled belt

Windbreaker: trademark name for a lightweight, waist-length zippered jacket with drawstring at or below waist, often with hood

TERMS REFERRING TO ACCESSORIES, HATS, UNDERTHINGS, AND SLEEPWEAR

Alpine hat: generally, a fedora with feather, tassel, braid, or brush trim

Ascot tie: a scarf with narrow neck-piece and wide, square ends meant to be folded over in a puffed effect and held in place with a pin

Boater: straw hat with flat crown and stiff brim

Briefs: fitted underpants

Cap: generally, a round cloth hat, fitting the head snugly; frequently with some sort of visor

Deerstalker: cloth cap with front and back visors

Derby (bowler): hard felt hat, dome-shaped

Fedora (Homberg): a soft felt hat, with the crown creased in the center from front to back

Four-in-hand: originally, a scarf with narrow neck-piece and somewhat wider ends, the same size and square; this was tied with a knot (now called the "four-in-hand knot") so that one end lay on top of the other; this is the forerunner of our modern necktie, with shaped ends and one piece wider than the other

Nightshirt: knee-length or longer one-piece sleeping garment, usually with a front-buttoned placket

Opera hat (gibus): a top hat with a collapsible crown

Panama (planter's hat): light-colored hat made from fine straw, usually with a fairly wide brim

Top hat (high hat): hat with a very high, hard crown, narrow, slightly rolled brim; usually made of black silk

Trilby: a soft felt hat, similar to the Alpine, but with a plush texture

Tyrolean hat: soft felt hat, similar to the Alpine, with a somewhat peaked crown

Union suit: one-piece suit of knit underwear; buttoned down the front, with long or short sleeves; knee-length or ankle-length

MENSWEAR LISTED BY TYPE AND PRICE

Accessories, scarf, rayon, fringed aviator-style, by Cisco, period ?, source: mail order, $18.00

Accessories, tie (wide), handpainted ship on burgundy rayon, 1940–49, source: mail order, $8.00

Accessories, tie (wide), with Salvador Dali design, 1940–49, source: store, $15.00

Accessories, tie, printed jacquard silk, 1940–49, source: store, $5.00

Hat, boater (straw), 1920–29, source: mail order, $35.00

Hat, derby (black), "Knox" label, period ?, source: store, $35.00

Hat, fedora (wool), 1950–59, source: store, $12.00

The first illustrations for mail-order fashions appeared in the Montgomery & Co. catalog of 1878, and by 1895, the Sears catalog was featuring fashions.

Hat, homberg (navy) with blue grosgrain band, period ?, source: store, $18.00

Hat, top hat, in original shaped traveling box with strap, 1880–99, source: store, *$125.00*

Jacket, blazer, cashmere, 1960–69, source: store, *$89.00*

Jacket, blazer, dark red cashmere, period ?, source: mail order, *$25.00*

Jacket, cutaway, black with satin trim, period ?, source: store, *$75.00*

Jacket, cutaway, natural-color canvas, 1910–19, source: individual, *$60.00*

Jacket, dinner jacket, gold and black brocade with narrow black satin shawl lapels, 1 button, 1960–69, source: store, *$45.00*

Jacket, dinner jacket, gold corduroy with black rayon shawl collar, cuffs, and pocket trim, period ?, source: mail order, *$10.00*

Jacket, dinner jacket, Hawaiian print, satin lapels, period ?, source: store, *$40.00*

Jacket, dinner jacket, white linen, double-breasted, 1940–49, source: mail order, *$25.00*

Jacket, dinner jacket, white, narrow lapels, 1960–69, source: store, *$35.00*

Jacket, flight-style, brown leather with sheepskin lining, ribbed cuffs and waist, front zipper, 1940–49, source: store, *$85.00*

Jacket, Mod-style, 4 buttons, unfitted, piped slash pockets, wide lapels, entirely lined with acetate print of stone-age cave paintings, 1960–69, source: store, *$12.00*

Jacket, sports, 3-button, unfitted, red sacking, red and white striped lining, period ?, source: store, *$22.00*

Jacket, sports, black/white wool tweed with red flecks, 2 buttons, narrow, notched lapels, 1950–59, source: store, *$22.00*

Jacket, sports, Continental styling, heavy cotton-satin, pumpkin color, 1950–65, source: store, *$25.00*

Leisure, dressing gown, floor-length rayon brocade, burnt orange with black shawl collar and cuffs, 1940–49, source: store, *$160.00*

Leisure, kimono, authentic Japanese, heavy printed silk crêpe, silk lining, 1930–39, source: store, *$240.00*

Leisure, kimono, authentic Japanese, patterned silk, cotton lining, period ?, source: flea market, *$50.00*

Leisure, pajamas, outrageous print cotton, 1950–59, source: store, *$22.00*

Leisure, smoking jacket, black silk velvet, heavy silk lining, 1 button, custom-made label dated "1904," source: store, *$85.00*

Outerwear, coat, Edwardian revival-style, black wool serge with caracul pocket flaps, nipped waist, flared skirt, knee-length, 1960–69, source: flea market, *$45.00*

Outerwear, jacket, high-school letter style, with sports patches, 1950–69, source: store, *$30.00*

Outerwear, jacket, homespun-type fabric, woven-in American Indian design, knit sleeves, front zipper, hip-length, 1940–49, source: flea market, *$33.00*

Outerwear, jacket, leather with long fringe, 1960–69, source: store, *$60.00*

Outerwear, jacket, motorcycle-style, black leather, with Harley-Davidson patch, 1950–59, source: store, *$365.00*

Outerwear, jacket, waist-length, wool, quilted lining, 1940–49, source: store, *$59.00*

"Harris tweed" is an especially beautiful and highly prized type of tweed woolen, entirely handmade on an island of the Outer Hebrides, off the western coast of Scotland. Though the name "Harris tweed" is now (since 1964) protected by Scottish law, and can only be accurately applied to tweed made on the Harris Island and approved by the Harris Tweed Association (it will have an HTA mark on the reverse side of the fabric), for many years before that, all sorts of tweeds—some excellent, some inferior—were sold under the generic name "Harris tweed."

Outerwear, overcoat, brown tweed, removable wool plaid lining, period ?, source: store, *$50.00*

Outerwear, overcoat, brown wool, ankle-length, double-breasted, with large notched lapels and very large patch pockets, 1940–49, source: store, *$65.00*

Outerwear, overcoat, camel hair, 1950–59, source: store, *$135.00*

Outerwear, overcoat, heavy blue wool, single-breasted, 1920–29, source: store, *$75.00*

Outerwear, raincoat, black London Fog, red lining, period ?, source: store, *$15.00*

Outerwear, topcoat, gabardine, 1950–59, source: store, *$55.00*

Outerwear, topcoat, gabardine, silk lining, 1940–49, source: store, $190.00

Outerwear, topcoat, houndstooth wool, Continental styling, silk lining, 1950–59, source: store, $150.00

Outerwear, trench coat, black horsehide, silk lining, 1940–49, source: store, $690.00

Pants, cotton clam-diggers, stripes down sides, Levi Casual (new-old), 1960–69, source: store, $20.50

Pants, fabric unknown, button-fly, 1910–19, source: mail order, $35.00

Pants, gabardine, double-pleated front, 1940–49, source: store, $11.00

Pants, polyester, bright pink and yellow plaid, slight flare, cross pockets, 1960–69, source: store, $15.00

Pants, sharkskin, iridescent cobalt blue, Continental styling, 1950–69, source: store, $15.00

Pants, suede, deep fringe down the entire sides and around the bottoms of the legs; belt loops and cross pockets, 1960–69, source: flea market, $10.00

Pants, wool, brown with pink flecks, pleated and cuffed, 1940–49, source: store, $9.00

Pants, wool, sailor-style, U.S. Navy, 13-button front, lace-up back, period ?, source: mail order, $5.00

Shirt, button-down, paisley print, narrow collar, Arrow, 1960–69, source: store, $10.00

Shirt, collarless, striped silk, 1920–29, source: mail order, $24.00

Shirt, formal, tucked front, white, 1940–49, source: store, $16.00

Shirt, Hawaiian (genuine), two pockets, hula-girl print, 1950–59, source: mail order, $35.00

Shirt, Hawaiian print rayon, 1940–49, source: mail order, $50.00

Shirt, Hawaiian, Kamehameha label, burgundy background with gray and white pineapple design, rayon, 1950–59, source: store, $75.00

Shirt, lumberjack-style, Viyella, 1940–59, source: store, $10.00

Shirt, sports, long-sleeved, gabardine, patch pockets, full-cut, 1950–59, source: store, $9.00

Shirt, sports, short-sleeved, flamingo-print cotton, 1950–59, source: store, $48.00

Shirt, Western-style, colorful floral print cotton, mother-of-pearl snaps, 1950–59, source: store, $39.00

Shirt, Western-style, gray rayon/acetate, embroidery, 1960–69, source: store, $69.00

Shirt, Western-style, yellow rayon with embroidery, 1950–59, source: store, $28.00

Shoes, boots, black kangaroo leather, ankle-length, period ?, source: store, $20.00

Shoes, boots, side-button, wool uppers, 1890–99, source: store, $65.00

Shoes, oxfords, white buck, period ?, source: mail order, $25.00

Shoes, wing-tips, brown and white suede (new-old), 1940–49, source: store, $65.00

Sports, bathing suit, black wool trunks, 1930–39, source: store, $20.00

Sports, bowling shirt, rayon, with lettering, 1950–59, source: store, $8.50

Sports, knickers, cream wool with brown geometric design, 1920–39, source: individual, $65.00

Sports, motorcycle pants, leather, 1920–39, source: individual, $115.00

Suit, double-breasted 3-piece, pleated pants, vest, navy gabardine, 1940–49, source: store, $85.00

Suit, double-breasted, navy blue wool, with light burgundy stripe (new-old), 1940–49, source: store, $175.00

> Said *Esquire* magazine in 1934, the English drape suit was "the way to dress if you are so sure of yourself under the New Deal that you are unafraid of offering a striking similarity to a socialist cartoonist's conception of a capitalist. Since a good appearance is about all that is left to the capitalist anyway, why not go ahead and enjoy it?"

Suit, double-breasted, peaked lapels, 6-button, pleated pants, blue window-pane plaid, 1940–49, source: store, $50.00

Suit, double-breasted, with pleated and cuffed pants, blue pinstripe, 1940–49, source: store, $55.00

Suit, Panama, cream-colored, double-breasted coat, pleated pants, "Palm Beach" label, 1930–39, source: store, $65.00

Suit, single-breasted, multi-colored wool tweed, button fly, 1930–39, source: mail order, $65.00

Suit, single-breasted, navy-blue serge, 1930–39, source: mail order, $35.00

Suit, single-breasted, sharkskin, blue two-tone, 1950–59, source: store, $40.00

Suit, tails, black wool, period ?, source: mail order, $55.00

Suit, tails, wool with faille lapels, striped pants, period ?, source: store, $120.00

Sweater, cardigan, argyle-patterned mohair, period ?, source: store, $15.00

Sweater, cardigan, handmade, ecru, large mother-of-pearl buttons, collar, period ?, source: store, $125.00

Sweater, cardigan, high-school-style, with lettering, 1950–59, source: store, $65.00

Sweater, pullover, brown wool, set-in crew neck, 1910–29, source: store, $15.00

> The sale of undershirts plummeted after Clark Gable revealed, in *It Happened One Night,* that he wasn't wearing one. Sales didn't pick up again until Marlon Brando made the undershirt a statement in *A Streetcar Named Desire.*

Underwear, boxer shorts, white cotton with heraldic pattern in gray and burgundy, Fruit of the Loom (new-old), 1950–59, source: store, $4.50

Vest, corded black satin, jet buttons, period ?, source: store, $35.00

Vest, satin, single-breasted, period ?, source: store, $20.00

Vest, silk brocade, 1900–09, source: mail order, $50.00

Children's Clothing

CONTENTS

All types of clothing worn by children from infancy to age twelve.

ARRANGEMENT

First by age, then by type of garment. "Infants" includes the first year, "Toddlers," two to four, and "Children," five to twelve.

A surprising amount of children's clothing is available (perhaps because of parental sentimentality!). Most frequently found are special occasion items—christening dresses, church clothes, party outfits, and the like—but everyday clothes are also to be found.

Though available, however, children's clothes are not necessarily easy to find. Many vintage clothing stores don't even carry children's clothing. Better hunting for older things may often be found in antique stores, where handmade baby dresses, children's bonnets, and the like are valued as decorative items. Flea markets are good sources, and later things—from the 1950s and 1960s—may sometimes be found in thrift shops.

Dating of children's clothing is difficult. The changes in children's dress that took place in the 1880s lasted well into the twentieth century, with styles such as the sailor suit and smocked dress continuing in fashion for decades, so in many instances, only fabric and construction hint at the period in which a garment might have been made. Handmade baby clothes, moreover, are often virtually undateable, since grandmothers and aunties were stitching, knitting, and crocheting them pretty much the same way in the 1940s as they had in the Gay Nineties.

Nevertheless, here are some of the highlights of children's fashions in the vintage century:

1880–1889

Skirts were generally below the knee for girls, and knee breeches were the usual rule for boys. Sailor suits for boys were extremely popular, and girls wore sailor blouses and dresses. Party dresses had low, sashed waists and tiers of ruffles. The princess line was popular. Coats for both boys and girls frequently had attached shoulder capes. Very young boys still wore dresses, frequently made like princess-style coats; the Little Lord Fauntleroy look was also popular at mid-decade. Knickers were introduced for boys, but were not widely worn until the next decade; the Norfolk suit appeared. Kilt suits were worn by young boys.

In the latter part of the decade, bustle effects were added to girls' clothing. Poorer children and children of the frontier or rural South usually wore the styles of earlier decades, with a natural waistline and full skirt for girls, plain, long trousers and shirts for boys. Infant dresses were generally very long and sashed throughout the decade; the extreme length was meant to allow for growth, and since children grow mostly in height (rather than width) for the first two years, infant dresses were often worn right through the toddler stage.

1890–1899

Girls' dresses continued to be worn below the knee, though a bit longer than previously; boys' pants also continued just below the knee, with dress pants sharply creased, and for casual wear, both knickers and the new jodhpurs were popular. Boys also began to wear long overalls. Sweaters, usually long and turtlenecked, were introduced for boys. Older girls might now wear culottes and "Turkish trousers" (very full pants banded below the knee) for cycling. Girls' fashion followed that of their mothers, with the addition of the new tailored shirtwaists and the development of very large sleeves; skirts were generally flat in front, with pleats at side and back, and the waistline was at or slightly below the natural waist.

The nautical influence continued strongly for both boys and girls, with the double-breasted reefer jacket very popular. Frilly blouses and velvet suits reminiscent of the Fauntleroy look were still worn by young

Children dressed for play in the 1890s.

boys. Infant dresses were very long, but now fell straight from the shoulders. Boys and girls were dressed much alike until the age of three, when boys began to be dressed in a more mature fashion, while girls continued to wear baby-style clothes until about five. Simple, short play dresses with cap sleeves and back ties were worn by many toddlers at home.

1900–1909

Basic styles continued to be the same, with some modifications that reflected adult fashion; but there were important additions to children's wear. With the development of waterproof pants, it became practical for babies and toddlers to be dressed in play overalls by day, one-piece, footed sleepers by night. Both boys and girls now wore overalls, and sweaters became popular for girls and infants as well as boys; romper suits were also worn. Dress for boys and girls began to be differentiated as early as six months. Among the new fashions for boys was the Buster Brown suit, and special clothing for such games as baseball and football was popularized; bell-bottomed trousers were introduced for the sailor suit. For girls, the sailor dress and the pinafore were extremely popular, as was a dress that fell in pleats from the shoulders and was worn with a low belt.

1910–1969

By the second decade of the century, all the basics of children's wear as we know it today were in place. Then, gradually, children's dress became more and more simplified. By the 1920s, very young girls were wearing short frocks, well above the knees, usually hanging straight from the shoulders or gathered to a yoke, and this style persisted into the 1940s; older girls wore the waist approximately where their mothers did—low in the 1920s, high in the 1930s. In the 1940s and 1950s, the natural waistline was defined in dresses for all ages. Throughout this period, for dress, young boys wore short pants, often buttoned to a top, or short suits made in one piece; by the mid-1940s, little boys were wearing long trousers with elastic waistbands for casual wear, and by the 1950s, little girls wore them too, with cotton knit tops. Older boys wore knickers into the 1930s, with blue jeans and other long pants becoming the norm by the 1950s, when they were worn with button-front shirts or cotton pullovers. Infants wore fewer clothes as the century progressed, and boys and girls were dressed differently from birth. By the 1960s, the clothing of infants and children was much as it is now.

Children dressed for school in 1922.

TERMS

Buster Brown: high-necked overblouse worn with knickers

Gertrude: a baby dress or slip, sleeveless, fastening at the shoulders with buttoned tabs

Guimpe: a short blouse worn under a jumper or dress

Kimono: a long baby wrapper, open down the front, held at the top with a tie

Little Lord Fauntleroy: frilly blouse with large soft bow at the collar, worn with velvet short pants

Romper: a one-piece play suit

Sacque: a short baby jacket, held at the top with a tie

Sailor-style: white or navy blue, with navy, red, or gold braid trim, and usually, a middy-style collar

Sleeper: one-piece, footed suit, originally with drop seat

CHILDREN'S CLOTHING LISTED BY TYPE AND PRICE

Infant, christening coat, white with yellow embroidery around hem and on cape collar, period ?, source: store, $35.00

Infant, christening dress, all hand embroidered, with lace, period ?, source: mail order, $65.00

Infant, christening dress, handmade lace and gathered handkerchief linen in alternating strips, with self-slip, 1900–09, source: store, $145.00

Infant, christening dress, ruffled neck, yoke, and sleeves, narrow lace trim, period ?, source: mail order, $28.00

Infant, christening dress, white cotton with lace and embroidery, 36″ long, 1900–09, source: mail order, $45.00

Infant, christening dress, white cotton, tuck-pleated bodice and skirt, embroidered floral patterns and openwork on bodice, cuffs, and skirt, period ?, source: store, $35.00

Infant, christening dress, yard-long, lawn, lots of tucking, lace, etc., 1900–19, source: mail order, $75.00

Infant, dress (short), windowpane weave batiste, period ?, source: flea market, $4.00

Infant, dress and slip (long), white batiste, cutwork trim, period ?, source: flea market, $18.00

Infant, dress with slip, handkerchief linen with handmade lace, tiny square mother-of-pearl buttons on belt, 1900–09, source: store, $65.00

Infant, gertrude, unbleached muslin, simple embroidery, 1910–29, source: flea market, $10.00

Infant, jacket, white wool crêpe with pink satin yarn crocheted around sleeves and front opening, embroidery on front, period ?, source: mail order, $4.00

Infant, long dress, of handmade filet lace, 1900–09, source: flea market, $75.00

Infant, sacque, cotton flannel print, handcrocheted edging, period ?, source: mail order, $8.00

Infant, sacque, short, French flannel with picot edging and embroidery, 1920–29, source: store, *$39.00*

Infant, sacque, long, 2 layers of long-staple cotton, picot edging, embroidery, 1920–29, source: store, *$49.00*

Infant, shirt, boy's corded cotton with contrasting collar and piping, embroidered toy train, 1950–59, source: mail order, *$2.50*

Toddler, coat, double-breasted, light blue wool with red wool lining, "military" buttons and embroidered insignia, period ?, source: store, *$59.00*

Toddler, coat, white piqué with crochet trim, 2-year-old size, period ?, source: store, *$18.00*

Toddler, dress, black cotton-satin 2-piece, Amish, size 2 or 3, period ?, source: mail order, *$40.00*

Toddler, dress, bleached muslin, with ribbon beading and candlewick embroidery, 1920–29, source: flea market, *$6.50*

Toddler, dress, navy coat-dress in rayon twill with lace-edged linen collar, double-breasted, pleated at waist, padded shoulders, toddler size, period ?, source: mail order, *$3.00*

Toddler, dress, white cotton batiste, drop waist, embroidery at neckline and edges of short sleeves, 1920–29, source: store, *$45.00*

Toddler, dress, white piqué, dropped waist with peach silk sash, lace bands at neck and waist, 1920–29, source: store, *$79.00*

Toddler, lederhosen, sueded leather, smooth leather straps and trim, carved celluloid medallion, period ?, source: flea market, *$20.00*

Toddler, play suit, 1-piece, cotton, 1950–59, source: store, *$24.00*

Toddler, slip, homespun wool, 1900–19, source: flea market, *$29.00*

Toddler, suit, boy's, pale yellow silk pongee, top with accordion-pleated trim, pants buttoned to top, size 2, 1910–29, source: flea market, *$65.00*

Toddler, top, blue wool sailor, period ?, source: store, *$29.00*

Child, coat, girl's white linen, shawl collar with satin-stitched floral pattern, size 7–8, period ?, source: store, *$37.50*

Fashion historian and collector Elizabeth S. Brown suggests this interesting care technique: lay a nylon screen over the garment and use a small vacuum through the screen to remove dust and loose dirt from the fabric.

Child, coat, gold velvet, brass buttons, large collar, period ?, source: store, $95.00

Child, costume, "Cisco Kid," wool with soutache scrollwork, about size 5, long-sleeved Spanish-style jacket, long pants flared at ankles, 1950–59, source: flea market, $35.00

Child, dress, handkerchief linen, 3-tier skirt with embroidery, pink ribbon sash, 1900–19, source: store, $240.00

Child, dress, homemade, floor-length prairie-style dress, high waist, blue cotton, size 4, 1890–1909, source: flea market, $28.00

Child, dress, Irish linen, short sleeves, natural waist, neckline and sleeves trimmed with Irish crochet, full skirt with 2 bands of Irish crochet, 1910–19, source: store, $135.00

Child, dress, lingerie style, white lawn with some lace, period ?, source: store, $190.00

Child, dress, novelty weave fabric, drop waist, short sleeves, good-quality lace collar and cuffs, 1920–29, source: flea market, $6.00

Child, dress, pink dotted swiss, 2-piece, hanging panels with black velvet trim, to fit a 10-year-old, 1910–19, source: mail order, $35.00

Child, dress, royal blue silk taffeta, drop waist, velvet trim, metal buttons, period ?, source: store, $125.00

Child, dress, sailor-style, white cotton with red pin-stripes, approximately size 6, 1910–19, source: flea market, $25.00

Child, dress, silk chiffon with embroidery and scalloped lace trim, short dress with short sleeves, sleeves and dress cut in one piece, gathered from neckline, no waist, 1920–29, source: flea market, $20.00

Child, dress, white batiste with lace trim, size 6 to 8, 1920–29, source: store, $50.00

Child, dress, white lace with lace inserts, dropped waist, short sleeves, approximately size 5, period ?, source: store, $190.00

Child, jacket, reversible gabardine zip-up, pink and gray, 1950–59, source: store, $55.00

Child, jacket, wool trimmed with black ribbon, 1880–89, source: mail order, $20.00

Child, nightgown, white cotton, cotton lace at edges, 1900–19, source: flea market, $25.00

Child, suit, boy's, long top with wide band at bottom, Peter Pan collar, knee-length trousers, cotton ticking, 1900–19, source: flea market, $20.00

Hat, baby bonnet, Amish, dark blue wool, 1930–39, source: auction, $25.00

Hat, baby bonnet, crochet, 1930–39, source: mail order, $8.00

Hat, bonnet, quilted velvet with satin ribbon ties, 1880–99, source: store, $28.00

Hat, brown velvet bonnet, floppy brim, high floppy crown, long ties, lace trim, 1880–89, source: flea market, $95.00

Hat, green velvet bonnet, high soft crown, soft brim, wide in front, ties, 1880–99, source: auction, $25.00

Hat, infant cap, handcrocheted of white cotton, in a pineapple pattern, period ?, source: mail order, $15.00

Hat, infant sunbonnet, very wide brim with parallel stitching, organdy crown trimmed with lace and buttoned to brim, long ties, 1890–1909, source: flea market, $6.00

Hat, velvet bonnet with heavy embroidery, ruching, lace, 1890–99, source: flea market, $85.00

P A R T
F O U R

Useful Information

Fashion is one of the last repositories of the
marvelous.

CHRISTIAN DIOR

A Quick Tour of Fashion History

❧

The following overview is intended in part to give a fast general understanding of fashion history, and in part to whet your appetite for more information. If you are inspired to track down some of the wonderful books available on the history of clothing and fashion, you'll find several of the best listed and briefly described in the "Books and Other Resources" section.

Before Fashion: From the Caveman to the Middle Ages

"Fashion" in clothes is actually something quite out of the ordinary, as far as history is concerned. We think of fashionableness—wearing long skirts or short skirts, padded shoulders or narrow ones, high heels or low, one sort of clothes for the neighborhood, another sort for the office—as an obvious part of dressing. But in the great scheme of things, this is an idea whose time has come only recently.

Up until the late Middle Ages (about the mid-fourteenth century), there were really only two shapes in use for garments: a tube of fabric that fell from the shoulders to the feet, and a basically circular sort of thing with a hole for the head to fit through (and maybe holes for the arms too). Clothing construction was based mostly on weaving or cutting fabric into large shapes, which were draped, hung, or bunched around the body in various ways.

Of course there were a multitude of variations on these two themes. These garments might have sleeves or not; they could be worn loose or belted in some way; they would be made of many different fabrics—

from crudely woven wool to the sheerest linen—left plain, or dyed any color of the rainbow.

Clothing was decorated, simply or elaborately. And garments of different colors, shapes, and motifs were mixed to create complex, multi-layered outfits. Long rectangular pieces of fabric were wrapped or swirled or tied in different ways to accent the basic garment. Capes were worn, and hats and ornaments of every sort.

So it's not that clothes were *dull* in "those" days. In fact, they were often far more splendid than much of what is worn today, in the age of the blue jean. But nevertheless, the clothes of the far past were not "fashionable." Societies adopted a few types of garments they found comfortable and attractive, and everybody wore those garments, generation after generation. Changes occurred, of course, but mostly in details—making some parts shorter, others longer, changing the draping, adding or subtracting layers, and so on. When major changes occurred, more often than not it was the result of another culture's influence.

Indeed, some societies which never encountered other cultures *never* changed their way of dressing. Probably only a few hundred of these people are left today, in the most remote parts of the world, but at the beginning of the twentieth century, there were still many traditional groups—like the nomadic Eskimos and the hunter-gatherer tribes of South America—who dressed much as their distant ancestors had in prehistory.

Based on the evidence of these traditional people, we know that in prehistory, people of warm climates probably wore very little, and most of what they wore was for the purpose of decoration. In cold climates, they wore a lot, and most of what they wore—though usually decorated—was worn mainly for the purpose of protection from the elements. Very simple.

But as civilizations developed, clothing, like everything else, became more complicated. Labor began to be divided (some worked in the fields, others in the houses, and so on), so different work clothes evolved for the sake of practicality; social classes developed—supervisors over the workers, officials over the supervisors, the aristocracy over the officials—and clothing became symbolic of rank. In ancient Rome, for example, only citizens were allowed to wear the toga, and the color of the toga and its trimmings reflected the status of the citizen, whether youth, senator, priest, or warrior.

Still, though, there was no "fashion" as we know it today. Century after century—through the rise and fall of the Roman Empire, through the Barbarian invasions, and through the Crusades—garments continued to be simple in construction, with variety achieved through the use of different fabrics and trimmings. Clothing was still basically hung, wrapped, or draped on the body. Until . . .

Silhouette: The Fourteenth Century

The different, daring idea that gave birth to the sort of fashion we know today was the concept of "silhouette"—that is, using the construction of the garment to create a line which would call attention to some parts of the body and obscure other parts. A dress with fabric gathered or tucked up in the back emphasizes the behind; a bodice drawn tight at the waist and puffed out above draws attention to the bosom; a man's breeches cut very tight give the figure a vertical line, while flounced, gathered, or baggy breeches create a different look altogether.

The beginnings of this idea seem to have occurred in the middle of the fourteenth century, when, rather suddenly, a new "look" sprang into being all over Europe. At first, men were more anxious than women to adopt new, fitted styles; they abandoned the long, shapeless gowns worn throughout the Middle Ages in western Europe in favor of short, snug jackets and tight hose. Women followed this change to a more fitted look, and bodices were cut closer to the body, hugging the bosom to below the waist, then flaring into full, long skirts.

Both men and women added a variety of under- and over-garments to their basic costumes, and adorned their clothing richly with fur and jewels. Fabulous fabrics—silks, cloth of gold, damasks—brought from the East during the Crusades had already begun to be a staple of costume during the Middle Ages, and once again they were increasingly popular. As Europe's own textile industries became more sophisticated (especially in Italy), the possibilities of costume design quickly multiplied.

These luxuries, of course, belonged only to the nobility; the working people had neither money nor time for fashion, and if they had, they would never have imagined dressing like their betters. But even the "betters," for all their rich brocades, lived in conditions which we would not care to experience. Witness this fact: a common item worn by the fourteenth-century fashion plate was a flea fur, intended to lure the ubiquitous vermin away from their human hosts by offering them a more lush playground.

Status: The Fifteenth Century

Once the concept of silhouette came into being, it gave rise to myriad possibilities. Silhouettes could be changed as social attitudes and values changed. Moreover, fashions in silhouette could actually distinguish one social class from another—and that fulfilled an increasingly important need, since the once rigidly separated layers of medieval society had begun to run together like a melting parfait.

Where once there had been only two main economic groups (those with inherited wealth and those with inherited poverty), now a new class, made up of merchants, was emerging. Indeed, the merchants were becoming rich—often richer than the nobles who ruled them—and the privileged classes were anxious to find ways of maintaining their distinct place in society. The aristocracy, by making their clothes increasingly more complex, extravagant, and impractical, sought to stay ahead of their middle-class rivals.

To reinforce the fashion superiority of the upper class, more "sumptuary laws" were passed to regulate dress. These laws were supposedly based on moral or religious grounds, but in reality, they were designed to prevent people from dressing above their station. A fourteenth century law, for example, had decreed that no one below the rank of gentleman could wear a coat so short that his buttocks were revealed—a breach of propriety which apparently was considered less offensive in a gentleman than in one of lesser rank!

The sumptuary laws preserved at least the appearance, if not the substance, of the old class system, and the upper classes made the most of their clear field in the fashion arena. If a rich merchant and his family tried to wear trains as long as a noble family's trains, or jewels as large, or trimmings as luxurious, they could be fined or even sent to prison. In the meantime, the nobles of northern Europe (Italy maintained a surprising degree of restraint) and England got themselves up in ever more elaborate outfits.

Dresses now generally had waistlines above the natural waist, and long trains; low decolletage was the rule in many places. Hairdos and headdresses took on a life of their own, with horn-like and heart-shaped effects popular during the first half of the century, and the tall, steeple-like affairs we associate with fairy-tale princesses all the rage in the second half. Men, too, wore elaborate headgear, along with short doublets over hose, dashing capes, and pointy shoes. But although these silhouettes prevailed, there was a great deal of diversity among the styles worn, for individualism was becoming a popular new attitude.

Pride: The Sixteenth Century

Once the concept of cutting and sewing fabric in different ways for fashionable purposes was established, the possibilities of clothing increased by many thousandfold. And of course, as soon as human beings discover that they *can* do something, they become *determined* to do it.

And overdo it. The most noteworthy fashion trend of the early sixteenth century was "slashing," a treatment (used most extensively in men's clothing) which featured slashed openings in the top fabric layer of a garment; the underlayer of fabric was either revealed through the slashes, or frequently, pulled through the slash to form a puff. Some outfits were slashed every inch or two, from top to bottom.

The idea behind slashing, of course, was to show off multiple layers of sumptuous material. A similar effect was achieved in women's clothing by outer sleeves turned back to reveal inner sleeves of another fabric, and skirts split down the middle to display rich brocade petticoats. But beyond just showing off their fabulous textiles, the ruling families of Europe had something more to prove through their clothing. In the sixteenth century, nationalism became an especially important force, in fashion as well as in politics.

Styles in clothing had varied from region to region in the fifteenth century, but these differences became more pronounced, and more insistent, in the sixteenth. Trends in fashion were set by the courts of the most powerful monarchs—and those trends often reflected the personal idiosyncrasies or physical characteristics of the rulers themselves. (For example, Elizabeth I was particularly proud of her small feet, and a few years after her accession to the throne, hemlines were raised to the ankle so that the Queen's dainty feet and elaborately jeweled shoes might be on display.)

In Europe, Italian styles—which were fitted, but still fairly natural—dominated for the first half of the century, but as the political fortunes of Spain rose, the dark, heavy Spanish styles began to be worn everywhere. Spanish fashions for both men and women were stiffly constructed, with the body compressed in some places by whalebone stays, and expanded in others—by padded bulges built into men's doublets (called the "peasecod belly") or by hooped petticoats ("farthingales") that held women's skirts out in varying directions. The essential result of the silhouette created by the Spanish was to make the body an assembly of geometric lines and shapes, rather than a natural form.

Only England was sufficiently powerful to oppose Spain, not only on the seas, but in the fierce world of fashion as well. During the first

half of the sixteenth century, English styles had fluctuated according
to the nationality of Henry VIII's latest wife, but from the beginning
of his daughter Elizabeth's reign in 1558, fashion ideas were taken
from many different national styles, the result being an elaborate
patchwork—bordering on a parody—of European fads. The basic
silhouette remained close to the Spanish model, but details were
worked out along lines which permitted a good deal more showing-off
of the body than was considered acceptable by the staid Spaniards.

France, meanwhile, had fallen to a low position in the ranks of
European nations, and accordingly, had lost a good deal of its fashion
influence. This was something of an irony, because the very monarch
whose foolishness ruined France's political status was the same king
whose passion for fancy dress pushed forward the development of
France's great textile industry, which laid the foundation for her later
domination over the world of fashion.

In the prideful arena of the sixteenth century, France was much
overshadowed, and no wonder, for Henri III's taste was bizarre at best.
One courtier reported the king wearing this unusual accessory: a basket of small dogs hung from a broad ribbon about his neck! That
fashion statement did not catch on elsewhere, and by 1589, the king
was assassinated (in fact, by a monk who objected to the ruler's sar-
torial self-indulgence) and his successor inaugurated a new era of somewhat more refined fashions, echoing what was happening throughout
Europe; jeweled trimmings gave way to ribbons and lace, extremes of
padding and hooping were softened, and the sixteenth century merged
more soberly into the seventeenth.

Status: The Seventeenth Century

Restraint did not last for long, however. By the early 1620s, the new
French monarch, Louis XIII, had turned the affairs of state over to
Cardinal Richelieu, and Louis then invested much of his energy in the
pursuit of fashion. At first, the king and his courtiers had free rein for
their fashion extravaganzas, and they went to great lengths to outdo
not only one another, but the rising middle class as well.

The sumptuary laws which had been passed to keep the middle class
in its fashion place by now were failing in their purpose, because the
merchants and bankers and professional folk had so *much* money that
they were perfectly willing to spend it in paying fines and wearing
whatever they pleased. In fact, very soon they began to outdo the

upper classes at their own game, and styles went to even further extremes. Throughout Europe—especially in France and England—necklines dipped almost to the nipples, and the most voluptuous fabrics and trimmings, imported from all parts of the world, were made up by legions of laborers into elaborate garments. Only Spain, meanwhile, clung stubbornly to its somber, old-fashioned styles.

In the political arena, the amazing Richelieu was hard at work recouping the fortunes of France, and in the process, he turned the fashion passion back to work in the economy. In 1625, he began to pass new laws forbidding the import of textiles, and the fashionable were forced to patronize their own textile mills and ribbon factories; the French fashion industry flourished. And at the same time, through Richelieu's brilliant political maneuvers, France was regaining a place of power in the world that was to make French styles dominant throughout Europe and even further abroad.

The style of dress which took shape during this period was very different from that of the previous century. Men's clothing was far more relaxed, with wide, soft lace collars replacing the stiff ruffs of the past, and unpadded, longer-skirted doublets worn over breeches that fell to the tops of soft, square-toed boots. Women's fashions, too, took a turn toward a more comfortable (comparatively speaking!) elegance. The rigid farthingale petticoat was abandoned in favor of skirts falling naturally to the floor, from a bodice which was usually boned rather than worn over a separate corset. Soft fabrics were favored, rather than heavy brocades.

By mid-century, when Louis XIII died, France was the virtual dictator of fashions for the rest of Europe (save Spain), not only in clothing, but in all of culture. And this power was only to increase during the long reign of the next Louis—number XIV—who was not called the "Sun King" for nothing. The glitter of his palaces and his courtiers was said to be blinding, and that accorded well with the new period of fashion extremism which began around the same time he came to power: men suddenly replaced their gently fitted garments with so-called "petticoat breeches" (puffed out to the width of skirts and reaching to the knee or below) and wore doublets cut away to reveal the lavish shirts beneath. (Both breeches and doublet were customarily adorned with ribbons—up to 250 yards to decorate a single outfit!)

Louis XIV encouraged this peacock revolution, but not out of idle vanity. On the contrary. The Sun King was a hard-working and determined monarch, who cleverly encouraged the nobility to spend all their time and money on court frippery rather than on politics and (possibly) rebellions. This policy saved Louis a good deal of trouble, and in the bargain, sent the French fashion industry into high gear, since the king firmly perpetuated Richelieu's ban on imports.

Women's fashions were less extreme than the men's, retaining the same basic shape as before, with the addition of a train, and some minor changes in necklines, sleeves, and so forth. Dresses were still generally made up in two pieces (bodice and very full skirt), the boat-necked bodice heavily boned and drawn down to a low, sharp point below the waistline in front. A loose boudoir gown called a "negligée" was introduced by one of Louis' mistresses, but on the whole, the trend was toward stiffer, more formal dress. And this tendency increased toward the end of Louis XIV's long reign, when women's court dresses were almost impossible to sit down in.

The Sun King left a curious legacy. His ambition for France paid off in some ways, but at the cost of nearly bankrupting the country. Louis XIV's policies ignored the welfare of the people, and made the French revolution inevitable. Yet the role of France as the fountain of fashion was carried to new heights, where it would remain almost continuously until the collapse of the couture two hundred and fifty years later.

Artifice: The Eighteenth Century

The influence of French fashion was obvious even in colonial America, where the founding fathers and their ladies wore slightly simplified versions of the same styles found in the cities of Europe. Too busy with subsistence to create their own culture, the American settlers borrowed most of their fashions—art, music, theater, and dress—from the countries they had left behind, adding only such innovations as were necessary to contend with the conditions of their new country.

Beginning a little before 1720, French fashion (and accordingly, European and American fashions) changed radically. The stiff formality of the previous period was left behind, except for the most elevated court occasions; in its place was a softer, more gracious silhouette. There were many different types of garments—a greater diversity of styles than ever before—but the most typical was the sacque, which was distinguished by a long, full back panel falling from pleats at the shoulders. (The French painter Watteau rendered these gowns, and the ribboned and flowered hats that accompanied them, so charmingly that the styles are called by his name to this day.)

At the beginning of its evolution, the sacque was full in front as well as in back, but within a few years, the front of the bodice became fitted. By mid-century, the sacque was transformed into the *robe a la française*—an open version (that is, with the skirt split down the front to reveal the petticoat) worn over hoops called "panniers," which were wide on the sides but virtually flat in front and back. This style of gown was made up in all sorts of fabrics and worn by almost all women for every occasion, well into the 1770s; customarily, it had a low, square neckline, with sleeves fitted to the elbow and ending in a deep, full flounce.

As the latter half of the century began, the fashion world as we know it today was beginning to take shape. For the past hundred years, modish styles had been circulated through Europe and even the colonies by means of "fashion dolls," which wore miniature gowns made up in the latest fabrics. (Rather like early cousins of our Barbie.) But in the 1760s, fashion journals began to appear all over Europe; they featured elegantly engraved plates which depicted the newest styles—and these began to change very rapidly indeed.

The 1770s brought one trend after another, most drawn from some foreign influence or fantasy, and each generally more comfortable than the last. The hoopless *robe a l'anglaise* provided a relaxed alternative to the *robe a la française*; the *polonaise*, with its curtain-like swags (drawn up and down on cords), was worn over small hoops, but it was short—often above the ankle. And a positively casual dress, the *robe a la creole*, was worn at home; actually an early chemise, the *creole* was made of gauzy material, worn without hoops, and gathered at the waist with a simple sash.

This seeming informality, however, was in reality more like frivolity. It was born of a desperate and perfectly correct feeling among the French aristocracy that their era of power was drawing to a close. As the political situation grew steadily worse under the well-meaning but ineffectual Louis XVI, fashion-mad France followed the example of Marie Antoinette, who alternately played at being a milkmaid and dressed up to a level of lavishness which was quite amazing.

Gowns in the 1780s were decorated until they had no more room for trimmings. Hairstyles were swept up to a height of a foot or more, this being accomplished by using pomade and flour to turn the hair into something like plaster of Paris, and decorated with all sorts of objects, from ribbons and flowers to miniature, fully rigged ships. But curiously enough, while the women went to ever more absurd extremes, men were steadily refining their costumes into straightforward, almost tailored affairs consisting of knee-length coat, vest, and fitted breeches, with a soft shirt flounced at neck and wrists.

Everything in Europe, including fashion, was to be changed after the French Revolution, which took place in fits and starts throughout the last decade of the eighteenth century. The revolutionaries, who included not only the poor but the middle class, rejected all the fantastic trappings of the aristocracy—including their clothes and the people who made them. The great textile mills were ruined, the seamstresses and hairdressers fled, and the French fashion industry was in a shambles as the century ended.

Extremes: The Nineteenth Century

And yet—nothing, it seems, could keep the French down when it came to fashion. On the eve of the Revolution, a simple English style, the chemise, had come to Paris; by the beginning of the nineteenth century, it had been transformed into the daring silhouette of the Directoire/Empire. The new look—a tubular dress, with very high waist, low-cut neckline, and small puffed or draped sleeves—was part of the French infatuation with the ideal of classical antiquity, and it spread, in somewhat less dramatic versions, almost everywhere. Its principal accompaniment was a large shawl, often necessary, because the dresses were so lightweight and bare that wearers grew chilly.

This simple, fluid, neo-classical style lasted into the second decade of the century, but soon began to be romanticized with fuller skirts, fancier sleeves, and frillier details. By the 1830s, waistlines were back down to their natural level, where they were belted, and bodices sloped off the shoulders, with enormous sleeves set into dropped armholes. In the 1840s, the waistline lowered and took on the distinctive Victorian point, while skirts widened toward the vast proportions that would characterize the fifties and sixties, when, with the coming of the Second Empire in France, a new wave of opulence in dress broke out.

A true—or perhaps mostly true—story from the middle of the nineteenth century comments on the absurd size of high-Victorian skirts. The Empress Eugénie, famed for her beauty and devotion to style, sent the Queen of Madagascar a gift: a fashionable gown (probably about ten yards around at the hem) and a crinoline (the enormous wire-hooped horsehair-covered frame that was intended to hold the gown at the proper distance from the body of the wearer). Madagascar's Queen Ranavanalona, coming from a less sophisticated but more sensible society, wore the dress, but thinking the crinoline must be a canopy designed to complement the dress, had it hung from a tree over her head!

Meanwhile, men's clothes continued to head in the opposite direction, becoming more and more restrained throughout the century. The famous fashion arbiter Beau Brummel started this trend in the first decade, when he decreed that status was best displayed through perfect cut and fine fabric, rather than through ostentatious use of color and decoration. Brummel's notion—which reversed centuries of fashion custom—took hold, and actually laid the foundation for the sophisticated couture of the mid-twentieth century.

To see how fashion fared between Beau Brummel and Christian Dior, you may want to return to Part Two for the quick tour of the nineteenth and twentieth centuries.

Some Sources of Vintage Clothing

Vintage clothing can be found in a wide variety of places, many of which are suggested in Part One. Every collector needs to develop personal and local sources as much as possible, but many collectors will also want to patronize mail order dealers, visit stores or dealers while travelling, and perhaps bid by mail at auction. The following listings are intended to expand your access to all these collecting resources.

Auctions

If you are interested in getting in on some auction action, your best resource is Christie's; they have fairly regular sales of costumes and textiles, which are handled by their Collectibles department. Each time there is a sale (several times a year in New York, more often in London), a catalog is published in advance, and if you wish to, you can place a bid by mail. The easiest thing to do is subscribe to the catalog series, and then you will receive a catalog two or three weeks before each sale. The catalog contains complete bidding instructions and a bidding form.

The catalogs also contain, of course, descriptions of the items offered for sale, estimated high and low values for each item or lot, and some pictures of the more significant offerings.

If you send in a mail bid, Christie's will treat that bid as your *maximum* offer. That is, they will bid for you up to the amount of your stated bid, and then quit (which means you could get the item at a lower price than your bid). If your bid succeeds, you'll be notified, and you will be expected to pay immediately the amount of the successful bid plus a small service charge and cost of shipment.

Whether or not you are a successful bidder, about two weeks after the sale, you will receive a list of the prices achieved, so you can see how much the items actually brought. Studying these prices is a great way to learn more about the vintage clothing market and how to bid in it effectively. To obtain a subscription, write to:

Christie's Publications
21-24 44th Avenue
Long Island City, NY 11101

They will send you a brochure describing all of Christie's publications, from which you can choose those you want to take. There are two catalog series which contain vintage clothing, both listed under "Collectibles." One is called "Costume and Textiles," and it's for the London (South Kensington) Christie's, where costume sales are more frequent, but also a bit more competitive; the other is called "Textiles, Dolls, and Toys," from Christie's East, one of their two New York locations. The price (in 1988) of the London series is $65 and the New York series is $35.

Should you decide you don't mind dealing with mail delays and keeping up with the price of the pound, try out the London market, but do study it carefully before you start bidding. In addition to Christie's, another London house, Phillips, also offers textile and costume auctions. For information about subscribing to Phillips' catalogs, write:

Phillips
Blenstock House
7 Blenheim Street
New Bond Street
London W1Y OAS, England

Whether New York or London, however, the obvious problem with bidding by mail is that you can't see the items beforehand. Looking at it one way, bidding by mail is like buying a pig in a poke; but looking at it another way, it's like sending away for a potentially wonderful surprise. The results can be exciting, particularly if you bid on the mixed lots described as "a collection of Victorian bodices" or "an assortment of beaded garments from the 1920s"! There's no telling what you may find in your grab bag, and if you've learned to bid effectively, you may get real bargains. It is not unusual to see a lot selling for less than half its lowest estimated price. (Many items, however, have unspecified "reserve" minimum prices, and won't be sold if there is no bid that meets the reserve.)

Auction catalogs may be purchased individually, by the way, if you know that an auction is coming up. A good way to keep up with the auction scene is by watching the antique and collectible periodicals which are listed in the chapter "Books and Other Resources." One magazine in particular, *Art and Auction,* is a rich source of auction news, though there may not always be anything in it about vintage clothing or costume in particular.

Stores and Mail Order

The list of stores and mail-order sources given here is only a brief sampling of the many that deal in vintage clothing. The explanation of why these particular ones are included is as follows:

First, I went through the current phone directories of about twenty cities scattered across the country to find stores that were listed, and I asked dealers I knew about other individual dealers *they* knew. I came up with more than a hundred names, and I sent them all questionnaires, asking for up-to-date information about their services. I also asked them to contribute descriptions and prices of about three dozen items they had available for sale at that time.

The dealers on the list below are those who took the time and put forth the effort to fill out the questionnaire. It was a lot of trouble for them to complete the questionnaire, and I know for certain that all the dealers who did it are serious about vintage clothing and really interested in developing their businesses. Judging from their helpfulness, and knowing the level of expertise that was required to fill out the questionnaire, I feel I can recommend these people with confidence.

If you should visit or correspond with any of the dealers on the list, it would be nice if you mentioned finding them in the *Official Identification and Price Guide to Vintage Clothing.* That way, they'll know that their efforts in behalf of the book are being rewarded.

Arizona, Phoenix
Honey Buns
Address: 5801 N. 7th Street   Zip: 85014
Tel: (602) 266–4353
Carries women's (and some men's) clothing from the 1920s through the 1950s, specializing in the 1950s. Regular hours Tuesday through Saturday. Most merchandise is in the $20–30 range.

California, Berkeley
Lacis
Address: 2982 Adeline Street   Zip: 94703
Tel: (415) 843-7178
Carries women's clothing and accessories from the Victorian period through the 1930s; also some children's. Specializes in lacy things. Regular store hours, Monday through Saturday. Offers restoration and conservation on wedding gowns and lawn dresses. Price range $200 to $1000.

California, Long Beach
Meow
Address: 2219 E. 4th Street   Zip: 90814
Tel: (213) 438–8990
Carries men's and women's clothing and accessories, 1940s to 1960s, as well as a few earlier things. Specializes in new-old stock. Price range $5 to $175.

California, Oakland
Lydia—The Purple Merchant
Address: 2368 High Street   Zip: 94601
Tel: (415) 532–9149 or 532–5177
Store hours Tuesday through Saturday. Carries all stock, but specializes in 1950s, with emphasis on poodle skirts.

Connecticut, Branford
Yesterday's Threads
Address: 564 Main Street   Zip: 06405
Tel: (203) 481–6452
Clothing from the early 1800s to the 1940s, mostly women's, though men's and children's are sometimes available. Also vintage accessories, and some restoration services. Regular store hours Monday, Wednesday, Friday, and Saturday.

Idaho, Jerome
Marian's Vintage Vanities
Address: 218 West Avenue 1, No. 44   Zip: 83338
Tel: (208) 324–3067
Carries all stock, 1900–1960. Primarily mail order, but will take appointments. Specialties include large sizes and vintage maternity clothes.

Illinois, Champagne
Carrie's Vintage Clothing
Address: 503 E. University   Zip: 61020
Tel: (217) 352–3231
A complete range of twentieth-century stock, through the 1950s. Regular store hours, Tuesday through Saturday; also, limited mail order.

Illinois, Chicago
Lost Eras
Address: 1511 W. Howard   Zip: 60626
Tel: (312) 764–7600
Women's and men's clothing, 1860–1965. Regular store hours every day; also mail order. Most stock under $100.

Illinois, Normal
Babbitt's Closet
Address: 104 North Street   Zip: 61761
Tel: (309) 454–7393
Men's and women's clothing and accessories, 1900 through the 1960s. Also creates accurate reproductions. Price range to $70. Regular store hours, Monday through Saturday.

Indiana, Culver
The Antiquarian
Address: 18989 Sunny Lane   Zip: 46511
Tel: (219) 842–3727
Carries clothing, 1860s to 1920s; also some 1930s lingerie. Primarily a mail-order business, but will take appointments. Price range from $40 to $350.

Indiana, Indianapolis
Modern Times
Address: 5363 N. College Avenue   Zip: 46220
Tel: (317) 253–8108
Women's and men's vintage clothing, mostly from the late 1940s to early 1960s. Stock ranges widely in price, but much of it is in the $10 range. Also carries some handmade clothing and new accessories. Regular store hours, seven days a week.

Indiana, Indianapolis
Red Rose Vintage Clothing
Address: 834 E. 64th Street   Zip: 46220
Tel: (317) 257–5016

Carries men's and women's clothing and accessories, 1900–1955 (emphasis on 1935–1955). Prices range up to $100. Regular store hours, Monday through Saturday.

Kansas, Topeka
Pastense
Address: 418 S. W. 6th Street   Zip: 66603
Tel: (913) 233–7107
Women's and men's clothing and accessories, 1910–60. Regular store hours except Sunday. Low prices.

Louisiana, Lafayette
Somewhere in Time
Address: 215 E. Convent   Zip: 70503
Tel: (318) 233–5077
Specializes in Victorian/Edwardian whites, but also carries day and evening clothing from the 1930s through the 1950s, as well as unusual accessories. Services include mail order and custom designs. Regular store hours Tuesday through Saturday, also by appointment.

Massachusetts, Boston
The Grand Trousseau
Address: 88 Charles Street   Zip: 02114
Tel: (617) 696–0070
Regular store hours except Sunday. Victorian through 1940; special emphasis on the 1920s. Large stock evening wear. Accessories, some men's and children's. Price range from $125 to $385. Also, made-to-order clothes from vintage fabrics and patterns.

Massachusetts, Cambridge
Vintage, Etc.
Address: 1796 Massachusetts Avenue   Zip: 02140
Tel: (617) 497–1516
Men's and women's clothing and accessories, late 1920s to late 1950s, specializing in formal wear and outerwear. Price range $12 to $100+. Regular store hours, seven days a week.

Massachusetts, Upton
Linda White Antique Clothing
Address: 1 Milford Street (Route 140)   Zip: 01587
Tel: (508) 529–4439
Specializing in Victorian and Edwardian clothing—men's, women's, and children's. Also accessories, linens, and some clothing up to 1940.

Regular store hours Wednesday, Thursday, and Sunday; also by appointment. Prices range from $50 to $450.

Michigan, Royal Oak
Passementerie
Address: 115 South Main   Zip: 48067
Tel: (313) 545–4663
Carries women's clothing and accessories, from the Victorian period to the 1930s. Also men's ties and hats, vintage linens, and a wide variety of trimmings. Prices range from $25 to $250.

Nebraska, Omaha
Diane McGee Estate Clothing Company
Address: 5225 Jackson   Zip: 68106
Tel: (402) 551–0727
Mail order only. Complete line, 1850s to 1950s; also carries old fabrics and trimmings.

New Jersey, Upper Saddle River
Pahaka
Address: 19 Fox Hill   Zip: 07458
Tel: (201) 327–1464
Carries all types of stock, 1880s through 1950s; typical price range $5 to $300. Mail order (three-day return policy); send detailed wants with SASE, or call. Also by appointment.

New York, New York City
Harriet Love
Address: 412 West Broadway   Zip: 10012
Tel: (212) 966-2280
Women's clothing and accessories, 1920s–50s; men's accessories and shirts. Expensive, but stock is high quality. Regular store hours, seven days a week.

New York, Troy
The Dressing Screen
Address: 2 Manning Avenue   Zip: 12180
Tel: (518) 274–2885
This wholesaler ships to dealers all over the country, and will also be glad to sell to individual collectors. Mostly women's clothing and accessories, 1860–1940.

North Carolina, Asheboro
Barbara Bulla, Antiques
Address: Box 282, Route 5   Zip: 27203
Tel: (919) 381-3554

Mail order only, women's clothing from 1900 to 1930. Stock ranges from $25 to $300. Also carries buttons and trims, other fashion-related items.

North Carolina, Clyde
Sharon Bramlett
Address: Box 535   Zip: 28721
Strictly mail order, specializing in women's wear, 1940s and 1950s; some men's and children's. Stock usually ranges from 1930s to 1960s, $5–30; accessories, but no shoes.

Ohio, Waldo
Fashions of Yesteryear
Address: 1780 Newmans-Cardington Road E.   Zip: 43356
Tel: (614) 726–2425
Mail order, or by appointment. Carries clothing (mostly women's) from 1840 to 1960, with a special interest in the 1920s. Style shows and slide programs. Price range $20 to $350.

Texas, Dallas
Puttin' on the Ritz
Address: 3113 Knox   Zip: 75205
Tel: (212) 522–8030
Women's and men's clothing, 1890–1960. All in mint condition or expertly restored. Accessories. Price range from $25 to $1500. Regular store hours every day except Tuesday.

Texas, Forreston
Bon Ton
Address: Highway 77   Zip: 76041
A huge potpourri of vintage items: men's, women's, and children's clothing and accessories, plus jewelry, old patterns and buttons, and lots of other fashion-related odds and ends. Open Thursday through Saturday. Prices moderate, trading welcome.

Texas, Fort Worth
Poor Little Rich Girl
Address: 7429 E. Lancaster   Zip: 76112
Tel: (817) 429–2084
Mail order, women's and some men's. Will search for requested items.

Museums and Collections

The major costume collections in this country are wonderful repositories of antique and vintage clothing, but for the most part, the many thousands of garments held in these collections are available for viewing to "serious" students and design professionals only. The space and personnel requirements for keeping a collection open to the public are just prohibitive.

Most collections do, however, mount public exhibitions periodically. If there is a costume collection near you, find out what they are up to; keep in touch or get on a mailing list if they have one, to make sure you know when a show is going on. Some also have lectures occasionally. When you travel, check with any collections you will be passing by, to see if there's a show up.

In addition to the collections listed below—which range from moderate-sized to enormous—there are also quite a few small, less formal collections scattered around the country. Check with your city or county historical society, as well as state and local museums, to see if they have costume holdings. You may be surprised at what you find.

While you're at it, find out if any nearby colleges or universities have fashion design departments. If so, they may have study collections, and they may also offer fashion history courses open to auditing.

Should you decide to approach any collection for viewing or study privileges, you will help your cause a lot by expressing specific interests (which have been well thought out beforehand). All but the most prestigious of the collections have small, overworked staffs, and while they may be willing to cooperate with serious collectors, they cannot accommodate people who just want to "look around."

Edward C. Blum Design
  Laboratory
Fashion Institute of Technology
227 West 27th Street
New York, NY 10001

Costume and Textiles
  Department
The Brooklyn Museum
200 Eastern Parkway
Brooklyn, NY 11238

The Costume Institute
The Metropolitan Museum
  of Art
Fifth Avenue at 82nd Street
New York, NY 10028

Museum of Art
Rhode Island School of Design
2 College Street
Providence, RI 02903

The Goldey Paley Design Center
  at the Philadelphia College
  of Textiles and Science
4200 Henry Avenue
Philadelphia, PA 19144

The Doris Stein Research and
  Design Center for Costumes
  and Textiles at the Los
  Angeles County Museum
  of Art
5905 Wilshire Boulevard
Los Angeles, CA 90036

Wadsworth Atheneum
600 Main Street
Hartford, CT 06103

The Museum of Fine Arts
465 Huntington Avenue
Boston, MA 02115

Chicago Historical Society
Clark Street at North Avenue
Chicago, IL 60614

Western Reserve Historical
  Society
825 East Boulevard
Cleveland, OH 44106

Detroit Historical Museum
5401 Woodward Avenue
Detroit, MI 48202

Indiana Fashion Design
  Collection
Indianapolis Museum of Art
1200 W. 38th Street
Indianapolis, IN 46208

Museum of the City of New York
Fifth Avenue at 103rd Street
New York, NY 10029

The Oakland Museum
1000 Oak Street
Oakland, CA 94607

The Arizona Costume Institute
The Phoenix Art Museum
1625 North Central Avenue
Phoenix, AZ 85004

Philadelphia Museum of Art
Benjamin Franklin Parkway
Box 7646
Philadelphia, PA 19101

Valentine Museum
1015 East Clay
Richmond, VA 23219

Missouri Historical Society
Jefferson Memorial Building
Forest Park
St. Louis, MO 63112

Historic Costume and Textile
  Collection
University of Washington
Seattle, WA 98195

The National Museum of
  American History
Constitution Avenue, NW
Washington, DC 20560

Books and Other Resources

The following list is focused mainly on books which are still in print, and available either at most bookstores or by special order from the publisher. But there are also some books which are so wonderful that I've included them on the list even though they are out of print and hard to find. (Where I know this to be the case, I've made some reference to the fact in the listing.)

If you are interested in obtaining out-of-print books on costume and textiles (and there are a *great* many which would be of interest), you will probably want to make contact with one of the following book dealers who specialize in these areas:

John Ives Antiquarian Books, 5 Normanhurst Drive, Twickenham, Middlesex, TW1 1NA, England.

R. L. Shep, Box C–20, Lopez Island, WA 98261.

Wooden Porch Books, Route 1, Box 262, Middlebourne, WV 26149.

As a rule, dealers will send you a list of available books from time to time; some will search for specific items. And don't overlook other sources of interesting material. Museum bookstores are always a good place to look, as are used bookstores, estate sales, library sales, and so on.

In addition to costume history books, look for sewing books, home economics textbooks, pattern books, mail-order catalogs, fashion and homemaking magazines; picture magazines such as *Look* and *Life* are also interesting sources of pictures that show real people wearing real clothes.

A note about British books: A great many of the books on costume available in this country were actually written in Great Britain, and they necessarily have a British point of view. While they are still very useful, it should be recognized that British and American fashion histories are by no means identical. Since British books are often published in the United States by American publishers, it is sometimes not clear that a book is British, so the listings below note specifically which books originated in Great Britain. If you are not sure of the origin of a book you're using, watch for the British spelling of words— like "colour" and "programme."

Generally speaking, there is a good deal of parallel between British and American high-fashion clothing, since both derive from Paris; the same is true of men's clothing up until World War II, because London was the fashion center of tailoring, just as Paris was for the couture. The chief differences in women's clothing are to be found in everyday and sports clothes, which were always a bit less formal in America; similarly, British men wore formal clothing a good deal more often than Americans.

During the war, however, both London and Paris were cut off as sources of fashion inspiration, and America began to develop its own styles. American tailoring asserted its independence with the "American shoulder," and men's clothing in this country took on a distinctive look, although the British model continued to have influence, especially among the conservative. Simultaneously, several American women designers created a uniquely American look called "sportswear," which has remained the staple of the American woman's wardrobe ever since.

As for children's clothing, there seems to be more difference here than in the other two categories. For one thing, progress toward comfort and practicality in children's clothing was made more quickly in this country, especially in the frontier West and the rural South. And for another, the influence of popular children's books, such as *Little Lord Fauntleroy, Alice in Wonderland,* and the Kate Greenaway books, was very strong in Britain, and reached these shores in a later and diluted form.

So—there are some American fashions which will not be found in British books, and some of the fashions described in British books were never current in America. *And* a given style may have appeared earlier or later in America than in Britain. Just a word of warning!

Fashion History and Theory

Batterberry, Michael and Ariane. *Fashion, the Mirror of History.* Greenwich House (New York, 1977).

An absolutely fascinating and first-rate overview of the development of fashion. Wonderful illustrations. (This book is also found under the title *Mirror, Mirror.*)

Bradley, Carolyn G. *Western World Costume: An Outline History.* Appleton-Century-Crofts (New York, 1954).
A compact standard. Basic information.

Kemper, Rachel H. *A History of Costume.* Newsweek Books (New York, 1977).
This beautiful book relates fashion to the political and cultural factors which have shaped history. An unusually thoughtful and wide-ranging book, yet very concise, covering the entire history of costume in 150 pages! (The chapter on the twentieth century, however, is very unsatisfactory.)

Laver, James. *Costume and Fashion.* Thames and Hudson (London, 1982).
This is a new edition of an old standard; it has been updated by the addition of a concluding chapter, written by Christina Probert. Concise, well-illustrated; very British, though it covers Western dress in general.

Mills, Betty J. *Calico Chronicle: Texas Women and Their Fashions, 1830–1910.* Texas Tech Press (Lubbock, TX, 1985).
Although the title sounds regional and limited, this book is full of interesting lore about life and clothes on the frontier. It's surprising, and a pleasure to read.

Nunn, Joan. *Fashion in Costume 1200–1980.* Schocken Books (1984).
This book covers a great deal of territory, and it is not conveniently arranged for reference, but it is interesting and readable. Pleasant sketches provide a well-organized visual catalog of styles for each period. Most useful is the fact that men's and children's clothing are treated, along with accessories. British.

O'Hara, Georgina. *The Encyclopaedia of Fashion.* Harry N. Abrams, Inc. (New York, 1986).
Handsome reference book covers designers and other figures of the fashion world (such as photographers and editors) well, and includes a respectable selection of fashion terms.

Picken, Mary Brooks. *The Fashion Dictionary: Fabric, Sewing, and Apparel as Expressed in the Language of Fashion.* Revised and Enlarged Edition. Funk & Wagnalls (New York, 1973).
There are more fashion terms explained here than you might think existed. Definitions are exceptionally concise and clear—and there

is a generous insert of odd but very instructive photographs. A great acquisition, if you can find one.

Russell, Douglas A. *Costume History and Style*. Prentice-Hall (Englewood Cliffs, NJ, 1983).

A nifty, no-nonsense college text for costume designers. Covers prehistory to the present, all in a very organized and helpfully illustrated manner.

Tranquillo, Mary D. *Styles of Fashion: A Pictorial Handbook*. Van Nostrand Reinhold Company (New York, 1984).

A useful book. It offers definitions and illustrations for a wide variety of garments, and also explains a good deal about construction details. All the information is easy to find and very concise. It is, however, oriented mainly toward contemporary clothing.

Wilcox, R. Turner. *Dictionary of Costume*. Charles Scribner's Sons (New York, 1969).

A motherlode of information! Every aspect of dress in every age, around the world, is mentioned here, though there is not a great deal of detail. Very useful illustrations.

————. *Five Centuries of American Costume*. Charles Scribner's Sons (New York, 1963).

One of the few books that really focuses on American clothing, as distinct from European styles. Unfortunately, however, it is not very useful on the twentieth century.

————. *The Mode in Costume*. Second Revised and Expanded Edition. Charles Scribner's Sons (New York, 1958).

A useful summary of fashion history, with handsome, informative illustrations by the author.

Worrell, Estelle Ansley. *American Costume, 1840–1920*. Stackpole Books (Harrisburg, PA, 1979).

Another of the few American-centered books, this one provides some very useful information, along with charming drawings. It is primarily addressed to theatrical costumers, and so focuses on typical styles of the periods. Too bad it stops with the 1920s!

Twentieth-Century Fashion

Barwick, Sandra. *A Century of Style*. George Allen & Unwin (Boston, 1984).

This British book explores twentieth-century fashion by focusing on fashionable women, several of whom are British aristocrats. Some interesting lore.

Bond, David. *The Guinness Guide to 20th Century Fashion.* Guinness Superlatives Limited (Middlesex, 1981).
Terrific pictures. Covers the 1960s much better than most books, and even skims the 1970s. British.

Cunnington, C. Willett. *English Women's Clothing in the Present Century.* Thomas Yoseloff (New York, 1958).
This book goes into amazing detail about the year-to-year progression of fashions in England from 1900 to 1950. One of its most interesting characteristics is the copious use of quotations from the fashion periodicals of the day. Well worth a look if a copy can be found. (Companion book, *English Women's Clothing in the Nineteenth Century* [same author and publisher], is equally interesting.)

Dorner, Jane. *Fashion in the Forties & Fifties.*

———. *Fashion in the Twenties & Thirties.* Arlington House (New Rochelle, NY, 1973).
British. Scrapbook-type compilations of advertisements, cartoons, magazine illustrations, and snapshots that give a very good feel for the real-life fashion ambience of these decades.

Ewing, Elizabeth. *History of Twentieth Century Fashion.* Barnes & Noble (Totowa, NJ, 1986).
Very British, and very interesting, because it goes into quite a lot of detail about the forces of fashion in this century. A nice, eclectic selection of illustrations.

Howell, Georgina. *In Vogue: Sixty Years of International Celebrities and Fashion From British Vogue.* Schocken Books (New York, 1976).
A fascinating trip through the fashion century, with many wonderful pictures and an intelligent commentary. Although the book is British in orientation, there is much reference to the role of the United States in fashion, providing an interesting, different point of view.

Mansfield, Alan and Phillis Cunnington. *Handbook of English Costume in the Twentieth Century, 1900–1950.* Plays, Inc. (Boston, 1973).
Lots of detailed information, useful drawings. This book is in many respects an updating and abridgement of the Cunnington book listed previously.

McDowell, Colin. *McDowell's Directory of Twentieth Century Fashion.* Prentice-Hall, Inc. (Englewood Cliffs, NJ, 1985).

A somewhat idiosyncratic, but very comprehensive, survey. Informative entries on virtually every fashion designer of the century, with
many good pictures.

Melinkoff, Ellen. *What We Wore: An Offbeat Social History of Women's
Clothing, 1950–1980*. William Morrow and Company, Inc. (New
York, 1984).
Just what the subtitle says. Fun to read and full of details, which is
especially helpful in the case of the 1960s, a decade which is given
short shrift in most books.

Torrens, Deborah. *Fashion Illustrated: A Review of Women's Dress 1920–
1950*. Hawthorn Books, Inc. Publishers (New York, 1975).
An unusual and entertaining book, presented as a series of yearly
seasonal fashion collections. Each collection includes photos,
sketches, and fashion magazine commentaries. Gives a good feel for
the diversity of styles which were seen during these decades. Although British, the book gives plenty of coverage to American
fashion.

Tyrell, Anne V. *Changing Trends in Fashion: Patterns of the Twentieth
Century 1900–1970*.
An unusual British book that includes simple, scaled patterns for
typical men's and women's garments from each decade of the period
1900–1970. This feature offers interesting insight into the construction of vintage garments. Equally valuable are the year-by-year sum-
maries of popular styles, colors, fabrics, trims, and accessories; these
even include hairstyles and fashionable postures. (A companion
book, *The Evolution of Fashion: Pattern and Cut From 1066 to 1930*,
by Margot H. Hill and Peter A. Bucknell, also from Batsford, per-
forms a similar function for earlier times.)

Useful Background Information

Cultural History

Gordon, Lois and Alan. *American Chronicle: Six Decades in American
Life, 1920–1980*. Atheneum (New York, 1987).
This book offers a fascinating array of highlights, year-by-year, from
every aspect of popular culture—including fashion. Very worthwhile.

Lucie-Smith, Edward. *Cultural Calendar of the 20th Century*. E. P. Dut-
ton (New York, 1979).

A wonderful book which summarizes the development of the arts and society year-by-year, from 1900 to 1975. Many illustrations reveal styles in painting, architecture, interior design, movies, and much more.

Martin, Richard. *Fashion and Surrealism.* Rizzoli (New York, 1987). See to believe!

Time-Life Books. *This Fabulous Century.* Time-Life (New York).
A splendid series of books, one for each decade of the twentieth century. Fascinating pictures and text. The original hardback series is now hard to find intact, but worth searching for, and the individual volumes are useful as well. A recent paperback reprint of the series is drastically reduced, but still interesting.

Weber, Eva. *Art Deco in America.* Exeter Books (New York, 1985).
Good illustrations and concise text make this book a fine introduction to the look and feel of Deco.

Couture

DeMarly, Diana. *The History of the Haute Couture, 1850–1950.* Batsford (London, 1980).
An interesting overview. This book covers the nineteenth-century beginnings of couture, as well as the more usually discussed twentieth-century designers.

Milbank, Caroline Rennolds. *Couture: The Great Designers.* Stewart, Tabori & Chang, Inc. (New York, 1985).
A beautiful and informative book. It has an excellent bibliography, too.

The following are a few of the growing number of lavish books picturing the work of major designers and offering insights into their lives and times:

Coleman, Elizabeth Ann. *The Genius of Charles James.* Brooklyn Museum/Holt, Rinehart and Winston (New York, 1983).

Deslandres, Yvonne. *Poiret: Paul Poiret 1879–1944.* Rizzoli (New York, 1987).

Giroud, Françoise. *Dior, 1905–1957.* Rizzoli (New York, 1987).

Leymarie, Jean. *Chanel.* Skira/Rizzoli (New York, 1987).

Morano, Elizabeth. *Sonia Delaunay: Art into Fashion.* George Braziller (New York, 1987).

Osma, Guillermo de. *Fortuny: Mariano Fortuny, His Life and Work.* Rizzoli (New York, 1980).

Topics for Collectors

Special Interest Areas

Boyer, G. Bruce. *Elegance: A Guide to Quality in Menswear.* W. W. Norton & Company (New York, 1985).
To quote the dust cover, "a book that is at once practical, delightful, and historical." I agree. A very good source of lore, though organized for leisurely reading, rather than reference.

Dyer, Rod, and Ron Spark. *Fit to be Tied: Vintage Ties of the Forties and Early Fifties.* Abbeville Press (New York, 1987).
Much fun to look at, and informative in the bargain. A stylish book, with extensive coverage of the topic.

Earnshaw, Pat. *Lace in Fashion: From the Sixteenth to the Twentieth Centuries.* Batsford (London, 1985).
More than you knew there was to know about lace and its part in fashion history.

Esquire's Encyclopedia of 20th-Century Men's Fashions. McGraw-Hill (New York, 1973).
A monumental book (nearly 700 pages!) which no collector of men's clothing should be without. Unfortunately, however, most will have to suffer the lack, since this book is long out of print and hard to find. Really a beauty, though.

Flusger, Alan. *The Principles of Fine Men's Dress.* Villard Books (New York, 1985).
Although this book is written from the contemporary point of view, it is full of very useful information about styles in men's clothing.

Holiner, Richard. *Antique Purses: A History, Identification, and Value Guide.* Collector's Books (Paducah, KY, 1985).
Covers mainly mesh and beaded purses, from the late nineteenth century through the 1920s. Lots of pictures (with dollar values), but unfortunately, there's not much information given about the purses.

Monserrat, Ann. *And the Bride Wore . . . A History of the White Wedding.* Dodd, Mead (New York, 1973).

A British book, but it conscientiously covers the whole world. Fascinating.

Probert, Christina. *Hats in Vogue: Since 1910.* Abbeville Press (New York, 1981).

———. *Lingerie in Vogue: Since 1910.* Abbeville Press (New York, 1981).
These two books bring together many fascinating illustrations from *Vogue* magazine; great for developing identification skills, and for just plain browsing. Also, a good source of ideas for display. There are several other books in this series as well, including *Brides in Vogue, Sportswear in Vogue, Swimwear in Vogue,* and *Shoes in Vogue.*

Steele, H. Thomas. *Hawaiian Shirt: Its Art and History.* Abbeville Press (New York, 1984).
Lots of lore, and great pictures.

Swann, June. *Shoes.* Drama Book Publishers (New York, 1982).
Everything you ever wanted to know about shoes—and more.

Taylor, Lou. *Mourning Dress: A Costume and Social History.* George Allen & Unwin (London, 1983).
Although this may seem to be a limited topic, the book is actually fascinating in its exposition of the relationship between society and fashion.

Worrell, Estelle Ansley. *Children's Costume in America, 1607–1910.* Charles Scribner's Sons (New York, 1980).
An absolute treasure. Packed with invaluable information for the collector of children's clothing. Extensive detail, lots of illustrations.

Zimmerman, Catherine S. *The Bride's Book: A Pictorial History of American Bridal Dress.* Arbor House (New York, 1985).
Interesting pictures and material, but the text is a little weak.

Vintage Clothing and Collecting

Antique Trader Price Guide to Antiques and Collector's Items.
A bimonthly listing of prices for a wide variety of antique and collectibles categories. Vintage clothing is covered only intermittently, but at $12 a year, it may be worthwhile to subscribe. P.O. Box 1050, Dubuque, IA 52001.

Antiques and the Arts Weekly.

A wonderful publication! It's like a large, fat weekly newspaper, except that all the news and all the ads are about antiques and collectibles. There is little news about vintage clothing, but there are often ads for auctions and large dealer markets that include vintage clothes, and besides that, it's just fun to read and really keeps you in touch with the excitement of collecting. A subscription is $32 a year. Write The Newtown Bee, Newtown, CT 06470.

Art and Auction.

A very slick publication, full of interesting articles and listings of the activities of major auction houses. Vintage clothing is not yet covered specifically in this publication, but reading it does make you feel "in touch" with the auction world. A year's subscription is $42. Address: 250 W. 57th Street, New York, NY 10107.

Costume Society of America.

This is a scholarly group devoted to the study and preservation of historical clothing. Most members are museum curators, costume designers, and so on, but anyone seriously interested in fashion history will find this a most interesting group to become involved with. There's a national convention every year, and in some areas regional groups meet more frequently. Members receive a newsletter and the annual journal, *Dress*, and dues are $40 a year for individuals. Further information can be obtained from CSA, 55 Edgewater Drive, P.O. Box 73, Earleville, MD 21919.

Doering, Mary D. "Clothing: Treasured Hand-me-downs." In *Encyclopedia of Collectibles: Children's Books to Comics.* Time-Life Books (Alexandria, VA, 1978). This relatively brief piece actually addresses antique clothing more than vintage clothing, but it's an interesting perspective.

Dolan, Maryanne. *Vintage Clothing: 1880–1960: Identification and Value Guide.* Books Americana, Inc. (Florence, AL, 1984). Lots and lots of useful pictures in this book—but the section on 1940–60 is really very inadequate. Value ranges given throughout the books appear to be similar to prices for near-mint condition items purchased from better dealers.

Fashion Historian: Elizabeth S. Brown.

Ms. Brown is a wonderfully knowledgeable lecturer and costume consultant. She presents a variety of programs on such topics as "Yesterday's Weddings" and "Dating Your 19th- and 20th-Century Clothes." Each program is "illustrated" with dozens of costume items from her collection. Ms. Brown also does appraisals and consultations on various aspects of collecting and conservation. For further information about fees and services, contact Ms. Brown at 45 Whippoorwill Way, Belle Mead, NJ 08505; (201) 359–3395.

Hildesley, C. Hugh. *Sotheby's Guide to Buying and Selling at Auction.* W. W. Norton & Company (New York, 1984).
This book offers a thorough introduction to the world of upper-crust auctions, and will tell you just how anyone can join in the fun.

Kennett, Frances. *The Collector's Book of Fashion.* Crown Publishers, Inc. (New York, 1893).
British, but nevertheless a very useful reference. Especially good on accessories, and even covers some ancillary collecting areas such as buttons and lace.

Love, Harriet. *Harriet Love's Guide to Vintage Chic.* Holt, Rinehart and Winston (New York, 1982).
A fun book, mostly oriented toward wearables. Useful details about many specific items, including care hints, and some good pictures of vintage clothes as they can look when worn fashionably today.

McCormick, Terry. *The Consumer's Guide to Vintage Clothing.* Dembner Books (New York, 1987).
This book is packed with helpful tips and interesting ideas, though they are not very accessible due to the narrative format. There are a lot of good suggestions for wearing vintage clothing successfully.

Roberts, Ralph. *Auction Action: A Survival Companion for Any Auction Goer.* Tab Books, Inc. (Blue Ridge Summit, PA, 1986).
Everything about auctions. Reading this book will make the first-time auction-goer much more confident.

Tarrant, Naomi. *Collecting Costume: The Care and Display of Clothes and Accessories.* George Allen & Unwin (Boston, 1983).
An adaptation of museum acquisition and conservation practices for use by the private collector. Very British, and thus some of the information is not especially useful in the United States, but there are quite a few interesting tidbits.

Vintage Clothing Newsletter.
This newsletter arrives six times a year, full of interesting notes about vintage clothing and the people who buy, sell, collect, and wear it. There are useful advertisements, too, along with news of books and shows. Well worth $15 a year. Write: Terry McCormick, P.O. Box 1422, Corvallis, OR 97339.

Whitis, Rose Freeman. *Starting and Operating a Vintage Clothing Shop.* Pilot Books (Babylon, NY, 1983).
    This is really a pamphlet, rather than a book, but it's a concise treatment of the considerations that go into acquiring and marketing vintage clothing. If you're thinking about becoming more than a collector, try to find a copy.

Care and Repair

Funaro, Diana. *The Yestermorrow Clothes Book: How to Remodel Second-hand Clothes.* Chilton Book Company (Radnor, PA, 1976).
    Although this book is primarily concerned with converting vintage clothing into "new" apparel, it is filled with useful tips about cleaning and mending, vintage fabrics, etc.

Robinson, Katherine. *The Clothing Care Handbook.* Fawcett Columbine (New York, 1985).
    Excellent all-around guide to techniques of clothing care.

Talas.
    Conservation supplies. There is a minimum order, but it's not too extreme. Send for free catalog: 213 W. 35th Street, New York, NY 10001.

University Products.
    Conservation supplies. No minimum order. Send for free catalog to: P.O. Box 101, Holyoke, MA 01041.

Index

313